I0879761

From Scenarios to Networks

performance works

SERIES EDITORS
Patrick Anderson
Nicholas Ridout

This series publishes books in theater and performance studies, focused in particular on the material conditions in which performance acts are staged, and to which performance itself might contribute. We define "performance" in the broadest sense, including traditional theatrical productions and performance art, but also cultural ritual, political demonstration, social practice, and other forms of interpersonal, social, and political interaction that may fruitfully be understood in terms of performance.

From Scenarios to Networks

Performing the Intercultural in Colonial Mexico

✦

Leo Cabranes-Grant

NORTHWESTERN UNIVERSITY PRESS
EVANSTON, ILLINOIS

Northwestern University Press
www.nupress.northwestern.edu

Copyright © 2016 by Northwestern University Press.
Published 2016. All rights reserved.

Printed in the United States of America

10 9 8 7 6 5 4 3 2 1

Library of Congress Cataloging-in-Publication Data

Names: Cabranes-Grant, Leo, 1960– author.
Title: From scenarios to networks : performing the intercultural in colonial Mexico / Leo Cabranes-Grant.
Description: Evanston, Illinois : Northwestern University Press, 2016. | Series: Performance works
Identifiers: LCCN 2016018951| ISBN 9780810133914 (pbk. : alk. paper) | ISBN 9780810133921 (cloth : alk. paper) | ISBN 9780810133938 (e-book)
Subjects: LCSH: Performing arts—Social aspects—Mexico—History. | Performing arts—Anthropological aspects—Mexico. | Mexico—History—Spanish colony, 1540–1810. | Mexico—Social life and customs. | Intercultural communication—Mexico—History.
Classification: LCC PN2312 .C33 2016 | DDC 791.097209032—dc23
LC record available at https://lccn.loc.gov/2016018951

For Arturo Echavarría, Luce López-Baralt,
and Mercedes López-Baralt

mentors, friends, islands

CONTENTS

PREFACE

First week of September 2013. Since I was unable to meet the people I am studying in this book, I had to interview their city. I was there now in the capital of Mexico, listening to the stones, the alleys, the ruins, the spectral remains of their past. It had been raining all afternoon. At the Zócalo, the vast expanse of the square looked like an improvised village made of orange and blue tents. Forming a series of meandering and intricate pedestrian passages in front of the cathedral, hundreds of *carpas* had been raised and tied to each other. Vendors displayed their merchandise on top of rugs or plastic curtains, selling clothes, figurines, and objects of all kinds and shapes, from plates to earrings and pots and food cooked on portable stoves. People walked and mixed in all directions, their voices and gestures swirling around in a variegated enjambment of accents, inflections, skin tones, and profiles that showcased the ethnic complexity of this country and our hemisphere. This alternative city in the plaza, so colorful and fragile, was built there as a protest against the education reforms proposed by the recently elected president Enrique Peña Nieto. I asked a man what exactly they were all rallying against. He explained to me that the government was trying to dismantle the power of labor unions; he also told me, with mesmerizing patience and vigor, that those in power intended to force experienced teachers to take examinations in order to keep their jobs. He was in his early fifties, probably, and although he was quite angry, he spoke to me in a calm and detached manner. After thanking him, I turned around and moved towards the museum of the Templo Mayor situated close by.

Once inside the excavations at the sacred precinct of the Mexicas, while looking at several monumental ramparts on top of which frogs and serpents had been skillfully carved, I suddenly found the site where the houses of the Avila brothers once stood. The Avila siblings are the main characters in the first chapter of this book, and they owe their relevance to the fact that they were accused of conspiring against the Spanish crown in 1566. Disguised as Indians, the brothers organized a masquerade that became one of the most incriminating pieces of evidence used against them during their trial. Their property was razed shortly afterwards, and the empty lots were covered with salt. Although I was aware the Avila siblings had lived near this area, it was quite surprising to discover how close their household had been to the remains of the Aztec temple. From where their homes once stood I was able to see now, just a few steps away, the precise spot where the notorious monolith of the goddess Coyolxauhqui was accidentally rediscovered five hundred years later. These two worlds—the center of the Aztec empire and the dwellings of two descendants of the conquistadors—are part of a conflicted intercultural conversation this book both addresses and intersects.

After leaving the Templo Mayor, I decided to follow the route utilized by a religious celebration organized in Mexico City in 1578. An analysis of this event is the point of departure for the second chapter of my investigation. The festival welcomed the arrival of a shipment of relics sent by the pope. The Jesuits were relatively new in town, and the Vatican provided them with an opportunity to impress their neighbors. The glory of God and the bones of martyrs were honored by Indian dancers and musicians, allegorical arches, several reliquaries covered with jewels, and a play. According to Pedro de Morales, who wrote a detailed account of this occasion, the multiple activities planned by the Jesuits took place at several streets that are still recognizable on the map of modern Mexico City (like Tacuba, Donceles, and Santo Domingo). While the urban topography has certainly changed since the sixteenth century, it was perfectly possible for me to retrace the procession's steps all the way to its final setting, the church at the Colegio Máximo de San Pedro y San Pablo. Today the Colegio is a massive building with a mostly flat, mustard-colored exterior. Since the church was started around 1576 and not finished until 1603, its precincts were still in their initial stages at the time of the festival. In 1822 Agustín de Itúrbide was sworn in as emperor of Mexico within its walls, and two years later the first Mexican constitution was debated and written here. The church of the Jesuits' Colegio now hosts the Museum of the Mexican Constitution. This overlapping of civil and religious functions experienced by the Colegio reveals cultural and political tensions—many of them inherited from the baroque period—that are still very much at work in contemporary Mexico.

The next day I strolled around in a more improvised fashion. Since the government closed the metro station at the Zócalo in a futile attempt to decrease the flow of protesters there, I ended up entering the old core of the city from Alameda Park. In front of the Palacio de Bellas Artes, at the intersection of Cinco de Mayo and Lázaro Cárdenas, I unexpectedly confronted a group of at least two hundred dancing males wearing only their *calzoncillos* or jockey shorts. Five drummers accompanied them (one of which was the only woman I could spot among the group). The shirtless, sweaty, mostly brown torsos—of all ages and shapes—sparkled under the cloudy afternoon. They called themselves the Movimiento de los 400 Pueblos (Movement of the 400 Communities) and they were demanding an *audiencia* or meeting with Manuel Mondragón y Kalb, the newly appointed secretary for national security. I talked to one of the men: he was middle aged, with a thin beard, and had a smiley photograph of Mondragón covering his crotch. He told me that the 400 Pueblos have been doing their stripped rallies since 2002. Forcefully evicted from their communities, these farmers from Veracruz were tired of being ignored and censored by a government that violates their rights. The third chapter of this work focuses on how drums, dancers, and songs enabled the Aztecs to articulate a dense and richly layered affective understanding of their history. A collection of poems known as *Cantares Mexicanos* includes compositions in which certain performative practices of the Mexicas enable surprising intercultural experimentations. To find these half-naked men gathering around their drums in order to reclaim their lands was both poignant and perplexing, a reminder of how the affective practices of the past impinge on the reclamations of the present.

The next day I visited the Universidad del Claustro de Sor Juana, a magnificent institution established among the restored remains of the convent of San Jerónimo where Sor Juana Inés de la Cruz professed and wrote her poetry, letters, and—among other *autos*—the sacramental play *The Divine Narcissus*, which is at the center of my fourth and last chapter. In her play, Sor Juana describes the first encounter between Indians and Spaniards by presenting a dance or *tocotín* that gradually changes its meaning in order to signal the conversion of the New World to Christianity. I am intentionally finishing this book with an example of baroque dramatic literature in an effort to integrate—instead of polarize—the methodologies of performance studies. Sor Juana's dancers are directly linked to the Avila brothers' masquerade, the Jesuits' procession, and the Aztecs' songs: they all belong to a performative genealogy that reenacts certain scenarios or foundational scenes in order to reconvene, solidify, or transform their history (a history that was, of course, their *present,* and is only *colonial* for us). What we experience now as testimony, document, and text was for the people living in the Viceroyalty of New Spain an ongoing process, a *being there* in which things were constantly emerging, moving, and vanishing. Looking at the ruins of Sor Juana's convent, the faded blue and green tiles attached to the walls that marked the places where the nuns lived, prayed, and waited for an everlasting inclusion in God's mercy, I craved an understanding of their past that is dynamic, embodied, and inclusive.

This book is a quest for such a living past—a past not merely lived and gone, but appreciated as *poiesis*, as labor—through an exploration of intercultural scenarios. Environments in which the constant intercultural exchanges of everyday life are intensified are particularly prone to exposing their own making—adjustments and compromises tend to be self-reflexive. My interest here is to revisit how modes of intercultural existence are worked out and experimented with; in other words, how those modes of existence rearticulate their *becoming* in order to actualize something new. How can we regain—at least partially—the motions of the past, the ways in which being was translated into action and redesigned by trade? How can we see both the specific event we are studying and the vast network of relations that made it possible? How can we catch an emergent identity while it is still taking shape, right before it acquires a definitive, recognizable form (if it ever does)? These are some of the questions this book proposes to tackle and unpack by mobilizing the ideas of Bruno Latour and his actor-network-theory. Latour offers a critique of the interactions among peoples, objects, and nonhumans that is both pragmatic and pliable, one in which becoming is conceptualized as *ergon* or collective work. It is only as collective work that a place like Mexico City—now or then—can be truly envisioned in its complexity, as a milieu, an *axis mundi*, an incessant process of unfolding and erasure.

It takes a network to write a book, and this one is no exception. To the staff at the libraries I personally visited—the Bancroft at UC Berkeley, the Archivo General de Indias in Seville, and the Library of Congress in Washington, D.C.—I owe many hours of support and help that I remember with enthusiastic gratitude. In Mexico City, Guillermo Morones Díaz and Pilar Moreno Jiménez and the staff at the Universidad del Claustro de Sor Juana welcomed me with extraordinary affection and made me feel at home. Professor Fermín Herrera's mentorship (California State University, Northridge) was fundamental for my understanding of the *Cantares Mexicanos* and the marvels of Nahuatl grammar and rhythm. Thanks to research funds provided by Dean David Marshall and the University of California (Santa Barbara) and the generous support of the Department of Chicano/na Studies, I was able to invite Professor Herrera to teach a Nahuatl introductory class on our campus. Osiris Gómez was particularly instrumental in organizing the administrative logistics of this class, and we remain *cuates*. I would like to thank the audiences that heard some portions of this book at the American Society for Theatre Research (ASTR) conference in Toronto (2010) and at the Department of Theater at the University of Texas at Austin (2012). I thank Ric Knowles and Penny Farfan for accepting for publication ("From Scenarios to Networks: Performing the Intercultural in Colonial Mexico, *Theatre Journal* 63, no. 4 [December 2011]: 499–520) a section from chapter 1 that won the Association for Theatre in Higher Education's award for Best Essay of the Year and an Oscar Brockett Honorable Mention from ASTR (both in 2012). Ric and Penny edited my work with care, rigor, and humor, and I learned from them lessons that are now part of my intellectual arsenal. Marlis Schweitzer and Joanne Zerdy included a section from chapter 3 in their collection ("Translocalized Drums: Mobilizing the Intercultural in the *Cantares Mexicanos*," in *Performing Objects and Theatrical Things*, ed. M. Schweitzer and M. Zerdy [New York: Palgrave, 2014], 214–27) and were incredibly generous and enlightening with their suggestions.

The *becoming* of a scholar is directly connected to the talent and kindness of his or her students, colleagues, and editors, and I have been extraordinarily lucky on that count. The graduate students in my two departments (Spanish and Portuguese, and Theater and Dance) have contributed to this book in innumerable ways by sharing their unlimited creativity and curiosity over the years. Kane Anderson has been particularly helpful both as a critical respondent and for his patient help in formatting this manuscript. My students are my ongoing education. Many of my colleagues at Santa Barbara (Jody Enders, Suk-Young Kim, Christina McMahon, Simon Williams, Nina Bennehaum, Christine Thomas, Jorge Luis Castillo, Juan Pablo Lupi, Suzanne Jill Levine, Antonio Cortijo, Ellen McCraken, Silvia Bermúdez) and other institutions (Catherine Cole, Emily Sahakian, Charlotte Canning, Jon Rossini, Lynette Hunter, Frank Wilderson III, Sue-Ellen Case, Susan Leigh Foster, Sudipto Chatterjee, Shannon Steen, Shannon Jackson) reacted to earlier versions of these materials with incisive and challenging commentaries. Sara Poot-Herrera's hospitality—both in California and in Mexico City—always provided a haven of joy and *amistad*. During the time I was working on the final version of this book my departmental chairs Jorge Checa (Spanish and Portuguese) and Risa Brainin (Theater and Dance) were incredibly generous in their constant advice and guidance. The anonymous readers and the editors at Northwestern University Press—Patrick Anderson, Nicholas Ridout, Michael Levine, and Anne Gendler—have been nothing less than amazing, and I thank them for believing in my project from its earlier stages. My husband Daniel Jaffe is the atmosphere that keeps me breathing, and if there is any sun and shine in this book, it belongs to him.

From Scenarios to Networks

Introduction

✦

Passing through the Network: Toward a New Historiography of the Intercultural Past

Poiesis and Becoming

This project is based on an elastic understanding of the word "poiesis," the process of making or doing something. As mobilized here, poiesis demands an account of the labors of becoming that actualize our experience, labors that we always perceive in terms of a relation between our body and an environment in which we interactively dwell. I believe that intercultural exchanges tend to increase the legibility of certain types of poiesis, the thick workings of production, maintenance, and exclusion that sustain our ecologies. I want to honor the full complexity of those entanglements of peoples, animals, objects, and geographies that both enable and disarray our living conditions. Shannon Jackson claims that "living beings . . . need their run crews."[1] The run crews of an intercultural milieu like the Viceroyalty of New Spain were dauntingly thick and multilayered; for that same reason, they offer an enhanced opportunity to grasp how a society creates and dismantles itself. But the scholar of run crews faces a double-edged challenge. If we aspire to track down every single path or hint, we run the risk of losing sight of fundamental trends and threads; at some point, we might feel an impulse to take some discursive short cuts (analogies, comparisons, summaries). Nevertheless, by occluding certain transitions and leaps, those selective readings will immediately simplify the events too.

In an intercultural setting, analogies are particularly attractive: they allow us to ponder approximations, familiarities, and proportions. Intercultural junctures can be analogically conveyed—there are *affinities* between certain masks and character roles in several theatrical traditions, for example—but those zones of convergence cannot be *explained* that way. Walter Benjamin alerted us to the fact that "relationship cannot be adequately inferred from either analogy or similarity . . . Analogy never provides a sufficient reason for relationship."[2] Any elements analogically linked—like those found in baroque emblems and allegories—are not truly connected; their semantic closeness is a mental operation induced by our thought, not an expression of their historical specificity. As Benjamin argues in his study of the German *Trauerspiel* (tragic drama), under such circumstances "any person, any object, any relationship can absolutely mean anything else."[3] Analogies mask difference and overlook power discrepancies. When we deem Soyinka to be the African Shakespeare, the analogy might be pedagogically effective but it also obfuscates the identity of both playwrights (and it assigns Shakespeare a *universal* function that Soyinka is being denied).

Ric Knowles observes that until recently many intercultural performances have been analyzed primarily as encounters in which two or more cultures find semiotic equivalences for each other. Although this is a valid approach, Knowles suggests that "what is needed is a model of scholarship that understands the multiple performances of difference, local and global, as *processes*, circulations of energy, in which previously marginalized cultures are seen to work *together* rather than *against*, constructing genuine, rhizomatic, and multiple intercultures that respect difference while building solidarity."[4] I agree with Knowles, although I recommend that we keep in mind that working *together* and working *against* are coexisting gestures, not alternative ones. Knowles's call for a processual hermeneutics of intercultural relations is indispensable, but abandoning our analogical proclivities is only a preliminary step. All becoming brings within itself an intensified simultaneity of motions and residues, an imperative to account for the fact that everything is constantly being interrupted and redeployed at the same time.

My insistence on the flowing nature of life is not just a sentimental recourse to the unrepeatable rivers of Heraclitus or the dialectics of the Hegelian *Geist* (spirit). We are *on the go*, and even when we claim to stop we serve as evidence for our movements. Under intercultural pressure objects and peoples move more than usual; they are dis-placed, re-located, and re-placed at a vertiginous—and often violent—speed. Recording those travails is our best way of avoiding any analogical shortcuts. Many of these changes are not exactly external, but epistemic: the *meaning* of the person or the object is reinstated, reversed, or dispersed. Confronting the past, we rely on those instantiations of meaning in which the inherent fluidity of becoming has been partially arrested or *slowed down*—ruins, texts, archives, bones, dances, archeological deposits, costumes. But as historians we crave more than that: we want to rescue the operations that *mobilized* those meanings. Which somatic and affective investments sustained the hands of artisans, scribes, actors, designers, and builders, the physical exertions of making things *happen*?

One of the reasons performance studies has leaned—from its inception in the 1970s and 1980s—towards ethnographic research lies in this intensified desire to be *right there* when things take place; an emphasis on the here and now of activity allows the scholar to become part of the journey, an attentive passenger instead of a distanced observer. Since my run crews in colonial Mexico have been dead for six hundred years, in this case I will have to pass. My advantage is that, due to the radical absence of the physical bodies I am interested in retracing, I have no choice but to look at a wider picture. Frequently enough (as I will discuss soon) intercultural criticism has been more focused on unpacking the reception and the ideological impact of our performances than in reconstructing the relational webs of labor and maintenance that keep those occasions going. When it comes to intercultural performances, this oversight can be deeply problematic since it has the potential to solidify a view of otherness as syncretic spectacle, an ephemeral mixing of practices that are *morphologically* similar to each other although wearing different clothes. This attitude also overlooks the most creative aspect of an intercultural performance: the establishment of new standards of identity that encompass and transform all the cultural materials involved *as they go along*. Intercultural meetings—voluntary or not—facilitate moments of *becoming-otherwise* in which foreign and domestic lines are blurred and even erased, thus confirming the fundamental hybridity of all manners of existence.

Homi Bhabha has placed hybridity at the center of his theorization of postcolonial identities, one that includes strong psychoanalytical and performative componenents,[5] and Anjali Prabhu has stressed how hybrid formations can become sites for resistance and negotiation.[6] In an influential book, Néstor García Canclini explains his preference of hybridity over *mestizaje* or racial mixing (a methodological decision particularly relevant in his Latin American context, as I will show shortly) by claiming that intercultural mixtures are not exclusively inflected by racial concerns and taxonomies. In his opinion, hybridity is the result of fractures in collective ideologies, an increasing deterritorialization of national cultures due to global redistributions, and the instantiation of what he calls "impure" practices.[7] My main concern with these insightful appropriations of hybridity is that they tend to localize the intercultural only when explicit ruptures within hegemonic discourses appear, or when an encounter *between* cultures takes place—an encounter that, more often than not, becomes legible only when the West arrives. But cultural differences—both ouside and inside the communities involved in such exchanges—are nodes of articulation that predate those encounters and actually enable or oppose them. Distinctions between pure and impure practices are not produced by intercultural relations—they are already *there* as part of a complex chain of networking operations that flow through, against, and because of them. Capturing the intricacies of these flows is one of the most demanding challenges an intercultural historiography confronts.

Once we realize that hybridity is not an exception, but the constitutive tissue of life, we are able to ask why we spend so much work hiding it under generic nouns like societies, nations, races, and genders. In this book I will not deploy hybridity as a philosophical tag, and one of my goals is to shake the implicit dichotomy signified by the term. Hybridity supposes that there is a non-hybrid state somewhere, a homogenous site that is suddenly being added to, contested, or broken down. This assumption privileges essence over becoming. Instead of biosocial plugs like hybridity or miscegenation, I want to develop a theoretical model in which intercultural differences and allocations are understood as *ergonic* and affective trajectories.

I am certainly not denying the records of racial and ethnic narratives, the extremely tangible forms in which certain contingencies—like skin pigmentation and geographic singularities—have been rigidified into taxonomies or manifested destinies. But these racial and national labels are never stable, and one of the radical signatures of any intercultural performance is to remind us that their history is still in the making. Attached to specific signifiers, peoples, and ecologies, we know these identities will be carried away and transported again, translocalized, and morphed. The shimmering transactions of everyday life are made of ripples, regroupings, tides, currents, and reversals that ensure their persistence by continuously putting it at risk through fragmentation, improvisation, and dissolution. How can we comprehend this coruscating heterogeneity without losing a sense of its momentum, the coeval pushing *from* and pushing *towards* that configures its performance?

In the field of Latin American studies, interculturality is not yet a very popular concept—other qualifications (baroque and neo-baroque, transculturation and coloniality, transnationalism and trans-americanity) have been critically preferred. It is not the task of this book to summarize the parameters of these discourses, but I would like to explain why I have decided to take a different route. More often than not, Latin American scholars have depended on an analogy between racialized models like *mestizaje* in order to develop a comprehensive theory of New World cultural identities. As a result, a biosocial category has become also an aesthetic and semiotic one; buildings, objects, and poems have been analyzed as *mixed* compositions, cross-fertilized signs that both express and amplify a communal mixing of bloods and phenotypes. This overlapping of racialized and heuristic categories has been quite fruitful, but it also contains serious limitations. Ilona Katzew, Susan Deans-Smith,[8] and Marilyn Grace Miller[9] have shown how, harnessed by nationalistic and corporatist agendas, *mestizaje* in Latin America has also served as an ideology of political assimilation that assumes and fosters a gradual lessening of indigenous, Asian, and African influences. This is a methodological trap I deliberately want to skirt here. Without entirely discarding some of the critical tools provided by *mestizaje*, I think an intercultural networking model like the one I am proposing can reduce or revise some of its most problematic dimensions. In this book I will tackle *mestizaje* as one mode of cultural classification that is coproduced *with and by* many other social discourses, not as a dominant hermeneutic principle.

Another potential setback of *mestizaje* is that it tends to essentialize racialized demarcations. As this book will attest, a certain degree of essentialization is necessary for the elaboration of intercultural concepts—but those concepts should always be seen as provisional or insufficient, not as definitive. A mestizo blend—one in which earlier Indian, African, Asian, and European factors are joined but still discernible—implicitly affirms that those previous factors were already either stable or fully decidable before they intersected each other. Our challenge is to recognize the blend without solidifying its materials into rigid genealogies and ancestries; new cultural combinations are not only modified versions of their past. A mulatto is not merely a variation of black and white antecedents—a mulatto redefines those antecedents while also positing a sense of self that inhabits its own epistemological space. As Claudio Esteva Fábregat,[10] Andrew B. Fisher, Matthew D. O'Hara,[11] and R. Douglas Cope[12] have shown, viceregal colonial authorities were occasionally quite sensitive to this predicament, and in Latin America the boundaries of racial identity were—while still tied to physical appearance—subjected to legal, gestural, and economic nuances. Joanne Rappaport argues that during the colonial period *mestizaje* was less a coherent social construct than a series of ethnoracial markers that were frequently blurred and oscillatory,[13] a situation that according to Ralph Bauer and José Antonio Mazzotti had a fundamental impact in the creolization of the Americas.[14] One of my aims in this book is to confront this notational volatility—the both/and of intercultural *mestizaje*—from a different perspective.

In her magnificent inquiry into the historiography of art in colonial New Spain, Alessandra Russo has come quite close to accomplishing a similar task. Russo articulates a critique of *mestizaje* based on the notion of the untranslatable. Since meaning was not easily transferred from one language to another, in New Spain cultural patterns and practices had to be juxtaposed and reassembled in highly unstable, unexpected ways. The semiotic density of the colonial setting led to the creation of objects that were not exactly syncretic or transcultural. In Russo's view, those objects (from feather mosaics to maps and even graffiti) were primarily material rearrangements of extremely local and pragmatic relations. Instead of classifying those objects along the lines of preexisting definitions of indigenous or European genres and traditions, Russo suggests that we should extract our own definitions *from* them. Every object "invites us to start from zero"; in order to understand them

> we will have to explore the material conditions and figurative traditions that allowed the creation of these images, the circumstances of their fabrication (time and place of production, iconographic choices), their immediate uses but also (for some of the artifacts) their displacements in order to grasp their progressive transformations. In other words, we have to return these objects and images to their *long durée*.[15]

Russo is requesting us to retrace the itineraries of each object, to acknowledge the diverse demands and *doings* involved in their formations. Her emphasis on the viceregal interactions between objects and their macro and micro histories not only aligns her work with recent projects about the Mediterranean sponsored by Peregrine Horden and Nicholas Purcell,[16] or the global panoramas of Jürgen Osterhammel,[17] but also with the holistic envisionings of contemporary Mesoamerican anthropology described by Susan Toby Evans.[18] As Leonardo López Luján indicates, this effort to study the deeper connections among objects, their function, and the networks of their production and comsumption has become particularly relevant in Mexico after the archeological discoveries made during the excavations that started at the site of the Templo Mayor in 1978.[19] This interest in assembling interactive cultural clusters has also been pursued by Diana Magaloni Kerpel in her detailed analysis of the production of the *Florentine Codex*. [20]

For Russo, the process of *mestizaje* is less about mediatory encounters between *authentic* cultural expressions than about the enactment of specific networks of collaboration and adjustment. By calling attention to how objects are reassembled and fabricated through the intensive labors of artisans and designers, Russo has made an impressive case for a methodology of intercultural affiliations without which my own work would not have been possible. It is surprising, then, that after effectively deconstructing the notion of *mestizaje* Russo herself returns to it by calling her book "a mestizo genealogy of objects" and "a mestizo history of art."[21] Once we realize that objects are their poiesis, the ways in which they are made *by* and *from* intersected narratives of cooperation and resistance, we are prepared to recognize that *mestizaje* itself is one of those objects. Should we pursue Russo's analogical pairing of *mestizaje* and *plurality*, or should we try to disclose how diversity itself is at the root of social labor? We never start from zero—we start from becoming. Insofar as the history of intercultural objects and performances has to be reactualized by an active revisiting of their process, it is their networking that needs to be prioritized. As we should see in the next section, an investment in the becoming of objects and events—what Russo has done so well in her indispensable book—is something many intercultural theorists are only recently beginning to consider more closely.

The Quest for the Intercultural

At the beginning of this introduction I stated that one of my goals is to articulate an approach to intercultural relations that takes into consideration their poiesis, the multiple ways in which objects, environments, and identities are tied together. As a first step in that direction I declared my intention to deemphasize the use of certain analogies—especially those that foster an equivalency among *mestizaje*, hybridity, and other forms of cultural expression. I am proposing instead that we see *mestizaje* and hybridity as networking devices, not only as ruptures or breaches in the alleged stability of what precedes them. Since cultures are constantly migrating and moving—and resisting those impulses too—they are at their core mixed templates, tentative renderings of a processual drive that remains open to unexpected turns and contingencies. Now we have to investigate if current understandings of intercultural exchanges contain the necessary tools to unpack and complicate these motions.

Sorting the full spectrum of intercultural discourses available today is an initiative I will not undertake here, but a succinct overview of some of the most influential trends in the field will allow me to situate my project under a clearer light. In the late 1970s, Richard Schechner and Victor Turner spearheaded an interdisciplinary call for an intercultural anthropology of performance.[22] Initially coalescing around the controversial work of Western directors like Peter Brook and Ariane Mnouchkine, many scholars conceptualized intercultural exchanges as liminal spaces—contact zones in which two or more preexistent, naturalized modes of ethnic or national interpellation transformed one another. Marvin Carlson counted at least seven degrees of interaction between the familiar and the foreign as a yardstick to measure how elements of different cultures are combined in specific intercultural events.[23] Patrice Pavis underlined issues of collaboration and authenticity.[24] For Bonnie Marranca, intercultural performance always had political undertones,[25] and Rustom Bharucha emphasized how, in their efforts to engage and utilize Eastern theatrical practices, Western practitioners tended to either recolonize or mistranslate them.[26] Eugenio Barba also developed a rich set of training techniques—called by him "theater anthropology"—based on a cross-cultural pollination of Western and Asian acting methods.[27] All these critical models posited hybridity as an *effect* of intercultural encounters, never as its source; as a result, they repressed the heterogeneous history of those same cultures, enforcing a strategic essentialization of them.

During the first decade of the new millennium, a second wave—so to speak—of intercultural discussions reacted to these foundational voices with their own demands. Recognizing the increasingly global entanglements facilitated by recent developments in communication and marketing technologies, and facing an international arena deeply divided along religious, political, and nationalistic lines in the aftermath of the 9/11 atttacks in New York City, intercultural critics had no choice but to recalibrate their methodological premises. Patrice Pavis introduced a methodology for the interpretation of non-Western performances—called "ethnoscenology"—in which complete actions are analyzed in terms of how different energies, embodiments, values, densities, and perceptions are distributed across global practices.[28] (This association of the intercultural with *non*-Western dramaturgies still identifies the cultural Other primarily in opposition to European lineages.) Counting on Lacanian models, Antony Tatlow analyzed the intersections between Brechtian and Chinese aesthetics as signs of an unconscious lack mutually repressed by East and West.[29] Mita Choudhury explored the impact of intercultural trade on the London stage during the eighteenth century.[30]

Julie Holledge and Joanne Tompkins provided a feminist and somatic slant,[31] and Christopher Balme focused on the dynamic transactions of syncretic performances.[32] Expanding and refining the links between postcolonial and intercultural discourses, Helen Gilbert and Jacqueline Lo introduced a comprehensive outlook acknowledging the existence of several forms of hybridity and the multiple spatiotemporal nuances of intercultural productions.[33] Although these authors were particularly aware of the economic inequalities sanctioned by neoliberal capitalism, and the uneven distributions of power between First and Third World theater practitioners, their efforts to improve upon previous ideas about interculturalism were still centered around readings of intercultural *representations*—in that respect, at least, they have not been that different from the critics studying intercultural performances in the 1980s and 1990s.

Under the leadership of Erika Fischer-Lichte, an international research center named "Interweaving Performance Cultures" opened at the Freie Universität in Berlin in 2008. In the 1990s, Fischer-Lichte copublished an important anthology of intercultural essays,[34] but her work in Berlin more than twenty years later reveals a deliberate and enthusiastic commitment to move beyond her earlier interventions. In response to cultural critics like Achille Mbembe and Abdelkebir Khatibi, in her most recent coedited volume Fischer-Lichte argues for an intercultural dialogue that avoids racialized binarisms and postcolonial strictures by promoting a deeper integration between artistic choices and their "ethical, social, and political implications in and beyond performance." In her view,

> interweaving functions on several levels: Many strands are plied into a thread; many such threads are then woven into a piece of cloth, which thus consists of diverse strands and threads . . . without necessarily remaining recognizable individually. They are dyed, plied and interwoven, forming particular patterns without allowing the viewer to trace each strand back to its origin. On the other hand, a process of interweaving does not necessarily result in the production of a whole. In it, mistakes, errors, failures, and even small disasters might occur when unintended knots appear in the cloth . . . That being said, it is all the more crucial to finally emphasize the *utopian dimension* at the very core of the concept of interweaving performance cultures . . . By permanently probing the emergence, stabilization, and destabilization of cultural identities, these performances can transfer their participants into states of in-betweenness . . . What is perceived as an aesthetic experience in these performances will be experienced as everyday life in the future.[35]

According to Fischer-Lichte, an aesthetic of interweaving manages to disclose how intercultural relations are *worked out*, emphasizing the transformative effects of performance and the ways in which cultures inflect each other into an imagined, rehearsed, and conjoined future. This commitment to the envisioning of an interwoven community is no doubt a response to increasing concerns about the shortcomings of multiculturalism in contemporary Europe (one already tackled, for example, by critics like Mark Terkessidis[36] in Germany and Charlotte McIvor and Matthew Spangler in Ireland).[37]

Fischer-Lichte also claims that an interweaving approach to performance cultures can take us *beyond* a pervasive methodological divide in which postcolonial discourses tend to grapple with ethical issues while intercultural discourses privilege matters of stylistic and aesthetic import. I personally believe that, at least in Latin America and the Caribbean, this alleged divide between the postcolonial and the intercultural has never been so sharply cut (as the work of Augusto Boal, Edouard Glissant, or Derek Walcott proves). In addition, I am less interested in advancing *beyond* certain critical discourses—a gesture haunted by linear, sublated, or positivistic narratives—than in repositioning those discourses (including hybridity and *mestizaje*) within a wider, more interactive and organic stance. Since my purpose is to revisit the colonial *past* of New Spain, I am inevitably writing from an archive that threatens me with the comforts of historical hindsight. I am (once all is said and done) writing *backwards*. If Fischer-Lichte's interweaving is mostly a proleptic mindset—or *utopian*—my networking has to be both retroactive and verifiable.

With its invocation of manual skills and everyday textures (cloth, fabrics) the metaphor of interweaving hails us to rethink intercultural experiences within the realm of labor. Nevertheless, for Fischer-Lichte labor is still primarily perceived in terms of mimesis (plays, events, spectacles). I will also depend on similar sources: public and private scenarios that were, from the start, ostensibly invested in intercultural transactions. The main difference between interweaving and networking is that for me those semiotic events are not the final destination of my analysis, but its actual point of departure. I want to restore the manner in which intercultural scenarios were relayed, attracted, reproduced, and reactualized by a convergence of objects, peoples, and materials that—at that *time* and in that *place*—were being experienced in the present tense through a masquerade, a procession, a danced poem, and even the rhetorical underpinnings of a dramatic text.

How can we grasp the intercultural *past* as instantiation, as becoming? Walter Benjamin's notion of the origin (*Ursprung*) can help us to confront this issue. For Benjamin, an origin is not a genesis but something that "emerges from the process of becoming and disappearance. Origin is an eddy in the stream of becoming." An origin is not a beginning, but an incision in the midst of things that has "to be recognized as a process of restoration and reestablishment . . . and precisely because of this, as something imperfect and incomplete." In Benjamin's analysis, originality is not merely the revelation of something new, but an instantiation of the unfinished quality of experience—and that unfinished quality "shows singularity and repetition to be conditioned by one another."[38] That unfinished quality, that *original* instant, is what we prefer to identify today as the *performative*: the twice-behaved, the now-again, all those *returns* that historicize the permanent collections of our change.

An intercultural scholar learns very quickly that God might have created the world ex nihilo, but we can only inhabit it in media res. The prefix "inter" encapsulates our predicament: we are supposed to be *between* cultures, but what we intend to study in this case was already taking place *within* those cultures before they met. When the Aztecs and the Spaniards fought in the flooded streets of Tenochtitlán, they were confronting each other out of their own multicultural *present*. Nevertheless, the prefix "inter" forces us to see each of these two preexisting, variegated cultures as if they were two finished vases that hit each other until their fabrics cracked. The intercultural historian is expected to explore as many scattered pieces as possible and then tease out how those pieces are gradually reglued by *mestizaje* into a third vase called contemporary Mexico. In such a vision intercultural enclaves are clusters of mediations that slowly obtain their individuality and self-sufficiency after a protracted period of starts, halts, syncretic adjustments, and political or semiotic naturalizations. From a postcolonial perspective, this condemns new cultures to live under the shadows of those mediations for the rest of their historical existence. With meridian clarity, Raymond Williams tells us how "it is virtually impossible to sustain the metaphor of 'mediation' (*Vermittlung*) without some sense of separate and pre-existent areas or orders of reality, between which the mediating process occurs whether independently or as determined by their prior natures."[39] The question here is not to find a way out of these derivative positions, but to realize that all cultures are mixed and unfolding articulations—they are constantly being *originated*, and we should not treat any of them as a completed object.

I am not looking for beginnings or mediations (although I will reserve a slot for *mediators* later on). What I define as intercultural in this book is a particular instantiation of Benjamin's *origin*, a citational moment in which elements from different cultures re-encode their relations and redirect their meanings. While still resembling their previous materials, these elements are no longer—if they ever were—semantically fixed or decidable. In their fusion, these elements are not duplicating themselves, but rehearsing a new standard of self. Their functionality has been altered and as a result they denote their becoming more ostensibly than they did before. An intensified intercultural setting reinserts history into hegemonic parameters of inclusion and exclusion: stories have to be reopened, archives have to be reorganized, and national and social plot lines have to be redrawn. This is what Deleuze and Guattari mean when they claim that "the minority is the becoming of everybody, one's potential becoming to the extent that one deviates from the model."[40] One of my proposals in this book is that intercultural subjectivities are detected as performative practices before being widely recognized as structures of feeling, and that we have to find pragmatic ways of marking these minoritarian gestures within the multifarious ebbs of social productivity. "Structures of feeling," says Williams, "do not have to await definition, classification, or rationalization before they exert palpable pressures and set effective limits on experience and on action."[41] But what exactly *prepares* us for the appearance of those structures? I will start responding to these and other questions by recasting Benjamin's *originality* as a search for emerging constructs, sites in which the twice-behaved becomes something *other* than what it was before through creative repetition, innovation, and networking.

Anaphora and Innovation

We have come to the realization that the closer we inspect intercultural formations the more we should wonder about the particularities of their poiesis, the types of labors involved in supporting the intensified manifestations of becoming brought to our attention by the arrival of new identities. Since I want to investigate intercultural conjunctions in terms of their emerging characteristics, I have intentionally resisted any exclusive reliance on analogy and hybridity as passwords for their description. I want to investigate the experiential unfolding of intercultural phenomena, mapping how they expand and fade while producing new relational entanglements along the course of their processual elaborations.

We should not assume that something *new* is always something unusual. A conceptual *slippage* between emergence and novelty is frequently committed, but the fact that something emerges is not necessarily indicative of a drastic change. It takes a lot of emergence to keep things going—otherwise the whole process of living will dissolve into indefiniteness. What I mean by *new* in this book is more a matter of grasping how cultural elements are relocated into significations they were not intended to have before; how identities that were considered rounded out are all of a sudden perceived as being made again. Michael North explores the conflicted philosophical models that from Plato to Thomas Kuhn have attempted to tame the tortuous contradictions tagged into Western discussions about novelty.[42] Is innovation a random effect, an arbitrary outcome, or something that is structurally embedded in nature? Is novelty an epistemic adjustment of our affairs (a change in the ways we tackle knowledge) or an ontological shock (a change in the substance of knowledge itself)? Is the new produced by recurrence, recombination, or inexplicable leaps? The *frisson nouveau* of modernism advertised by Baudelaire and turned into a slogan by Ezra Pound is quite different from the scientist's quest for new hypothetical blueprints that would make the foretelling of certain reactions viable. I will not participate in any of these controversies, but since innovation is at the core of my focusing on intercultural emergence, the least I could do is to recognize that the concept is not exempt from its own uncertainties.

It should be clear that my emphasis on innovation does not indicate any nostalgia for romantic swells or avant-garde manifestos, but an interest in cultural rearrangements. The task of tracking down emerging forces faces undeniable expressive demands. Emergence is easier to reproduce kinetically than verbally. I am aware that some of my sentences might seem at times too serpentine and overloaded with hyphens, but as soon as we access the mechanics of process we take the chance of increasing the opacity of our language. Before the West contacted them, Mesoamerican and East Asian builders were already raising façades in which bodies, animals, flowers, and objects collapsed into each other, reaching out for their *next* shape. It is only during the baroque period that Europe caught up with those architectures of imminence, those ebullient solids so eagerly envious of the plasticity of water. The baroque period during which my case studies took place was fully cognizant of these challenges, and it reacted accordingly by forcing words and matter to bend and melt and measure every twist of shape and wit. The New World was one of the unexpected sources of information—like the microscope and the telescope—that contributed to the emergence of baroque culture and its aspiration to include everything.

An emergent event recomposes its antecedent materials into new relational patterns, but origins are not entirely discernible. There are always segments of an emergent organization that cannot be accounted for—as a rule, innovation exceeds its determining factors and alters the horizons of its own reception. How are we expected to distinguish between distracting serendipities and transformative innovations? My idea of emergence is based on a critical alertness to the *alterative* reshuffles of repetition, how performances *change* things by bringing them back. Becoming (the passing from the virtual to the actual) is signaled by pervasive ambiguities and ambivalent leads. But in what sense is emergence a disclosure of something *new* if the world around us remains, after all, quite recognizable and available?

John H. Holland advises that although it is "tempting to take the inability to anticipate—surprise—as a critical aspect of emergence," our priority should be to spot the regularities that forge an emerging process, discarding "any incidental and irrelevant details."[43] Nevertheless, Holland himself thinks that in an emergent system, "the interactions between the parts are nonlinear, so the overall behavior [of such a system] *cannot* be obtained by summing the behaviors of the isolated components."[44] But how are we supposed to select which parts are *less* relevant for the maintenance of the whole? Holland acknowledges that "even when the simplest persistent patterns are infrequent in a generating procedure, they will eventually occur if the system runs for any length of time."[45] I will claim that it is precisely due to their nonlinear travels that behaviors reveal themselves to be not isolated at all. To say it differently: every emerging incident has its own specific inclinations, but it also replicates the complexity of the environment that mobilizes it. It is only as a result of our descriptive shortcomings that we forget that regularity is nurtured and performed by variations and contingencies.

Contrary to Holland, I want to recuperate the *incidentals* of intercultural traffic. My definition of emergence is closer to Étienne Souriau's view of process as intensified *work*. Souriau suggests that becoming is primarily experienced as labor, a cumulative sequence of modifying repetitions that slowly shape our objects, techniques, and personal styles. What we call existence is an incremental perception of our *doings*, the multiple ways in which we are constantly testing our sense of being. For Souriau, fiction and science built their becoming through different practices, but they are both examples of *instauration*, an effort to achieve a presence within the world. As a trope for instauration Souriau selects *anaphora*, a concept tinted with rhetorical, grammatical, and religious resonances. From the Greek for "carrying back," anaphora can refer to the strategic repetition of certain words or clauses along a text, the offering of bread and wine during the liturgy in Eastern Christianity, or the act of replacing a noun with a pronoun. In linguistics, anaphora is a structuring operation that enables the long-distance binding of related words.[46] Anaphors include "gaps (or empty categories), pronouns, reflexives, names, and descriptions."[47] It has been suggested that anaphoric chains are similar to some of the cognitive wirings that modulate the functions of our brain.

Souriau's anaphoric model for innovation is an efficacious strategy that defines emergence as networking. Anaphora expands its range by reappearing at different locations; it creates lines of continuity by introducing variations and informative transfers. Metonymy amplifies proximity; metaphor mixes and conflates its elements; anaphora *moves away* in order to *come back*. The intercultural scenarios studied in this book are anaphoric gestures, reassemblings of former relations into new emerging factors.[48] When a group of disgruntled descendants of the conquistadors decided to cut their ties to Philip II in 1566, they borrowed an indigenous dance that reproduced the first meeting between Cortés and Motezuma and disguised themselves as the same Indians they wanted to control. This masquerade was not just a reenactment of a previous event, but also an echoic *binding* between a past event and the quite present labors of the indigenous towns those Spaniards aspired to keep under their jurisdiction.

As I will explain later in chapter 1, repeating a colonial scenario allowed those rebellious *encomenderos* to traverse again the full praxis of their intercultural milieu, the productive alignments that actualized the emergences of their wealth. We can analyze their performance as a hybrid *show*—and it certainly was—but what strikes me the most about it is the expansive scope of their masquerade, the enormous social distances that were linked and alluded to in order to make their statement legible. Those are the anaphoric excursions I would like to retrace, and in order to do so I will tap into processual theorizations by William James, Pierre Bourdieu, Niklas Luhmann, Michel Serres, and Bruno Latour in order to describe how our communities support and reproduce themselves.

Boundaries and Performations

Intercultural scenarios—like the masquerade just mentioned in the previous section—are anaphoric genres; they leap forward by returning to themselves. In that sense, they can be mapped, retraced, traversed. We have to imagine their emergence not as a detectable point in space, but as a dynamic mingling of retroactive and proleptic tensions. After receiving a gift of relics from the pope, the Jesuits organized in 1578 a celebratory festival that harnessed most of the material resources of Mexico City. In chapter 2, I will show how during those festivities several reliquaries were covered with luscious jewels, some young Indians sang a poem in Nahuatl, and at least one actor wore a costume in which indigenous and European clothes were either contrasted or fused. Every singular instauration motivated by the Jesuits during the festival relied on the productive cycles that actualized the viceregal capital as a whole: the reliquaries, the dancers, and the costumes were areas of intentionality carved into—and *from*—the collective energies of the city. Paraphrasing William James, we can say that each of these activities was both an *all-form* and an *each-form*. Performation (the *all-form* of communal networks) preceded and continued through all those performances (the *each-form* of specific events).[49]

According to William James, "what really exists is not things made but things in the making." Following James's recommendation—"put yourself in the making"—I wonder what kind of critique will be able to address intercultural poiesis as social labor.[50] How can the *making* of a scenario be described and assessed more accurately? What is an intercultural scenario *doing*? In *The Logic of Practice* Pierre Bourdieu claims that we are always part of a *habitus*, a conditioned environment that includes our bodies and all those structuring orientations—rituals, language, sex, objects, laws—that are available to us. Many of these semantic frames have been so successfully naturalized that we hardly notice them.[51] Within their habitus, scenarios tend to play a double game: while reaffirming the past, they also reveal how that same past was once—and still is—generated. Each intercultural scenario reopens its origins to the variables of process: taking a habitus for granted is precisely what these scenarios work against.

Is an intercultural scenario something similar to what Niklas Luhmann defines as a system? Luhmann observes that all systems are self-referential: they "have the ability to establish relations with themselves and differentiate those relations from relations with their environment.[52] Systems are autopoietic—they monitor themselves from within, and their emergence is both an interruption of former states of organization and a realization of new states of complexity.[53] Systems can be preconditioned, but not predetermined; contingency provokes options and deviations, and any system will be unable to sustain itself if all its elements are rigid or fully stabilized. Nevertheless, no system can exist without zoning its boundaries either. Boundaries—like membranes—modify communication without shutting it down. Systems are also areas of containment (structures), but their process is sequential; as a result, their becoming is irreversible. Only as structures can systems be moved around, retold and reshaped into adaptable narratives and repertoires.[54] As for the rest—it flows, it passes away, and it never moves backwards.

If we accept Luhmann's view, we have to conclude that what makes historiography possible is our ability to recognize systems—to catch certain *structures*—within the vast ecological flows of our existence. We can tell our stories because we abstract our structures out of their passing in order to reutilize them. On the other hand, the history of process cannot be told because its configurations are always new—we would have to start again as soon as we try to describe it. If process is always innovation, my efforts to develop a critique of intercultural scenarios in terms of their becoming will flounder as soon as I focus my attention on any of their structural features. It all boils down again to the conflict between the all-form and the each-form: once you buy a ticket for one of them, you are immediately expected to give up the other.

This is a potential methodological impasse that for a long time stopped my research in its tracks. Is becoming more a matter for poetry than for academic scholarship? Can we actually analyze change and durability together? The book you are reading is a response to this impasse—and hopefully a philosophical passage out of it. What is usually overlooked is that some practices assume the function of addressing poiesis itself. Intercultural scenarios are *structures* reassembled in order to expose the historical process of their habitus. They allow communities to put themselves into their making, and are not delimited by their boundaries: on the contrary, scenarios intentionally replicate those boundaries in order to re-encode their networks. Intercultural scenarios are systematized transit zones in which we rediscover that nothing stands still, and their emergence has to be grasped—if at all—through a theorization of their pliable belongings and their potential to intersect other travelers.

Michel Serres has formulated a few conceptual principles that can lead us to a more efficacious unpacking of the *togetherness* of singular and collective labors. First of all, Serres is enthusiastically cognizant of the need for discourses of pliability and belonging. He starts with a basic question: how is it that we manage to live together (*all-form*) while still being so deeply installed in our own self (*each-form*)? The leap from person to collective (from *each-form* to *all-form*) is never transparent or fixed. Where exactly is our body located when we are exercising, waiting, or eating? And then there is another matter at stake—where exactly are the other bodies while we are circulating among, against, or with them? Bodies never move *just* by themselves either: they participate in multiple forms of transportation (like trains, cars, airplanes, dreams, santería) and they are never entirely isolated from objects, obstacles, mountains, rivers, and animals.

How can we explain, then, the passing from being into relation? Serres responds to this apparent riddle by denying any enduring correspondence between functions and entities. Subjects and objects are *quasi*-positions; their applicability fluctuates depending on the "network of passes"[55] through which they become and coexist. Serres compares the experience of becoming to a swimmer who "knows that a second river runs in the one that everybody sees, a river between the two thresholds [of departure and arrival], after or before which all security has vanished."[56] Serres knows that his swimmer still betrays a dualistic bent by thinking that there are only two rivers when in fact there are many. Redefining boundary as portability, Serres posits a *quasi*-world in which "the real passage occurs in the middle."[57] An indigenous example can illustrate this type of portability. When Aztec men played *ulamaliztli*—a rubber-ball game—they hit the ball with their knees, hips, and buttocks. Each side of the masonry ball court had a vertical ring attached to it: if a player managed to score through one of those rings, the game was over and he was declared the winner.[58] We know that Motezuma II and Nezahualpili (the lord of Texcoco) played a ball game in order to decide if a comet recently observed in the eastward skies was an omen announcing the demise of the Aztec Empire. Nezahualpili believed so, but Motezuma denied it—and he lost the game. [59] Were the indigenous rulers following the rubber ball, or was the rubber ball following them? Was the outcome of the game the result of chance, luck, or the will of the gods? A ball is a *quasi-subject* (it needs a person handling it in order to become the game), but the other players would be lost without it, too (they are *quasi-objects* since the ball, once thrown away, is orienting their bodies on the court). The competition takes place *within* these shifting positions—in the middle of a moving coordination between function and action. For Serres, "the quasi-object, when being passed, makes the collective, [and] if it stops, it makes the individual."[60] For Motezuma and Nezahualpili, the solid *quasi*-ball made of rubber was both the *quasi*-person hitting it back with a hip and the *quasi*-person intercepting it again with a knee, and all the spaces traversed *in-between* were the potential *future* of the Triple Alliance. Aztec history was being played out in the *middle* of the game.

We are not enclosed by our habitus and our systems; we are carrying them while they are carrying us. Serres utilizes *quasi*-objects and *quasi*-subjects to stress how portable our identities are, how much of our sense of existence is inflected by relational patterns that work—when they do—due to their potential for elasticity and adaptability. We occupy many intersections at the same time, and our roles tend to shift along the way. The concept of *quasi*-entities authorizes a critical discourse in which hybridity is treated as an enabling function, not as a deviation from some kind of primordial essence that is being dismantled or canceled. I feel that neither Bourdieu nor Luhmann make enough room for a robust description of how networks move from one connection to another. Both authors recognize the becoming of social interactions, but once they start to study those interactions they almost freeze them into highly specific moments or settings. Bourdieu and Luhmann are not sociologists of the *while*—their models explain outcomes, not transitions. For a methodology of transitions more in tune with Serres's *quasi-* we will explore the ideas of Bruno Latour, a philosopher of science whose work lies at the core of this book.

By Means of Latour: Actors, Translations, Mediators, and Scripts

I firmly believe that Bruno Latour's actor-network theory is an excellent point of departure for an intercultural critique invested in paying attention to the emergence of new identities. Some readers might find my engagement with an author mainly known as a theorist of science intriguing, even risky. What exactly has Latour to do with intercultural scenarios? Since his work includes forays into philosophy, politics, sociology, religion, aesthetics, and anthropology, it will be difficult to anchor him exclusively to any of these practices.[61] Latour's engagement with the works of Machiavelli, Hobbes, and Carl Schmitt has been considered controversial, and his defense of institutional reforms over more radical political options is well known.[62] Nevertheless, the motivation for my interest in Latour is quite precise: he has been able to build a refreshingly pragmatic approach to social transitions.[63] Contemporary debates on becoming have been almost monopolized by the conceptualizations of Deleuze and Guattari—and I myself will count on them in my final chapter—but I argue that Latour offers an epistemic tool kit that is equally useful and certainly more concise then theirs, one in which each-forms and all-forms are blended from the start.

Since the 1990s, Latour has been developing a methodological project that aspires to reveal the conceptual contradictions of modernity. In *We Have Never Been Modern* (1993), Latour indicates that normative distinctions between nature and culture—so central to traditional scientific and humanistic discourses—are based on a persistent disregard for the *in-between* modalities of life. Latour also points out that modernity's insistence on validating either/or models of knowledge actually increases the number of hybrids that actively challenge those same dualistic imperatives. Latour defines this ironic predicament as a contrast between translations (the transfers that make the circulations of meaning possible) and purifications (a tendency to introduce sharp separations between things, persons, and animals). Purifications prefer binary constructions—like human/nonhuman and object/subject—while translations tend to expand and proliferate as they "shuttle back and forth" through their networks.[64] To occlude these translations is, in Latour's opinion, one of the main characteristics of the modern mind, one that leads—curiously enough—to a misleading understanding of "every hybrid as a mixture of two pure forms."[65] Restoring those translational textures denied by purification is one of Latour's most urgent demands.

We Have Never Been Modern revamps the axiological foundations of modernity by reminding us that neither science nor nature are objective realms that can be isolated from our own attitudes—objectivity is, after all, our own invention. Latour thinks that objectivity has its gains and its losses—it has a *quasi*-status, not an absolute one. Latour's positing of a critical discourse in which hybridity remains constitutive—neither exceptional nor ever erased—allows him to propose an anthropology of mediators, "actors endowed with the capacity to translate what they transport, to redefine it, redeploy it, and also to betray it."[66] A network moves because its relations are elastic; objects and subjects are distributive functions, not permanent states.[67] There is a plurality of *quasi*-options, metamorphic transfers, and translational permutations that cannot be forced into rigid schemes. And we don't behave like mediators all the time; at some points we are more like *intermediaries* and we passively convey our meanings without drastically altering them—until we become mediators once again.

Borrowing from Michel Serres's work, in *We Have Never Been Modern* Latour encourages a conceptual outlook that emphasizes exchange over certainty, but it will take him several years to refine these arguments into a more subtle exploration of networking. It is not until *Reassembling the Social: An Introduction to Actor-Network-Theory* (2005) that Latour offers a detailed disclosure of how relations can be studied. He begins by resisting dominant definitions of the social. A society exists only to the extent that certain connections are being acted out—the social is not a basic substance or an ingredient that can be isolated from its motions. When we feel that our society is guiding us with an invisible hand this only means that we are not being specific enough. The productive vectors that keep us moving are always there to be followed or adumbrated if we are patient and willing to restore them: "to the convenient shorthand of the social, one has to substitute the painful and costly longhand of its associations."[68] Society—like religion, like capitalism, like theater—is something that has to be restored and reassembled.

Latour elaborates a cartographic modeling of networks, one based on the shifting gradients of activity that articulate our relations. Each network has to be carefully recuperated in order to become legible again. To be consistent with this approach, Latour introduces a series of categories or uncertainties that promote an investigation of how networks are to be retraced. Some of these categories are defined by a convergence of vectors (directional flows) and relays (sites of exchange). Groups, for example, are provisional gatherings of conflicted tendencies and they are qualified by noise, contradiction, and unpredictability. Actions are never individual or autonomous: they are more like knots or nodes of entangled agencies. While we are used to seeing groups and actions as indexes of volitional exertions, Latour also welcomes objects and inanimate elements as participants in the becoming of networks: "any thing that does modify a state of affairs by making a difference is an actor—or, if it has no figuration yet, an actant."[69] Objects have no will of their own—although future technologies might change this—but they indeed facilitate our narratives through their circulation and by assisting us in the anaphoric instaurations of labor. (For Latour, an *agent* is something or someone that modifies a relation.) As we will see in chapter 3, drums were quite important objects for the Aztecs;[70] through them they coordinated long-distance communications with their neighbors, and drumming was part of a pedagogical system that trained Indian dancers to see themselves as trans-localizing bodies, portals for the transports of a created world that was not unlimited and had to be refurnished by our affective interventions.

Latour recommends that when deploying any of these categories we should emphasize their performative capabilities.[71] A network is not something we can grasp while at rest; networks have to be caught in the act, and most of their features can be relayed, taken over, and replicated by other means. Latour believes that both scientists and post-humanist scholars can find common critical grounds through an informed unpacking of the collective performations all their performances emerge from. His epistemic preference for actors has a dramaturgical slant: "an actor on stage is never alone in acting. Play-acting puts us immediately into a thick imbroglio where the question of who is carrying out the action has become unfathomable."[72] Latour likes actors for the same reason that J. L. Austin didn't: their statements and their deeds are neither true nor false—but they influence us nonetheless.[73] Actors are more than one person and one function; they work both as subjects and objects. Actors do *quasi*-things for a living; in Schechner's words, they are *not* their roles and *not-not* their roles.[74] It is this liminal condition that Latour wants to place at the center of our research, a prescriptive alertness to the boundaries we inhabit while we are traveling.

Latour is adamant about insisting that a network is not an entity but "a string of actions where each participant is treated as a full-blown mediator . . . If an actor makes no difference, it's not an actor." What we call the social is nothing less than the residue of translations that are already slipping away. Networks are "not made of nylon thread, words or any durable substance but [are] the trace left behind by some moving agent."[75] In spite of this emphasis on the shortcomings of our knowledge, Latour is far from claiming that our positional uncertainties make the acquisition of reliable facts unreachable. After all—and the example is mine—if one jumps off a cliff the options available to our falling bodies are quite evident and hard to negate. But matters of fact don't tell their stories by themselves; facts obtain our interest and their coherence under certain circumstances and only when they are perceived as matters of concern. Our standards of appreciation qualify our data, and those standards are fabricated within a network of associations that prioritizes them in a particular fashion. Empirical investigations can still be exact, but our concerns will obscure some details while rehabilitating or revealing others.

A field of uncertainties, mediators, translations, and moveable functions: such is the picture Latour draws for us in *Reassembling the Social*, one I will utilize to refocus our concerns about intercultural negotiations, looking at certain historical facts from a different perspective. What kind of description can convey the polyrhythmic beats of a network? Can we really write about it? Latour himself has experimented with fictional devices in his *Aramis or the Love of Technology* (1996), a text in which a Parisian transportation system becomes a character among many other voices and institutions.[76] I will not go that far, but in chapter 4 I am taking the step of treating a play as if it were a *fact*, a piece of evidence for intercultural matters of concern in colonial Mexico. Sor Juana Inés de la Cruz wrote the sacramental play *The Divine Narcissus* towards the end of the seventeenth century. Intended as a theatrical exposition of the miraculous gifts of the Eucharist, the play audaciously mixes an Indian dance, an Ovidian myth, references to the Old and the New Testaments, and a masterful command of poetic diction in order to produce a circum-Atlantic dramaturgy. One of my objectives in the last chapter of this book is to reanimate the skills of textual analysis that performance studies has tended to relegate—albeit never entirely—to the back corridors of our academic departments. Latour says that "novels, plays, and film from classical tragedy to comics provide a vast playground to rehearse accounts of what makes us act,"[77] and I don't see any reason why we should not consider a dramatic text as another form of relay.

Elusive, faster than us, a network is in a constant state of transition while we float on it, flow with it, and emerge as part of it. The currents of a network are multidirectional and their vectors can be localized when they meet other vectors and a particular relay is actualized—then everything moves on again. Latour challenges us to keep all those motions at hand, to see groups, actions, and objects in their kinetic, interactive becoming, as they reach another *origin* and then vanish. The network is not a substance nor an essence: we can find it only to the extent that we are able to refigure it, and our selected facts will be deeply inflected by the matters of concern that spurred our initial questions.

Latour has considered other potential names for his actor-network-theory (or ANT, as it is also known): "actant-rhyzome ontology," "sociology of translation," or "sociology of innovations," and even "associology."[78] His latest methodological contribution is probably his most ambitious one. *An Inquiry into Modes of Existence: An Anthropology of the Moderns* (2012) is both a synthesis of his previous work and an attempt to replace ANT with a more inclusive model. Although my book is mostly a response to ANT, a panoramic overview of Latour's new proposals can expand our understanding of networks. Latour admits that ANT's quest for a flat, horizontal—as opposed to a vertical or hierarchical—display of vectors and relays was devoid of a nuanced analysis of how performation and performance solicit each other. How are mediators attracted, played with, overlooked, carried away? Why do some translations seem to be more lasting than others? Why, in spite of our uncertainties, are we still capable of determining certain domains of knowledge, specialized cultural practices like theater, law, science, and religion? We live within the becoming of all these discourses, but their porous boundaries are signified by contrasting values that seem to *survive* the discontinuities of their materialization often enough.

Are our epistemic labels really as fluid as we claim them to be?[79] Our contingent world is not exactly a chaotic one—although it can do *unexpected* things.[80] When we observe our becoming across long spans of time and space, stability and instability look more like strange bedfellows than adversaries. It might be excusable if we occasionally believe—like the Sicilian prince played by Burt Lancaster in Visconti's film of the novel *Il Gattopardo*—that everything has to change in order to remain the same. A typical reaction to the infinite variety of perceptions and values that configure our experience has been to conceptualize them as partial aspects of a common substance that grounds everything, something Latour describes as a "pluralism of representations" expressing a "monism of being."[81] The result of this implicit attitude is that we *talk* about process but we still structure our scholarly insights by *suspending* it.

We frequently analyze *inter* cultures as *mixed* representations of their monistic predecessors—and we do so because the emergence of new identities is the result of continuities and discontinuities that are almost impossible to describe simultaneously. In *An Inquiry,* Latour tackles this ontological problem by eliminating the concept of substance altogether—there is no common ground, only *beings* that pass through each other in order to persevere and maintain themselves. Recruiting Souriau's ideas about modes of existence, Latour argues that "in order to exist, a being must not only pass by way of another . . . , but also in another manner . . . by exploring other ways, as it were, of altering itself."[82] Since "subsistence always pays for itself in alteration," value fluctuations denote sites in which networking is being intensified.[83] Latour asks us to imagine that we are taking a hike up Mont Aiguille, a high limestone mesa formation south of Grenoble (France). We are following a map of the region. The map is not a representation of the mountain—the topography lying ahead of us has been rescaled, translated to a different code that has its own rules. The map is not a substitute for the mountain (or vice versa). At its best, the relation between the chart and the mountain is based on an emphasized chain of references that make sense under very specific conditions. The map and the mountain stand for two different protocols of veridiction, two different standards of efficacy. It is precisely because they are not equivalent to each other that we can place ourselves between the chart and the limestone bulk in order to get *there* from *here*.

By enacting a translation between the mountain and the map we have earned our *quasi*-role as mediators. If we rush to analogize the chart to the mountain, we will be missing our intervention, the creative hiatus that transformed the terrain into such a map. Our personal connection to both sources of information is ambulatory; our eyes move back and forth between chart and land, two different axiological systems that allude to each other by endorsing "a form of transubstantiation" in which "the signs inscribed on the waterproof paper are gradually *charged* . . . with certain properties of Mont Aiguille."[84] The connections between Mont Aiguille and our map are anaphoric, not merely mimetic. Imitation is *translational*: the chart is reproducing the being of the mountain *through* the being of another medium.

Latour's efforts to re-encode repetition as reproduction opens the possibility for a non-analogical critique of emerging intercultural values. In an intercultural situation two or more states of being rescale each other, translating their former modes of existence into new forms of togetherness.[85] Although not discussed in this book, the Virgin of Guadalupe is a well-known example of this process. When the hill of Tepeyac on the outskirts of Mexico City was remapped as a Catholic sanctuary, a local intercultural overlapping of the Indian goddess Tonantzin and the Virgin Mary was certainly taking place. But as Jeanette Favrot Peterson has shown, the dark-skinned Guadalupe was not only replacing and merging two previous motherly images.[86] Many Mesoamerican deities combined traits from several indigenous cults, and the black Virgin was a medieval figure closely associated with the wars of the Spaniards against the Arabs in Extremadura. The hybridity of Guadalupe was not just beginning in Tepeyac—it was *continuing*.

I would like to consider intercultural translations as modifiers of veridiction, instaurations of new modes of attachment—like the Virgin of Guadalupe—in which cultures *pass* through one another. While intercultural scenarios *verify* alterative standards of belonging, their discontinuous reassembling is both supportive of and supported by the continuities of social performation. Aztecs and Europeans were thus *re-produced* as New Spain through the slow confirmations of masquerades, processions, dances, and plays. The Virgin of Guadalupe marked a moment (among many others) in which Indians and Spaniards realized that their performations were unmistakably entangled: they were no longer able to perform anything without each other. The Guadalupe became a figuration for that new state of being, a prepositional script that has *oriented* Mexican history from the wars of independence until the present day.

Each intercultural scenario analyzed in this book traces a similar transition from relay to prepositional script. A scenario navigates and shapes its networks very much like a ball that is being passed from player to player, varying its meaning with every move. The ball and the persons who disrupt and direct its trajectory are reassembling their game together. Subjects and objects merge, follow each other, and carry along their boundaries while showing flexible gradients of *quasi*-specificity. According to Latour, "scripts obtain duration through what does not last."[87] Scenarios are reassembled in order to actualize a *passing*: one of their functions is to ensure movement, to translate. Once scripted, intercultural scenarios are experienced as statements of veridiction, embodied constatives of a shared origin that has to be readdressed. Their processual circulation re-encodes contingency as genealogy while offering, once more, an occasion for emergence.

Reassembling the Past: Scenarios and Networks

Horizontal vectors, transitory relays, flattened relational patterns linked by their portable boundaries, mediators vested with *quasi*-roles that oscillate and jump around without being either entirely dissolved or entirely fixed, scripts with prepositional capabilities: Latour's networks are translational engines that are constantly in motion and passing from one form to another. I find Latour's actor-network-theory attractive because it portrays the social as poiesis, a series of labors. ANT provides a methodology of transitions, a critical discourse in which cultural structures are manifestations of flow, not closure. Change and continuity are equally recalcitrant, and the challenge for the scholar is not to choose one over the other, but to travel along with both of them. Intercultural scenarios demand a historiography of emerging identities because their repositions are primarily motivated by a desire to re-actualize the past in terms of today's work.

Graham Harman tenaciously postulates that Latour is *not* a philosopher of becoming. According to his argument, Latour defends the radical singularity of every entity. The characteristics of each actor (human or nonhuman) are only sustainable within a highly specific set of relations. If those relations change, the actor changes with them. Once transformed, the new actor is as unique as the previous one. Like the individual frames in a film, each singular actor occupies a self-contained instant. Harman claims that our error is to believe that there is a projector somewhere (a *process*) that helps every frame to become part of a *moving* picture. The fundamental concreteness of every actor has to be *breached* in order for any relations to appear and inflect how actors are linked. In Harman's view, the reason so many mediators are needed is that no actor is automatically close to the other actors—the gaps between beings have to be translated into a relation every single time.[88] Networks *seem* fluid because their relational configurations are constantly being reinvented.

Harman's debunking of becoming is logistically impressive and it made me pause on more than one occasion. Does this mean that I have been wrong all along? I find Harman's understanding of becoming too cinematic and restrictive. I am willing to accept that process is not a primordial substance, a fluid that contains and grounds all our motions. Still, our affective life is not experienced as a series of snapshots. We *feel* like swimmers. My work with drums, mugs, feathers, and scripts should not be seen as an engagement with the object-oriented critique recently spearheaded by Harman himself[89] and other thinkers like Levi R. Bryant[90] and Jane Bennett.[91] My book is an epistemic exploration of intercultural scenarios, not an ontological inquiry. Besides, I am still doubtful of any attempts to talk about objects from an *impersonal* point of view, as if those objects were somehow unmediated by our intentionality. I am more inclined to keep myself in the picture—since I am part of it through the networks I am passing through while I write—and my approach is closer to the phenomenological attitude of someone like Sara Ahmed,[92] or Paul Connerton's[93] view of objects as expressions of expanded embodiments.

In his book about Latourian metaphysics, Graham Harman pays relatively little attention to *Reassembling the Social*, a book in which Latour develops a veritable poiesis of collective labor based on how networks move around. And both Latour and Harman are not too interested in how affect influences their actors and motivates them to translate. This allows both of them to evade the *specifics* of culture (gender, class, race) too easily, a serious flaw in a methodology that aspires to explain how mediators *work*.[94] Harman's and Latour's emphasis on relational forces is also strangely devoid of a complementary theorization of power. What really matters is to remember that becoming is not a container that encloses our actions, but a series of translations that reorganize our vectors and relays. If we remain within these translational parameters, ANT can still offer relevant pragmatic cues for the intercultural scholar.

Some readers might speculate why I am dancing to Latour's tunes while other conceptual implementations of becoming are available, especially in the indispensable work of Manuel DeLanda.[95] DeLanda has provided a comprehensive theorization of social interactions based on assemblages that include both functional and expressive elements. For DeLanda, assemblages are made of external relations, not internal links. Every connected part can be relocated without losing its singularity. All the components of an assemblage are thus detachable, and a network is shaped by their recurrence and adjustment. DeLanda explicitly requires that we pay less attention to how things emerge—their *origins*—in order to describe in detail the maintenance operations that sustain each assemblage.

As persuasive as I find many of DeLanda's arguments, his ideas are heavily indebted to Deleuze's ontological ruminations, and I have intentionally preferred to access my materials from a position that emphasizes their *performative* characteristics, a dimension Latour's ANT underlines quite consistently. In the end, though, neither Latour nor DeLanda have vested their philosophical care on explaining how an assemblage can be experienced as an affective zone of innovation in which external relations *coalesce* into alterative forms of belonging. Supplementing that gap with an analysis of intercultural scenarios is one of the primary goals of this book.

The most important lesson I have learned from ANT is that in order to analyze a network we have to reassemble it. Like one of those blurred rooms drawn by Alberto Giacometti, a network emerges out of a swirl of traces, a bundle of crisscrossing vectors and relays that are constantly adopting different shapes and directions. Objects, humans, and nonhumans are all actors—they modify each other incessantly. Nevertheless, Latour has to be *fleshed* out, and to compensate for some of his flaws I will bring to the conversation—among others—the voices of Giorgio Agamben, Alfred North Whitehead, David Graeber, Brian Massumi, Susan Leigh Foster, Gilles Deleuze, and Félix Guattari. It should be evident by now that this book owes an incommensurable debt to Diana Taylor and her pioneering conceptualization of scenarios. All my networks are intercultural scenarios, and this book proposes four distinctive types of translational approaches to them: prepositional analysis (chapter 1); figurative interpretation (chapter 2); affective entrainments (chapter 3); and geochronic discourses (chapter 4). These approaches supplement each other, but can also be deployed on their own; they respond to Latour's ideas but also depart from them when necessary.

The first chapter ("Networking the Scenario: The Avila-Cortés Insurrection") takes as its point of origin (in the sense Walter Benjamin gave to this word) a rebellion against Philip II planned by two brothers of Spanish extraction in Mexico City. In 1566 the Avila siblings were accused and ultimately sentenced to death for their participation in a conspiracy that attempted to turn the Viceroyalty of New Spain into an independent kingdom. The most important piece of evidence held against them during their trial was a masquerade organized in honor of Martín Cortés (the son of the conqueror of Tenochtitlán with his second Spanish wife). What makes this masquerade so intriguing is the fact that most of its elements were borrowed from an indigenous dance or *mitote* that by that time was already closely associated with the first encounter between Emperor Motezuma and Hernán Cortés. I am proposing that the masquerade was not only a mimetic representation of Indian customs but also a reproduction of the economic structures that united Indians and Spaniards to the *encomienda* or land distribution system established during the first decades after the conquest. The Avila brothers intercepted a series of objects, costumes, masks, and even mugs to indicate the sources of their wealth and to allure others to join their ambitious agenda. By seeing this *mitote* as a vectorial scenario in which gestures and objects can be read as *prepositional* props—markers of specific goals, social labors and orientations—I am able to extract from the descriptive details of the event a relational map that uncovers the complex performations involved in the assembling of the masquerade.

If chapter 1 emphasizes the study of vectors, chapter 2 underlines the function of relays. "Reassembling the Bones: The Festival of the Relics" focuses on a procession organized by the Jesuits in Mexico City in 1578 that celebrated the arrival to the viceregal capital of a shipment of relics sent by the pope. The Jesuits were relatively new to their city, and this festival was a grand opportunity to mark their space within it. My discussion of the festival centers on the wide variety of reproductive actions that accompanied the procession, from the creation of luxuriantly made reliquaries to enthusiastic—if not particularly inspired—literary contests. Of all the activities enacted during the festival, I pay special attention to a group of young Indians that danced to the tune of a song in Nahuatl, a hagiographic play written by the Jesuits, and an allegorical dress. What all these performances have in common is how they instantiate incipient alterations of both Indian and European practices and perceptions. I suggest that new identities can be experienced first as *figures* of becoming, performances that bring into visibility—sometimes fleetingly, sometimes for longer periods—the ergonic and transformative processes that sustain their intercultural environment.

Chapter 3 ("Indian Weddings and Translocalized Drums: Mobilizing the Intercultural in the *Cantares Mexicanos*") centers on an investigation of objects as agents or *mediators*. The Aztec song-dances preserved in a manuscript collection of poetry known as the *Cantares Mexicanos* are justly famous for the outstanding beauty of their images and the almost perplexing capacity of their language to merge and connect a wide variety of references to warriors, flowers, animals, places, and historical memories. I read closely one specific song that tells the story of a group of travelers that crosses the Atlantic, survives a hurricane, and then pays their respects to the king of Spain and the pope in Rome before returning to Mexico, thus signaling the emergence of a circum-Atlantic network. This song was part of a kinetic regime that among the Aztecs reproduced the energies of creation by passing a common substance from form to form. Their commitment to cosmic recycling motivated the Aztecs to institutionalize a system of affective entrainments in which drums and bodies were collaborators in a process of moving around—or *translocalizing*—the powers that supported the material world.

The Aztecs saw their dancing bodies as portable boundaries through which things and peoples traveled while redefining the meaning of their time and space (a portable, pliable effect that I have called *geochronicity*). Chapter 4 ("Geochronic Scripts: Sor Juana Inés de la Cruz and *The Divine Narcissus*") expands this category to the study of a dramatic text. It is my belief that scripts are also relays, and as such we can network them by observing their vectorial operations. In *The Divine Narcissus* the Mexican nun Sor Juana Inés de la Cruz adapts the quintessential Western myth of self-contemplation into a figure for the role of geography in the expansion of Christianity. The play is an *auto sacramental* that praises the spiritual gifts of the Eucharist by introducing a group of Indians singing a *tocotín*, an indigenous dance related to rhythms and poetic images very similar to those found in the *Cantares Mexicanos*. Deploying a rich metaphoric tapestry made of echoes and replacements, Sor Juana manages to reproduce the origins of New Spain by designing a text in which the transportations of sound replicate the becomings of intercultural history.

Although each chapter deals with a different scenario, Aztec dancing ended up having an anaphoric function that traverses the complete book. The Avila brothers incriminated themselves in front of the colonial authorities by imitating a *mitote*; a song in Nahuatl was danced to in the middle of the festival of the relics; besides their ceremonial drums Aztec dancers and singers actualized their own chains of translocalized referents; and Sor Juana Inés de la Cruz started her religious play with an indigenous *tocotín*. I am not a dance scholar, but networks are choreographies of becoming, and the ubiquitous presence of moving bodies in this book is not serendipitous. My aim has not been to study dance per se but to visit some intercultural instaurations in which emerging identities have been tried out.

Echoing Dwight Conquergood, I excavated my documents very closely in order "to recuperate the *saying* from the *said*, to put mobility, action, and agency back into play."[96] Intercultural scenarios are instaurations of an innovative *now* based on a comprehensive reassembling of the communities that nurture them. The four chapters illustrate ten conceptual *axioms* that contribute to emphasize this fact: (1) networks are made of nonlinear vectors and relays that circulate by means of translational operations; (2) in a network, singularities (performances) always emerge within collective efforts (performations); (3) networks are primarily mobilized by mediators or intermediaries; (4) in a network all positions—human or not—are partial (*quasi-*) agents prone to participate in several trajectories and entanglements; (5) in a network boundaries are portable zones in which flows increase their gradients of pliability; (6) within networks, intercultural scenarios reproduce themselves through anaphoric citations, not only mimetically; (7) intercultural scenarios are reassembled figurations; (8) intercultural scenarios are nodes of experiential veridiction and innovation; (9) intercultural scenarios reinsert process into narratives of identity; and (10) intercultural scenarios provoke an effect (geochronicity) in which time and space are affectively transformed and/or intensified.

I could have circumscribed this research project to the five categories wisely selected by Charlotte N. Canning and Thomas Postlewait for the historiography of performance (archive, time, space, identity, narrative).[97] I actually address all of them in this book, but these are general categories for the *representation* of the past, and intercultural scenarios are not only recording something that already happened—they are *becoming* it again. It is important to keep in mind that while these four chapters engage some of ANT's uncertain categories, they also call attention to some conceptual aspects that Latour's theories are also neglecting. As a scholar of the baroque, I find ANT's dynamic approach extremely empowering, since it provides the instrumental bones for a general reconstruction of remote scenarios. Nevertheless, the limitations of ANT are also quite evident: the bones are still too bare. What exactly turns some vectors into relays? Why are some relays revisited so often that they mutate into scripts that can be followed and recycled? Attractions and rejections are not automatic, and not every relevant historical event ends being reassembled as a scenario. Values are standards of appreciation; in order for those standards to be worked out scenarios have to be capable of eliciting responses that are both pragmatic and affective.

ANT rarely deals with the affective dimensions of networks, and my book is in part a reaction to this lack. One of the most salient characteristics shared by Mesoamerican and European cultures was their commitment to the artistic vestments of political spectacle. As documented by Enrique Florescano[98] and Roy Strong,[99] public demonstrations of power were lavishly programmed and enhanced on both sides of the Atlantic. Jacques Rancière has described this becoming-together of politics and aesthetics as a "system of self-evident facts of sense perception that simultaneously discloses the existence of something in common and the delimitations that define the respective parts and positions within it." Politics borrows from the arts "what they have in common: bodily positions and movements, functions of speech, the parceling out of the visible and the invisible."[100] Since both politics and aesthetics implement highly specific regimes of perception, they are modes of existence with strong translational affinities. Chapters 1 and 2 are particularly invested in showing how vectors and relays depend on highly *aestheticized* labors in order to mobilize their networks.

Another issue hardly touched by ANT is how vectors and relays encode time and space. The anaphoric nature of scenarios provokes a reorganized perception of temporality. Scenarios actualize chains of reference that are both retroactive and proleptic. While recalling the aftermaths of the past, scenarios rehearse an imagined future by harnessing the networks of the present. This chronological density furnishes every scenario with a potential to enclose drastic ideological disparities. A scenario can be both a survival strategy and an enforcer of techniques of oppression, an effort to protect conservative agendas and a channel for utopian messages. Even when attached to a single place and date—like Pierre Nora's memory spaces or *lieux de mémoire*—scenarios enact subtle proxemic manipulations. A performed scenario sanctions a translational ethos in which bodies and objects are invited to participate in several narrative lines simultaneously, thus occupying deeply elastic deictic vectors (right *here* and over *there*). It is through their aggressive interpellation of these spatial and temporal boundaries that scenarios manage to access the full spectrum of their historical becoming, and it would be a serious oversight not to ponder how *quasi*-subjects and *quasi*-objects are both semantically and kinetically carried on by them. Chapters 3 and 4 tackle this question by developing an intercultural category (geochronicity) in which *time-as-space* and *space-as-time* are tightly fused.

How much the music of the networks will replace the music of the spheres remains to be seen. Networks probably sound more like Elliott Carter than Franz Schubert. In Carter's second string quartet, the four instruments play together (more or less) but none of them serves as accompaniment for the others. The listener has no traditional melodies to hang onto; nevertheless, a splendid emergent world is being actualized through daring collisions of pitch and pulse. I think intercultural scenarios are regimes of affective entrainment, heuristic zones in which new identities are figured out, gathered, and tested. Rebinding their communities by means of a guided reproduction of their origins (a political performance if there is any), intercultural scenarios reveal a disposition to match bodies, objects, and practices quite closely (a process that emphasizes their aesthetic capital). Persons, reliquaries, feathers, costumes, drums, and even mugs can serve as *ergonic* indicators, rescaled signifiers of the collective performations each event intersects in order to emerge.

Although this propensity of objects and peoples to stand in for the forces involved in their material reproduction is far from being exclusive to intercultural scenarios, one of the aims of this book is to prove that within those scenarios this potential becomes especially prominent. This book utilizes ANT as a springboard, not as a dogma, but I expect my readers to follow my scenarios while they are moving, and to rehearse a new intercultural methodology based on prepositional vectors, relaying figurations, affective entrainments, and *geochronic* scripts. I believe our becoming will disclose its networks to those that reimagine them creatively (like poets and musicians) while conceptualizing them with axiological precision (like philosophers and scholars). As Franco Moretti says, "theories are nets, and we should evaluate them, not as ends in themselves, but for how they *concretely change the way we work*: for how they allow us to enlarge [our] field, and re-design it in a better way, replacing the old, useless distinctions (high and low; canon and archive; this or that national literature . . .) with new temporal, spatial, and morphological distinctions."[101] Our intercultural predecessors and the objects they lived with can still talk to us if we are willing to accompany them.

Chapter 1

✦

Networking the Scenario: The Avila-Cortés Insurrection

This one starts with an arrest. On July 16, 1566, Martín Cortés y Zúñiga, second Marquis of the Valley of Oaxaca, was invited by three *oidores* or functionaries of the Audiencia—the king's council—in Mexico City to read with them in their headquarters a document they falsely claimed had been recently received from Spain. Cortés entered the Audiencia and was immediately ordered to relinquish his sword, because of his supposed participation in fomenting rebellion. The marquis expressed his surprise while walking to his cell.[1] Less than twenty years after the death of his legendary father, the legitimate heir of Hernán Cortés was imprisoned in the same lands his ancestor had conquered. The events that unfolded after his detention include a series of interrogations, tortures, and executions that seriously compromised the civic stability of the capital, inciting Philip II to tighten his vigilance over the Viceroyalty of New Spain.

My interest in this circum-Atlantic crisis is based less on its thriller-like features than on the fact that a substantial number of the accusations directed at the marquis and his presumed collaborators were based on the observation of several public performances. Masquerades, pageants, and even the perambulations of Cortés himself through the streets of Mexico City were reinterpreted as deliberate displays of secrecy that enabled the conspirators to test the waters of opinion and to recruit supporters while playing cards, drinking heavily, and organizing mock battles. The so-called Cortés insurrection had a plein air quality that both baffled and mesmerized its investigators in the sixteenth century—and afterward. The rebels organized some of their activities as probes into emerging social significations, tentative tryouts that invested bodies, clothes, and other everyday objects with an experimental quality. I want to conjure up the manifold ways in which several gatherings of friends and relatives were encoded as proleptic acts (they hinted at situations yet to come) and facsimilar convocations (they purposely echoed past scenarios). The rebels knew that forms of entertainment are also forms of attachment that have the capacity to insinuate new political allegiances.

Theatricality became in their hands a clever and in some instances lethal instrument to sponsor semiotic and affective uncertainties. The conspirators wanted to impose a new identity on the Viceroyalty of New Spain, but it was their misfortune that their attempt at a coup d'état was mainly successful only as a coup de théâtre.

I also see the Cortés insurrection as an opportunity to tease out some theoretical questions about how performance works, and to what extent current critical models in the field of performance studies, such as Diana Taylor's scenarios, can actually increase our understanding of how intercultural relations are enacted. As we know, performative events are truly graspable only while they are happening. A performance is constantly emerging, rolling, vanishing. Theory and practice are tied together, in this case, by a shared anxiety: the need to understand *process*. It is by working itself out that performance becomes legible. My main purpose is to explore the possibility of finding an analytical language that honors, as effectively as possible, the *becoming* of performance itself. After highlighting some of the most salient events related to the Cortés insurrection (and taking my lead from Bruno Latour's actor-network-theory), I will argue that intercultural scenarios are better served by a methodology that supplements their critical unpacking with a careful remapping of the relational ties that made them viable.

Like other expressions of liminality, like *métissage* or hyphenated nouns, "intercultural" relies heavily on a grammar of lineage that spotlights the mediatory role of certain performances (their location between cultures), at the expense of exposing how those performances are also engines of emergence (sites for new positions, bodies, and voices) and deconstructive gestures (they recall tensions still at work within cultures). Cultures are moving targets: the prefix "inter" should emphasize their becoming, not their decidability. At what point does a cultural collage become what Brian Massumi defines as an "economy of belonging," in which living in-between is experienced not as mediation, but as self?[2] More often than not, in-betweens are denied their in-themselves: they are presented as amalgamations of static materials, as if they were being built with Lego modules. Which are the intersections of human labor that sustain an intercultural structure of feeling? How are new histories instituted for and by the actualization of intercultural networks? I am invested in understanding how intercultural exchanges modify and make history, how certain performances contribute to the management and reevaluation of social identities.

One of the effects of intercultural exchange is to foster the apparition of subjectivities and discourses that traumatize normative narratives of ethnic closure. An intercultural event instantiates multiple and intersecting materials, semiotic and economic heterogeneities that display their components in myriad directions. Intercultural performances promote social sites in which the co-belonging of certain categories (for example, space and time, past and present, local and global, we and them) becomes extremely acute. The core of my argument in this chapter is that scenarios in which the networking of intercultural relations is exposed tend to incite a scanning effect that discloses how identities are construed and parsed out in unexpected ways. Intercultural performances are relapsing machines that re-singularize their labor chains, calling attention to how cultural materials were created in the first place, and bringing into scrutiny the new alignments that are transforming them.

Una Chaudhuri suggests that interculturalism has been treated more as "a practice confined to matters of display and presentation" than as "a property of certain *texts*, something inhabiting the deep structure of a work." Chaudhuri proposes that "a *practical* interculturalism would not simply reproduce already established (and hence politically coded) images of cultural difference; instead, it would *produce the experience* of difference."[3] According to her, an intercultural critique will disclose how encounters between cultures motivate changes, contestations, and readjustments within each culture's hegemonic sense of identity. Chaudhuri's recourse to a morphological grasping of the intercultural process can easily fall back into a milder though still obtrusive essentialist posture, but it offers the rudiments for a rearticulation of the intercultural in which issues of representation and reception are expanded into a wider recognition of the relational webs that made them tangible. All renditions of intercultural performativity need to be conceptualized as narratives of coeval, and frequently evanescent, networks. One of our tasks as scholars is to catch up with those networks, not to simplify them.

Cast of Characters: Mexico City, Martín Cortés, Alonso de Avila, and the *Encomenderos*

It is important to remember that in 1566 Mexico City was still an island in the middle of a system of lakes.[4] Ten years earlier, Robert Tomson observed how

> the said citie of Mexico hath the streets made very broad, and right, that a man being in the high place, at the one ende of the street, may see at the least a good mile forward, and in all the one part of the streets of the North part of their Citie, there runneth a pretie lake of cleare water, that every man may put into his house as much as he will, without the cost of any thing, but of the letting in.

Water was such a central feature in the life of the capital that there was also

> a great cave or ditch . . . that commeth through the Citie, even into the high place, where come every morning at the break of the day twentie or thirtie Canoas, or troughes of Indians, which bring in them all manner of provision . . . which is made, and groweth in the Countrey, which is a very good commoditie for the inhabitants of that place.[5]

Martín Cortés's presence literally thickened a space that was already semantically dense. Intercultural frictions and exchanges in the area certainly predated the arrival of European explorers,[6] and the Aztecs had created a social environment in which everyday activities were closely connected with cosmic calendars and divinatory cycles.[7] As Viviana Díaz Balsero has shown, the semiotic turbulence provoked by the conquest led to a series of intercultural protocols in which Nahuas and Spaniards tested each other's boundaries: on the one hand, the missionary campaigns of the Franciscans promoted a dramaturgy of conversion in which Indian and European elements were adapted to their goals; and on the other, the Indians managed to preserve many of their own beliefs and practices within the seams of Catholic evangelization.[8] Although large numbers of Indian objects and other materials were destroyed,[9] friars like Bernardino de Sahagún combined pioneering ethnographic zeal and verbal virtuosity in order to describe and translate indigenous customs and languages.[10] All the events discussed here took place around a very small area, the main square of Mexico City, also known today as the Zócalo. The ruins of Aztec temples, the foundations of the new Catholic cathedral, and the palaces built by the conquistadors were extremely close to each other. The inhabitants of this quadrangle were not facing the "blind mobility" that Michel de Certeau ascribes to the modern pedestrian;[11] on the contrary, the downtown city center offered Martín Cortés and his allies a scenography of recycled and tentative materials, a half-designed intercultural stage in which the past was still too close and the future was not close enough. The city's layout had been rebuilt under the supervision of his own father, and the son felt entitled to retrace it.

Born in Mexico in 1532, Martín Cortés accompanied his father to Spain in 1540 and subsequently served Philip II both as courtier and soldier. He came back to New Spain with nothing less than an arrogant and confrontational attitude.[12] By the time he entered Mexico City on January 17, 1563, his behavior was already getting mixed reviews. Hidalgos and friars alike were startled when he used the pronoun *vos*—traditionally reserved for servants or subalterns—to address them. After enjoying the hospitality of a rich landowner, the marquis initiated a legal complaint against him. Some of the reasons for Cortés's aggressive stance predated his journey, and were closely linked to the litigious relationship that his father had established with the monarchy. From the start, Hernán Cortés's intention was to gain patronage powers over his territories, including civil and criminal jurisdiction. The conquistador was awarded the title of Marquis of the Oaxaca Valley on July 6, 1529, and the title was to be inherited perpetually by his family. His lands included twenty-two Indian towns and access to two ports—Veracruz on the Atlantic, and Tehuantepec on the Pacific. The administrative center was in Cuernavaca.[13] Cortés wisely distributed his lands along trade routes that were already active during the Aztec rule. As for vassals, Charles V granted him 23,000 tributary Indians.[14] From the beginning, Hernán Cortés saw his *marquesado* as a self-reliant unit that promoted its own economic program.

The *marquesado*'s main source of revenue was human labor: the tributes and services extracted from his Indian subjects.[15] Indians were also involved in most construction projects sponsored either by the conquistador or by the mendicant friars in charge of their religious instruction. Nonetheless, the *marquesado*'s prominent position in New Spain was the exception, not the rule. In the New World the crown preferred to reward the conquistadors with *encomiendas*, not with territories. An *encomienda* granted Spaniards the right to require from the Indians personal services and tributes that otherwise belonged to the monarchy. The *encomendero* was expected to supervise and promote the Christian welfare of the indigenous population. What in principle was an endowment became something more akin to a patrimonial privilege in the minds of the conquistador's descendants. In the late 1550s, the king started to reform the distribution of Indian services by developing the *repartimiento*, an arrangement under which the Indians were considered free subjects of the crown who provided compulsory, low-waged labor. The monarchy was trying to replace an economic system based on vassalage with one centered on enforced paid work, but the *encomenderos* wanted their Indian allocations to be conceded in perpetuity to their families.[16] Article 35 of the New Laws of 1542 ordered that the *encomiendas* were to be gradually reverted to the crown in exchange for a pension.[17] Upon his arrival in New Spain in 1550, Viceroy Luis de Velasco actively started to implement the New Laws, and in 1552 the *encomiendas* were reduced to two generations. By the time Philip II became king in 1556 it was dawning on the *encomenderos* that their privileges were now seriously threatened.

It is out of this intersection between the marquis's aspirations and the *encomenderos'* fears that the specific profile of the insurrection would slowly take shape, including Martín Cortés's friendship with Alonso de Avila Alvarado. In his mid-twenties at the time of the conspiracy, Alonso de Avila was either admired or resented for his amatory adventures and his splendid taste in expensive fabrics, furniture, and jewelry. His house—located just a few blocks north of Cortés's palace—was noticeable enough to be mentioned in surveys of Mexico City,[18] and in a letter to Philip II, Archbishop Fray Juan de Zumárraga observed that Avila's home was decorated with silks and tapestries as splendid as those favored by the empress.[19] The chronicler Juan Suárez de Peralta comments on Avila's handsome features, saying that he was particularly proud of the fairness of his skin, and that many women envied the elegance of his countenance.[20] His *encomiendas* amounted to approximately 20,000 pesos and included lands in Cuauhtitlán, north of Mexico City. Charles Gibson states that the Cuauhtitlán *encomienda* was made of four towns, or *cabeceras*, and had at least 5,000 tributary Indians. As early as 1561, the crown wanted some portions of this *encomienda* back, but Avila ignored the ruling.[21] Alonso's brother, Gil González de Avila, was a recent widower, and everybody considered him a reserved, more private man. The siblings were nephews of a conquistador also named Alonso de Avila. The Avila brothers belonged to a generation of Spaniards that were heirs to the conquistadors, but lacked their exploratory ambitions. Writing to the king at the end of 1567, a citizen blamed the insurrection on the fact that Mexico City was mainly inhabited by these younger, inexperienced males.[22]

Replacing the Viceroy's Body

Since the marquis was the only creole figure who owned anything comparable to a medieval fiefdom, it was inevitable that the *encomenderos* would look up to him as an ally.[23] Once in New Spain, the marquis surrounded himself with a festive atmosphere that motivated competition and masculine solidarity. The home of Cortés became a center for card games and expensive dinner parties that included drinking contests in which guests challenged each other to toast into exhaustion. (Those who declined to participate saw their *gorras* or caps taken and slashed with knives.) This practice was introduced in Mexico City by the marquis, and it became one of his most distinctive forms of entertainment.[24] The homosocial intensity of the drinking sessions held at the marquis's residence was accompanied by a relish for impromptu masquerades dedicated to the courtship of women. These displays of sentimental playfulness brought to Mexico City a note of informality, an ostensive relaxation of the strictures of social protocol that forced into visibility—and hearing—the role of the marquis as a local leader. In the streets Cortés was accompanied by a page wearing a helmet and brandishing a lance quite similar to a royal standard. The marquis's insistence on parading his personal charms implies an effort to reassemble Mexico City as a locus that was tightly inflected by his physical exertions. He was actively performing his position as a figure who challenged and even replaced the viceroy as the hierarchical axis of the capital. Cortés's relations with Viceroy Luis de Velasco were initially cordial, but Velasco's reputation as a committed protector of the rights of the Indians was not exactly something Cortés was inclined to appreciate.[25] The marquis went as far as suggesting in a letter to the king that under Velasco's administration the crown had been deprived of at least two million pesos of revenue. Following Velasco's request, in the summer of 1563 a *visitador* or special envoy named Jerónimo de Valderrama came to New Spain to investigate the situation.

It was at this juncture that Cortés decided to openly upstage Velasco.[26] As a special envoy from the king, Valderrama was to a certain extent the viceroy's supervisor. The viceroy invited Cortés to welcome Valderrama as part of the official retinue, but the marquis got ahead of Velasco—page, helmet, lance, and standard included—and met the *visitador* outside of Mexico City. Velasco was flabbergasted by this act of rudeness and notified Cortés that personal standards were not allowed when the king's standard was being carried by the official authorities. Cortés was offended by Velasco's words, and the viceroy prepared himself to persuade the marquis by force if necessary. Valderrama intervened, and the mystified page was asked to follow the group from a distance. Although Valderrama had already decided to stay with Cortés before arriving in Mexico City, it is easy to imagine that after this incident, Velasco assumed that the *visitador*'s choice of lodgings was far from neutral. Extant documentation proves that Valderrama was highly critical—for quite valid reasons—of Velasco's administration.[27] By royal command, both the viceroy and the members of the Audiencia were expected to abstain as much as possible from developing close links with other Spanish families, but Velasco's close collaboration with the religious orders and his own circle of friends and relatives compromised his objectivity and the ability of the *oidores* and other civic officers to oppose his decisions. While partial to the marquis on several occasions,[28] Valderrama's priority was not to protect Cortés but to strengthen the financial gains of the crown.

It is important to realize that the viceroy was not only a symbolic stunt man for the actual monarch: he *was* the monarch, embodied through another person. What was done to the viceroy was done to the king. The king's physical absence validated a transferential network, in which even material objects were considered participants in the monarch's substance. Velasco and Cortés were actually involved in another quarrel that included such an object. To stamp his own administrative provisions, the marquis committed the indiscretion of ordering a silver seal that was almost the same size as the royal one used by the Audiencia. Cortés's seal included a small crown, his coat of arms, and a logo that proclaimed "Martinus Cortesus primus hujus nominis Dux Marchio Secundus" ("Martín Cortés, first of the name, second marquis"). Cortés was pushing the envelope, since "Dux" could be read both as "second" or "Duke," a title he insisted belonged to him in spite of the fact that Philip II ignored his frequent claims. A bureaucratic official reviewing some tax documents sent by Cortés to the Audiencia got alarmed when he saw the stamp and cautiously confiscated it while informing Velasco about its existence. The viceroy informed Philip II and the king prohibited Cortés from utilizing the seal again.

As Alejandro Cañeque explains, when a king died, the old seal with the royal coat of arms kept by the Audiencia was melted and the silver was taken back to Spain while a new seal was sent:

> On its arrival to Mexico City, the seal was received in the same way as the King or the Viceroy was: the *audiencia* and the *cabildo* [municipal council] would go to meet it and ride back to the city with the seal, place it on a horse or mule, between the president of the *audiencia* and the senior *oidor*. Thus, the ritual of reception of the seal made the King "present" at the same time that it reactivated his power.[29]

By closely matching the size of the royal seal with the size of his own personal stamp, the marquis knew exactly what he was doing. Marking his territory one gesture at a time, Cortés managed to institute a state of uncertainty in which Mexico City became open to be reenvisioned as different from Spain. Cortés was fostering a provisional environment that allowed some *encomenderos* to rehearse their view of New Spain as something truly new. As the seal incident shows, the marquis facilitated a situation that we can compare with what Michael Taussig calls a "public secret": "that which is generally known but cannot be spoken . . . [an] invisible border waiting to be crossed, tempting but dangerous, even cruel, guarding some secret awaiting release."[30] I would like to claim that Taussig's positing of public secrecy as something that is both recognizable and hidden—thus familiar and uncanny at the same time—can be an efficacious tool for scholars trying to trace the emerging profile of intercultural transformations. New cultural constructs are perceived gradually, in unexpected or unpredictable circumstances—and, occasionally, as secrets waiting to be disclosed.

The marquis's contestation of the colonial chain of command was both somatic and iconic. Cortés tried to relocate or to displace the viceroy's body. If nothing else, in 1563, the conquistador's son was a clever but undiplomatic manager of his own spectacle, one that became a game of cat and mouse three years later. Cortés was experimenting with the possibility of a different New Spain—one built around the aura of his wealth, his nobility, and the still loud clarion sounds of his father's legacy. His actions had a double edge: he was simultaneously recasting himself as an alternative to the viceroy and as an autonomous, *quasi*-feudal lord. His public exhibitions served as a recruitment tool, a call to others to recognize the potential gains to be derived from an *altered* community. His theatrical advertisements give us an opportunity to ponder how the performative intervenes in the disclosure—and planning—of emerging intercultural rearrangements.

Remapping Mexico City

On June 22, 1564, Velasco wrote a letter to Philip II in which he defended his work as viceroy and notified the king that he thought the marquis was blatantly increasing his personal tributes and adding subjects to his patrimony. A few weeks later, on July 31, Velasco died. As soon as the viceroy passed away, Valderrama moved from Cortés's house to the Casa Real where Velasco had been living. After a painstaking reappraisal of the value of many Indian properties, towns, and assets, the *visitador* began to implement a comprehensive reform of the tributary system prevalent under Velasco's tenure. Valderrama eliminated some tributary exemptions conferred on the Indians—especially those living close to Mexico City—and tried to minimize the illegal interference of caciques and clerics that in his opinion were abusing their access to the communal funds of their villages. As usual, a transitory juncture was seen by some as an opportunity to introduce potentially lasting changes in governmental structures. By the end of August 1564, there was a proposal asking Philip II to replace the post of viceroy with a different administrative arrangement: an Audiencia with a president (Valderrama) and a captain-general (the marquis). Both the *visitador* and Cortés candidly recommended themselves to the king, but Philip II ignored their generous disposition to serve the monarchy. The marquis also sent Diego Ferrer—his former preceptor—to scout for him in Spain.

The bureaucratic vulnerabilities produced by Velasco's death were precisely what Cortés needed to intensify his performative quest for social domination. When friends and acquaintances encountered Cortés riding his horse across the city, it became customary for them to join the marquis and stay with him all the way back to his house. Not everybody complied with this new ritual. Those who found it excessive or had a grudge against Cortés kept their caps on their heads when they saw him, an intentional breach of politeness that at least on one occasion led to a public fight. Meeting the marquis readjusted the pacing of other people's schedules, encouraging them to suspend their everyday routines for the sake of his leisure. To control time is also to re-encode space: escorting the marquis through the city became a daily procession that marked the urban landscape with his influence, turning the city into a backdrop for his political prowess.

The ambulatory amusements of the marquis embodied a new communal contract in which the recognition of his authority was paramount. To casually intersect his traversing motions through Mexico City forced both creoles and Spaniards to participate in the emergence of an alterative social order that was not fully institutionalized yet. These encounters, strategically improvised by Cortés, actualized a state of uncertainty that exposed the seams of colonial power. He reinstated a sense of timing into the hierarchical layers of a city that was expected to incarnate the demands of imperial obedience. The formative and naturalized relations that grounded Mexico City became perilously tangible and open-ended when the marquis impelled his friends and detractors to reposition themselves in the streets as actors in the public performance he was sponsoring. The King's Council was notified by an informant that there were talks about the marquis becoming king of New Spain and that some theologians had declared his aspirations to such a crown to be legitimate.

Mexico City in the 1560s was incredibly tight in terms of social lacings. A few families, supported by a contested *encomienda* system or by their influence within the administrative bureaucracies commanded by the viceroy and the church, monitored the jetsam and flotsam tides of New Spain's wealth. Between April and June of 1565, there were at least three violent incidents that confronted Martín Cortés with some of his opponents in the streets of the capital. The *encomenderos* were divided among themselves into two factions:

the Bocanegra family was on Cortés's side, while members of the Cervantes family and their friends were openly challenging the marquis.[31] Rumors had it that Cortés was fond of the Bocanegra clan because he was courting the wife of one of them, named Marina. Since Marina was also the Christian name of Hernán Cortés's interpreter—also known as Malinche—this piece of gossip has to be taken with a grain of salt. Was this a coincidence, or was this Cortés's attempt to replicate the erotic details of a paternal scenario so closely related to the conquest of Mexico?

In the summer of 1565, Cortés organized a tournament at Tocubaya to honor his wife. This mock battle was a display of military power that included "a force of harquebusiers and about seventy horsemen carrying lances and banners" and was widely attended by Indians and Spaniards.[32] In spite of these revels, 1565 turned out to be a frustrating year for the marquis. On August 1, a letter from Spain sent by Diego Ferrer explicitly told Cortés that perpetuity for the *encomiendas* was not favored at court. On September 28, Cortés received a *cédula*, or letter, ordering him to address his legal disputes in Spain, either by going there himself or by selecting another person to represent him. The king gave him six months to make his preparations. A notification forbidding him the use of his silver seal also arrived around that time. According to some witnesses, by the summer of 1565, the marquis was already discussing plans for an insurrection with Alonso de Avila.

A careful reading of the *cabildo*'s proceedings reveals that in 1566, Alonso de Avila was absent from his duties during most of February. His name resurfaces in March, when Valderrama's approaching departure to Spain incited a flourish of discussions and meetings among the *encomenderos*.[33] Avila decided to organize a masquerade that was probably one of the last festivities Valderrama attended in Mexico City. During his later interrogation, Avila himself offered some intriguing details about his masquerade:

> We were twenty-four horsemen, and we organized a masquerade and we disguised ourselves with Indian costumes and masks that imitated Indian faces and we carried roses in our hands that are called *suchiles* by the Indians and we brought food to the *Marquesa* . . . We wanted her to see how the Indians celebrated their festivals . . . and that night I placed a garland made of feathers on the Marquesa's head as the Indians do.

His brother Gil confirmed most of these facts.[34] Juan Suárez de Peralta says that during the masquerade, "some mugs were served, called alcarrazas, and some jugs made of clay, and they were all made in Alonso de Avila's town, in Cuahtitlán, because there is a lot of mud there, and in order to ornate them it was commanded to inscribe them with some ciphers, in this way: a double RR and a crown on top."[35] This masquerade, of course, was not happening in a vacuum. Victoria A. Vincent deftly summarizes the increasingly convoluted sequence of private meetings and informant reports that led to the arrest of both Cortés and Avila.[36] Echoing Jody Enders, it is valid to imagine in this case that Cortés and Avila realized too late that theatricality can also be assumed as an index of intentionality;[37] actors and citizens can find themselves being held accountable for what they thought they were merely rehearsing or staging.

Redirecting the Flows

Peggy Phelan reminds us that performance is an agonistic practice in which the pursuit of presence is always confronting its ephemeral effects. If, according to Phelan, performance is that activity that constantly collapses into tracelessness, writing about it introduces nothing less than a phenomenological distortion of our experience.[38] For the historian of the sixteenth century, the evanescent qualities of performance are frequently and poignantly underlined by one's inevitable reliance on archival materials over embodied manifestations. Since a substantial amount of my inquiry into Cortés's insurrection is based on somebody else's accounts or on legal records made under highly coercive circumstances, my critical access to the bodies and the actions involved has been severely compromised from the start. The best I can do is to interview dead people. Fortunately—as any reader of Juan Rulfo's *Pedro Páramo* knows—in Mexico, the dead like to tell stories. I would like to suggest that Avila's intercultural scenario rearticulated the rift between representation and disappearance in order to increase the traceability of the social relations that enabled it. We can supplement and profit from his choices if we study them as networking. But first, we have to conceptualize both what networks are, and how scenarios can be retraced within them.

Diana Taylor argues that a scenario is a morphological template that reproduces the structural features of a foundational event. The once-againness of the scenario activates a series of semantic transfers and variations that modify and adapt its meaning to new historical predicaments. Produced at a particular point in history, the scenario offers a conceptual model that has enough cultural specificity to be locally significant, and enough paradigmatic force to be translated into wider postcolonial variations and retellings. Scenarios have to be reembodied and recontextualized in order to access their narrative functionality. As her analysis of Coco Fusco's and Guillermo Gómez Peña's performance as a caged native couple shows, Taylor's utilization of the scenario in *The Archive and the Repertoire* privileges a multidisciplinary approach that includes aesthetic, ethnographic, and semiotic readings.[39] Her preferred areas of inquiry are issues of representation and reception. In her opinion, a scenario is "often banal because it leaves out complexity, reduces conflict to its stock elements, and encourages fantasies of participation."[40] But this is only partially correct: sometimes the power of a scenario resides elsewhere. Most colonial scenarios are embodiments of intercultural networks, and it is in their capacity to reassemble those networks that a substantial part of their political and affective attraction lies.

Scenarios are relational switchboards, bundles of convergent heterogeneities. My claim is that the implicit intercultural impact induced by any reposition of a colonial scenario can be more effectively evaluated through a retracing of the uncertainties and labor investments that enable it. We need to support our analysis of intercultural scenarios with a wider acknowledgment of the productive vectors that articulate them. Bruno Latour reminds us that "the object of a performative definition vanishes when it is no longer performed—or if it stays, then it means that *other* actors have taken over the relay." According to Latour, it is precisely through the phasing of these performative relays that a society becomes detectable: "There is nothing more difficult to grasp than social ties"; the social "is traceable only when it's being modified . . . No new association, no way to feel the grasp."[41] Latour argues that communal interactions are not that different from staged ones: they both become traceable as performances, in the midst of their doings and alterations. As part of a relational network, a person—like a character in a play—tightens or releases a bundle of functional roles that are *acted out* as much as they are *acted upon*. Instead of congealing those roles into abstractions that predetermine their movements, our challenge as critical observers is to follow them in their perpetual rearrangements and resignifications.

For Latour, performance is not something that reflects or illustrates a social network: performance *is* the armature of the network itself. In Latour's view, what we call "the social" is never something that is being given, but something that is constantly being worked out, remade. The social is our shorthand for a performative *becoming* that accelerates, proliferates, or slows down according to how its actors realign their connections. For the actors involved, the singularity of each relation is always more relevant and acute than any panoramic design used to systematize society as a whole. It is at those junctures—the highly localized intersections between actors and roles—that the uncertainties of the performative process are more dramatically intensified.

While Taylor rightly calls for an understanding of intercultural events in terms of how they provoke moments of translation, she also invites us to embrace the opacity of the Other, the right of all cultures to resist transparency.[42] On the one hand, the imperative to translate can lead us to a rushed dismissal of fundamental axiological differences between cultures; on the other, our respect for opacity can inadvertently encourage a more refined version of the exotic. In my view, a poetics of networking enables an intercultural critique that is both cautiously translational and ethically responsible. Cultures are neither completely accessible nor absolutely impermeable: at all points, human and nonhuman elements are being reentangled and transcoded.

A historiography of intercultural scenarios should try to catch these local and relational relays as they emerge and oscillate, instead of consolidating them too quickly into encompassing, retroversive narratives.

Performance studies can expand its historiography and its methodology by focusing on what I define as a *prepositional analysis* of events and scenarios. Grammatically speaking, "a preposition expresses a relation between two entities . . . Place and Time are the most prominent and easy to identify."[43] In the pages that follow, I will explore the extent to which Avila's scenario was also a prepositional grid, in which certain objects expressed an intercultural network of relations. I want to deploy a clearer understanding of the labor investments that made the masquerade possible in the first place. Manuel Castells defines a network as "a set of interconnected nodes. A node is the point at which a curve intersects itself." Networks are "open structures, able to expand without limits, integrating new nodes as long as they are able to communicate within the network, namely as long as they share the same communication codes."[44] Which were the actual boundaries of the masquerade, and how many nodes were imbricated within its scope? General categories like scenarios tend to subsume all contingencies into a centralized narrative thread, but I want to focus instead on the relational nodes that kept Avila's scenario *going*. Without discarding Taylor's ethics of reception and representation, my prepositional analysis of the masquerade will try to posit a distribution of overlapping vectors that will give us a glimpse of how the masquerade reassembled the intercultural community that supported it.

Objects and People: Masks, Flowers, Feathers, and Mugs

What type of scenario was Avila's masquerade reactivating? I suspect that Avila and his friends were imitating in their own fashion an Aztec dance or *mitote* based on the first encounter between Emperor Motezuma and Hernán Cortés.[45] In 1645, a Jesuit historian named Andrés Pérez de Ribas described in his book *History of the Triumphs of Our Holy Faith amongst the Most Barbarous and Fierce Peoples of the New World* a

> *mitote* dance that they name after the Emperor Motezuma . . . The company of dancers comes out in the costume and the adornment of the ancient Mexican princes. The mantles, or cloaks, are of two fabrics, the outer one transparent, so that the embroidery and beautiful flowers on the inner one can show through; and these they wear hanging from their shoulders . . . On their heads they wear diadems that rise above the forehead in the manner of a pyramid . . . and this is adorned with the richest gems and gold that they could obtain—and such was the style of the crowns worn by the Mexican Emperors.[46]

That *mitotes* of this kind were performed in Mexico City quite often at the time of Avila's masquerade is documented by the fact that Indian farmers were complaining about them. On March 2, 1564, several Indians from Mexico City presented to *visitador* Valderrama a legal request in which they accused their own caciques and their Spanish officers of collecting communal money to pay for feathers and other ornaments in order to dance and get drunk together.[47] For many *maceguales*, or Indian commoners, this abuse of the *mitote* implied a complicity between their caciques and the Spaniards: the dance was already signaling an emerging reclustering of cultural formations.

As French philosopher Michel Serres says, "Relations are, in fact, ways of moving from place to place, or of wandering . . . It's better to paint a sort of fluctuating picture of relations and rapport" and to think vectorially.[48] Avila's masquerade was a *prepositional scenario:* its goal was to revisit an ensemble of relations, to retrace the intercultural nodes of the *encomienda* itself. The masquerade included at least four vectorial objects—masks, flowers, feathers, and mugs—that served as material tokens of the *encomenderos'* financial prosperity. Although we don't know exactly which types of disguises were utilized by Avila and his friends, it is undeniable that their choices were influenced by Indian clothing and that their masks replicated Indian features. Covering their Spanish faces with Indian faces, the *encomenderos* unabashedly conflated their identity as potential vassals of Cortés with an impersonation of their own indigenous subjects. By reinserting their bodies into the scenario of the conquest, the *encomenderos* were not merely reinterpreting the past; they were actually performing the materiality of their wealth.

It is possible that by covering their faces with Indian masks, the *encomenderos* were obliquely evoking recent indigenous acts of resistance against the king's fiscal reforms. The *Annals of Juan Bautista*—a Nahuatl account that covers events from the 1560s to the 1580s—gives a vivid description of how the Indians reacted to Valderrama's efforts to extract monetary tributes from them.[49] The Indians protested, saying that they were already paying their tributes by providing labor, artifacts, and agricultural produce. To add money on top of those contributions was considered excessive. Among the Indians, services to the community were linked to personal merit and social standing; an artisan's tribute was measured by the quality of his craft. The *visitador* was asking the Indians to abandon a tributary system based on the evaluation of personal skills for a tributary system based on the redistribution of personal salaries. The increasing unrest produced by the interventions of the *visitador* underlined the Indians' awareness of their situation as conquered subjects, and between 1564 and 1565, a series of riots, arrests, and other violent occurrences ensued. To wear an Indian mask in this volatile context was not devoid of political ambiguities.

Avila's attaching of his personal heraldic emblems and some ingenious short poetic compositions to the rose bouquets distributed during the masquerade was another example of transcultural plagiarism. For the Aztecs, flowers and poetry were always metaphorically paired. *Suchiles*, or flower arrangements, were prominent in Aztec religious ceremonies, and they can also be thematically linked to the notion of "flower wars," ritual battles dedicated to capturing soldiers in order to offer them as sacrificial victims. Max Harris analyzes how the "flower war" was one of the templates for *The Conquest of Jerusalem*, a performance organized by the Tlaxcalans in 1539 in which an actor impersonated Hernán Cortés dressed as an eventually defeated Sultan of Babylon.[50] In an insightful study of this performance, Patricia Ybarra claims that plays like *The Conquest of Jerusalem* paraded Indian skills in order to submit them to a public process of conversion that was both religious and economic.[51] The masquerade can be seen as a secularized, inverted version of this approach: the Spaniards were symbolically converting themselves into Indians as a way of exposing and defending their sources of revenue.

Feather headdresses were especially admired during flower war combats; to the Spaniards' advantage, Aztec soldiers were proud of turning themselves into easy targets by wearing them. The *guirnalda de plumas*, or feather garland, that Avila gave to Cortés's wife has been compared to a *copilli*, a feather headdress worn as a sign of authority and prestige. As Inga Clendinnen explains, the Aztecs appreciated plumes both for their aesthetic import—colors, textures—and for their semantic associations. Feathers were also concrete markers of the Aztecs' sphere of territorial domination: they were brought from Guatemala, the lowlands close to the Gulf Coast and the Pacific shore. Due to their exquisite and vibrating palette of blues and greens and their naturally stylized length and design, quetzal feathers were at the top of the Aztecs' tributary list.[52] As Sahagún and his informants attest, Aztec feather workers lived in separate wards or neighborhoods, and they tended to marry among their own families.[53] Sahagún specifies how feather officials, or *amanteca*, had their own rituals and even sacrificed slaves. Feather workers were both male and female, and they created shields and other weapons.

In the *Osuna Codex* the litigants emphasized how expensive the feathers were:

> [The] alcaldes and regidores often request money from the officials of each neighborhood, in order to produce feather arrangements and other feather-made objects for the *mitotes*, and each piece costs up to sixty pesos, and these feather ornaments are then rented and given to many young males so they can impress the women that are watching them during their *mitotes*, and then the same young men offer money and wine from Castille to those same alcaldes and regidores during their festivities and this is how the money that belongs to the macehuales and officials ends being used.[54]

Most of the witnesses called to participate in the legal inquiry testified that *mitotes* were quite popular among Indians and Spanish alike, and that feathers were particularly coveted. Since the feathers were paid with communal funds, they were supposed to be used for public occasions, but they ended up being rented for private festivities. During the trial interrogations, the feather garland provided by Avila was compared to a crown.

Although it can be claimed that feathers and flowers were elements taken directly from traditional *mitote* celebrations, the earthenware mugs and jugs that were used in the masquerade were by all means Avila's choice, and they invite us to guess what their functions were in this particular case. Each mug was inscribed with a crown and the letter "R" for "Reinarás" ("You will rule"). Specially made for the occasion in his *encomiendas* of Cuauhtitlán, the mugs were a direct reminder of the contributions of indigenous craftsmanship to the daily routines of the ruling families of the viceroyalty. Avila intentionally used handmade wares, not wheel-thrown majolica imported from Europe. Displaying European pottery was seen by many as a sign of sophistication, and Spanish earthenware workshops in Mexico tended to restrict the presence of indigenous workers to menial tasks. But by the 1560s, Spanish artisans were fully aware that their indigenous counterparts produced excellent ceramics that were as good or even better than their own.[55] (Once the Manila trade route was established, both groups had to deal with an increasing preference for Chinese porcelain.)[56] It would have been easier for Avila to buy plates, water jars, and other ceramics at the market of Mexico City's Plaza Mayor, but he was trying to make a point. Avila's choice was a deliberate touch of local color aimed at underlining the services rendered to him by *his* Indians.[57] Cuauhtitlán was celebrated for the quality of its clay, and the area was still a major center for the manufacture of ceramic ware and other forms of pottery at the end of the eighteenth century. Shaped by Indian hands out of mud collected in his Cuauhtitlán towns, Avila's jugs were prepositional objects, portable pointers that invited other people to retrace the productive interactions that sustained his *encomiendas*.[58]

When Avila asked his potters in Cuauhtitlán to fabricate special mugs for the masquerade, he was intentionally alluding to certain jurisdictional demarcations: those jugs were, to a certain extent, made out of what he considered *his* inheritance.[59] The *encomiendas* tended to use the original Nahua *altepetl* as their basic unit. As James Lockhart explains, an Indian *altepetl* was defined by common territorial and ethnic affiliations, a *tlatoani*, or ruler, and a set of smaller parts or household nodes called *calpolli*. Aztec cities—a European concept more than an Indian one—were conglomerations of these modular blocks.[60] Although *encomienda* lands were never supposed to be owned by the *encomenderos*—with the exception of Cortés's family—their aspiration to keep their territorial assignations for perpetuity would have turned those lands into a personal legacy. One of the most frequent complaints that Indians addressed to the marquis was that he was usurping communal lands to plant sugarcane without paying for it.[61] (As we saw earlier, the *macehuales* also protested against how their communal feathers were being rented for private profit.) For us, the metonymic impact of these mugs is hard to avoid: Avila was asking Cortés and his guests to hold what he considered *his* alleged property in their hands.

Toward a Prepositional Analysis of Intercultural Scenarios

If we approach Avila's masquerade mainly as the encounter of certain actors and audiences mediated by a scenario, the deeper complexity of his intervention will completely escape us. Like any deictic, each of the objects just mentioned had a directional function. Through the introduction of these objects, Avila brought into the picture an anaphoric reminder of the latticed relational transactions the *encomenderos* wanted to perpetuate. What was being performed was not only a scenario, but the *network* that sustained it—feather workers and pottery makers. Even the masks were prepositional devices that instantiated the operations of colonial capital: dressed as Indians, the *encomenderos* were acting out the indigenous resources that comprised their own economic abundance.

Avila's masquerade took place at a moment when the economic patterns of New Spain were undergoing a gradual process of adjustment. Aztec military exertions were primarily oriented toward the accumulation of tributary wealth. Conquered territories were coerced into sending to Tenochtitlán a diverse array of fine objects and foods, but they were not expected to assimilate into Aztec culture. The lakes around Tenochtitlán made it easier for the city to receive goods from agricultural lands located beyond their shores. The *tlateme* (portage worker) and the *pochteca* (long-distance trader) articulated a radial system that, aided by canoes, flowed into the weekly markets that were the true centers of Aztec material life. Although the Spaniards took their cue from indigenous market practices, Ross Hassig explains how the introduction of new modes of transportation like the horse and the wheel-cart accelerated and increased the volume of trade.[62] Certain items saw their value drastically altered or modified. As the resentment of the *macehuales* and the artisans in the *Códice Osuna* testify, it is evident that feathers were becoming props for *mitotes* and drinking bouts, in which Indian and Spanish elites misappropriated communal funds. But those *mitotes* were more than just the prelude to viceregal hangovers; they were also emerging, anaphoric signs of a transcultural shift.

How do we account for the process that turns multiple individual experiences into the accruings of a new cultural sense of being? The leap from ontogeny to phylogeny is always hard to localize and document, and it involves both material and emotional factors that are not easily quantified. My argument is that, when studied as networks, intercultural scenarios reveal a reassembled space, in which these sedimentations are made available for retracing. One of the things a scenario enables us to do is to experience that retracing as the emergence of incipient cultural variations and differences.

Prepositional objects like the mugs reviewed earlier are transformative conductors: they locate the flows of exchange that mobilize a network. An object is prepositional because it helps us to delineate a chain of interactions. I claim that it was exactly for this vectorial effect that Avila so ostensibly included his water jars in the masquerade.

Avila's masquerade was presenting to Cortés and his wife both a testimony of the *encomendero*'s wealth and an affective call for their support. More importantly, the masquerade was actualizing an altered New Spain that at that moment could only be envisioned as a theatrical act. Avila enforced the traceability of his intervention; he wanted his audience to know where the food and the mugs were coming from. His introduction of masks, flowers, and feathers recalled the *mitotes*, in which Indian caciques and Spaniards showcased their ascendance over *macehuales* and artisans. As soon as we start looking at the masquerade prepositionally, it becomes clear that its impact was based on its vectorial proficiency. The mugs and feathers were prosthetic (that is, they supplemented or transformed the bodies of their users) and capillary (by alluding to highly localized economic activities). These vectorial objects were part of an ongoing process, reassembled elements in a network that was passing and unfolding through the masquerade.

One of the advantages of Latour's actor-network-theory is that it depolarizes normative oppositions between nature and culture, human and nonhuman factors. Latour denotes this depolarization by adding the prefix "*quasi-*" before the words "object" and "subject" alike. (Brian Massumi prefers to say "part-object" and "part-subject.")[63] To the extent that objects and subjects facilitate the relays of a network, their functional role within that network will fluctuate. Positionality is more a matter of degree than a matter of essence; the pliable circulation of *quasi*-objects and *quasi*-subjects is germane to the network's existence. As Bruce Clarke states, in Latour's reasoning, hybridity is operational, not exceptional; any semblance of network stability is nothing less than illusive.[64] Since the performative (either as network or as theatricality) is reassembled behavior, it can be apprehended only as an actualization, in real time, of its own process. The fluid and blurring boundaries of the performative are not incidental, but concomitant and portable.[65] Performance discloses the fluidity of a network, exposing it as a tissue made of *quasi*-conditions, incessantly shifting and metamorphic.

Quasi-, in Latour's dictionary, signifies translation. He suggests that we are constantly trying to pin down a reassembling pull that is always moving ahead of us. The current investment of performance studies in the skills of interventional witnessing—ethnography, audience reception, production analysis, and the preference of event over text—signals a radical effort to honor the phenomenological *quasi-* of its object, an object that, like networks, is only there *now*. When I propose that we read Avila's masquerade prepositionally, I am trying to reinstate the becomings of that *now* into my archival records. While Taylor's focus on scenarios represents a delicate balance between textual interpretations of the past and recent reenactments of that past, I am more concerned here with finding a way to reenergize the reading of vanished intercultural performances.

Scenarios are restated both for maintenance (namely, they serve to solidify and adjust hegemonic agendas) and for emergence (instantiating the presence of new formations, deviations, and alliances that are yet to be fully recognized). Scenarios are thus both effective and affective. The fact that most of my primary materials are written documents does not mean, of course, that my subjects had only their language as a tool to perform themselves. Following John Moreland's advice, I have tried to read my textual sources as if they were archeological fragments, artifacts imbued with networking evidence.[66] People accessorize their actions in order to reassemble their scenarios: wearing a crown of feathers morphed the body of the *marquesa* into a figuration of a prospective queen. Reported embodiment like the descriptions provided by Suárez or the interrogations of the Avila brothers can lead to the prepositional reading I have essayed here, a reading that recuperates the vectors that made Avila's masquerade moveable and visible as a potential mode of existence.

In *Cities of the Dead*, Joseph Roach invites us to study how societies "have invented themselves by performing their pasts in the presence of others."[67] But Cortés and Avila were also trying to pre-perform their future—and how they expected to pay for it with the labor of others. Even the number of men included in the masquerade had a political implication. The twenty-four horsemen mentioned by Avila probably reminded Cortés that several cities in Spain—like Seville—had a municipal council made of twenty-four functionaries. The masquerade's success as a scenario depended on its audience's competence to recognize the vectorial itinerary of certain objects, costumes, and gestures. A demand for this enhanced traceability is deeply embedded in the armature of most intercultural scenarios; in Avila's case, the *encomienda* was hypostatized as a series of Indian-made objects drastically severed from the Indian bodies that produced them.

The semiotic miscegenation that articulates the masquerade has been afforded in an intrinsically ironic way. Since the Indians are mostly *represented* at the masquerade by the results of their work—earthenware, food—their physical absence from the *máscara* certainly reenforces their subaltern positionality. But while the sweat of Indian bodies joins the masquerade primarily as reified matter, another subtle performative relay emerges into legibility. Objects valuable to the Indians—a feather garland, a *suchil*—now acquire a different function. Cortés's actions were primarily narcissistic and expository—look at me, notice me, rally around me—but Avila's masquerade was more inclusive and can only be read in transcultural terms. Avila's recall of the scenario of conquest fuses and maybe confuses Mexican and European signifiers. The *encomenderos* were asserting their agency by probing the signs of the Indian culture they aspired to keep under their domination; by grasping and circulating those Indian objects, the *encomenderos* were already altering their own history. The masquerade's retracing of the economic singularities of potters and feather workers and the semiotic impact of flowers and masks within a *mitote*-like spectacle both reflected and furthered the intercultural *becoming* of a society in which Indian and Spaniard increasingly blended.

I am not suggesting that objects acquire their own volitional capability. The performativity of vectorial objects lies in the fact that, due to the particulars of their circulation, they become a reminder of the process that assembles them. Although we are imagining Avila's scenario from the point of view of certain objects, we should not forget that *we* are still the ones selecting the objects in question. (Like it or not, our scholarship cannot entirely avoid some basic degree of anthropomorphic entitlement.) My tenet is that certain scenarios are recycled—among other reasons—to highlight some objects and resignify them, calling attention to their function as links within an intercultural network that otherwise would be ungraspable. Both Cortés and Avila were activating scenarios of conquest in order to provoke what Arjun Appadurai defines as tournaments of value, "calculated diversions that might lead to new paths of commodity flow."[68] The masquerade re-singularized these objects—mugs, flowers, masks, feathers—in order to posit a potential adjustment of the forces that compounded the *encomienda*. While Indian labor was being festively reconquered, the *encomenderos* engaged another, less conspicuous plot line: their own transculturation into a group of Spaniards that could only efficaciously represent themselves as Indians.

There is also another aspect of these objects that calls attention to one of Latour's most intriguing limitations. Latour leaves almost no room in his actor-network-theory to account for the functionality of desire in the process of reassembling relational connections. Objects, nonetheless, are frequently effective in linking people due to their affective value. Alice Rayner says that "it is through the intersections of objects and their narratives that history can be written, not in terms of authenticity or of recording what may or may not have happened, but in terms of commentary, often ironic, about such recording of history . . . An object is destined to travel."[69] I think Avila reassembled certain objects in order to enhance and mobilize their affective dimension for the *encomenderos*. The objects in the masquerade are vectorial not only as pointers of material destinations, but also as signifiers of attachment and emotional capital; their anaphoric quality invests them with a power to re-encode absence as relation. Avila's objects, framed by the intentionality of his scenario, were experienced as *mediators*. What we have been learning from Avila's masquerade is that an intercultural scenario emphasizes its traceability as an affective strategy: scenarios from the past are selected to the extent that they provide an opportunity to re-network the present. If performance sooner or later has to confront the failure of embodied practices to remain visible, Avila's scenario actually works because that failure was counted on from the start. By simultaneously indexing the exclusion of Indian bodies and their own political dependence on them, the *encomenderos* confronted the contradictory range of their political predicament.

The efficacy of a scenario relies on what Marvin Carlson defines as "an audience's binocular vision—its members' familiarity with the previous treatment of this same material and their ability to draw comparisons between that and the new, rival treatment."[70] Actively ghosting the first encounter between Cortés and Motezuma, Avila's masquerade introduced a dense temporal layering in which past, present, and future were compressed into a state of synthesis.[71] Like the elastic timings of prophecy, the chronological referents of this scenario are simultaneously serial and disjointed. In such a context, things that have not happened yet (like a *quasi*-insurrection) can be affectively experienced without being effectively actualized: fiction morphs into virtual history.[72] But virtual history is still anchored in the operational networks that metabolize human activity, networks that tend to be intercultural in nature if not in name. Scenarios are genealogical spectacles, engineering fantasies that reposition an existing chain of relays in order to summon their capacity for transformation.

Scenarios are engines of *origins*, receptacles in which change can be rehearsed and planned. A scenario is propelled by what Tracy C. Davis describes as performative time, a realignment of chronologies that is "crucially dependent upon citationality." Davis explains how the iteration—or the reassembling—of specific performative events "calls attention to the question of who has agency to convey history, as well as how evidence for history is generated." Performative time "may reverberate indefinitely" because it manages to reproduce actions and scenes out of sequence, thus authorizing a multiplicity of overlapping spaces, stories, and temporal vectors.[73] As we have shown in our discussion of Avila's masquerade, virtual histories—scenarios that are replicated in order to be translated into new meanings and potentialities—also generate unexpected reframings of identity.

The important thing to keep in mind is that the malleable sense of time implicit in each scenario has to be reassembled out of the irreversible labors of performation. The most salient characteristic of the events unfurled in 1566 by Cortés and the *encomenderos* is their incremental recourse to public networking activities. For three years, the marquis focused on a proxemics of personality, a recasting of urban spaces centered on his physical proximity and crescive power to reorganize or unsettle alliances and rapports within creole and European elites. Avila's masquerade evoked the *encomienda* itself: the food, the cups, the clothes, and the reposition of the first encounter between Hernán Cortés and Motezuma were all genealogical references that reproduced the formation of the *encomiendas* and the tangible circulation of their tributary riches. What all these objects and actions have in common is that they were surrogates for the outcomes of Indian labor the *encomenderos* aspired to exploit. Avila's masquerade was nothing less than the deployment of a relational, intercultural network—the *mitote* was an activity that enabled him to reassemble certain patterns of behavior and production, to retrace and readjust them.

Scenarios always render our *process* visible. Avila's scenario was both a representation of the *encomienda* and a reproduction of some of its constitutive elements. It proclaimed the *encomenderos'* political status as a self-appointed local aristocracy, and it also underlined the radical hybridity of their situation. Shortly after Avila's masquerade, an official report against the rebels was presented to the Audiencia by Luis de Velasco—son of the deceased viceroy—and two more informants. While rumors about the potential insurrection had been circulating at least since the beginning of that year, after this denunciation the *oidores* decided to prepare themselves for an eventual fight.[74] On May 27, an emissary from Martín Cortés told the members of the *cabildo* that the marquis had received a letter from Spain advising him to drop any demands for a perpetual assignation of *encomiendas*.[75] The *encomenderos* were now running out of patience.

At the time of Avila's masquerade in late March, Cortés's wife was pregnant. On June 30, 1566, the couple baptized their recently born twin children, Catalina and Pedro. An elevated walkway made of flowers, trees, and triumphal arcs was built from the marquis's house all the way to the church, and a mock fight between knights preceded the ceremony. Artificial glades, meadows, and forests were prominent in Indian ritual ceremonies dedicated to deities like Tlaloc and Xochiquetzal. These human-made, transient ecologies were very popular in New Spain. In 1539, for example, a play included nothing less than a complete landscape built in the central plaza of Mexico City.[76] On that occasion, two squadrons of *salvajes* or savage fighters and a cavalcade of male and female riders wearing masks shared this topographic replica, and it seems that Hernán Cortés himself was the leader of a group of Christian soldiers that defeated a group of faked Turks.[77] It was certainly not lost on Martín Cortés in 1566 that he was enjoying his own artificial forest almost on the same location on which his father had made a cameo appearance as a conqueror of infidels two decades earlier.

The *oidores* thought the baptism festivities were an opportunity for the rebels to attack, and they were prepared to defend themselves.[78] Nothing happened at that time, but by now the Audiencia had reasons to fear the arrival of another date: the feast of San Hipólito. Since the Aztecs were defeated by the Spaniards on San Hipólito's day—August 13, 1521—these celebrations occupied a special place in the colonial calendar. Avila was supposed to carry a standard or *pendón* during these festivities in 1565, but he suddenly excused himself. Nevertheless, a year later he was expected to have a leading role in San Hipólito's feast again. On June 21, 1566, the *cabildo* promised to cover some of his expenses; this decision was ratified on July 8. At that point the Audiencia decided to strike first and arrested Martín Cortés and the Avila brothers. On August 2, the *cabildo* acknowledged that Avila was in prison and requested a different person to take charge of the standard for San Hipólito's day.[79] Soon after that, the Avila siblings were declared guilty of treason, and sentenced to death.

Sadly enough, our *quasi*-insurrection ends with an execution. On August 3, 1566, at seven in the evening, Alonso de Avila and his brother were beheaded. A few years later, their house was razed, adding another layer to the phantasmagoric accumulations of viceregal Mexico. Martín Cortés was forced to return to Spain, and he never saw his American lands again. Avila, of course, did much more than lead a masquerade: he certainly conspired with other people, or at least talked about it quite seriously in the privacy of his and his friends' homes, but his turning of these private conversations into a public secret through the playfulness of a scenario speeded up his demise. His scenario of choice was radically intercultural. To change New Spain, he decided to replay the conquest of its native laborers, but in the process of doing so he also transformed that scenario into a compressed reassembling of some aspects of a colonial network that was already neither Indian nor European, but both. The *encomenderos'* intercultural scenario was performing, at a very high cost for some of them, the emergence of New Spain's own Otherness.

As we have seen, performance is *reassembled behavior*; twice-behaved behaviors and scenarios are better understood as reassembling opportunities. What makes them *performative* is not just the repetition of recognizable acts, but the relational relays those acts percolate and redistribute. Intercultural transformations can only be apprehended when we retrace the network; if we focus only on the reception of scenarios, we are emphasizing actors and audiences over labor. If we study scenarios as reproduction—and not mainly as representations—the full spectrum of their impact will become clear. The prepositional analysis I have been proposing here aims at revisiting as many vectors as possible, envisioning intercultural scenarios as an ensemble of dynamic, lateral relations. The remaining chapters of this book will explore three different ways of observing these vectors: as relays or translational figurations, as affective environments, and as *geochronic* settings in which time and space are historicized.

Chapter 2

✦

Reassembling the Bones: The Festival of the Relics

In 1575, a ship bringing a cargo of relics destined for the Jesuits of New Spain floundered in the vicinity of the fortress of San Juan de Ulúa near the port of Veracruz. In the pillage that followed when the spoils were washed ashore, the reliquaries that contained the sacred bones were stolen and dispersed. While many of the thieves became ill—a sure sign of God's displeasure—most of the documentation identifying the relics got lost or mislaid, thus rendering the bones unusable for devotion. Since nameless skulls were less attractive than skulls associated with a particular martyr or saint, the Jesuits were extremely disappointed. A relatively recent presence in the viceroyalty—their first mission had arrived there in 1572—they were counting on the relics in order to organize a public festival that would consolidate their influence in the religious life of New Spain. In a generous show of support, Pope Gregory XIII sent a new shipment of relics for the Jesuits in 1578. This one made it to Mexico City, and the partisans of Saint Ignatius of Loyola welcomed it with one of the most sumptuous public celebrations ever recorded in the history of the capital.

The festival of the bones was nothing less than a transient but impressive reassembling of the economic and human networks of Mexico City. The splendid and costly preparation of sermons, literary contests, processions, dances, and multiple examples of ephemeral architecture sponsored by the Jesuits implied a deliberate effort to remap their surroundings. Focusing on their own buildings and schools, the Jesuits redrew the axiological balance of their urban landscape, turning the capital into *their* city. As opposed to the Franciscans and the Dominicans, the Jesuits were quite new to the place, and at the time of the festival they were still learning to understand Mexico. Inserting themselves into the productive networks of the viceroyalty, the Jesuits were also provoking some new vectors of their own. Cultural agency has been envisioned by Bruno Latour in terms of two functions: intermediaries (forces that circulate "without transformation[s]"), and mediators (forces that modify what they transport).[1] These positions are quite fluid and can change at any time: relations move around thanks to constant relays and regroupings. The fact that the Jesuits were actively adapting to their new surroundings implies—in a Latourian sense—a deliberate effort to mediate, an avid desire to avoid the apparent neutrality of the intermediary.

As I already pointed out in chapter 1, Latour's categorizations are not particularly helpful when we attempt to understand the affective connections that bring certain forces together: he is not interested in grasping performative relays in terms of their cultural specificity. As presented in *Reassembling the Social*, there is not enough room in Latour's actor-network-theory to concede that networks are also the result of attractions and dismissals that are efficient due to their semiotic and ideological input. As historians, we still have to figure out what moves some agents to do things in a certain way, and not another. Granting Derrida's point that context is an elusive matter, we also know that cultural expressions do not come out of nowhere. In Latour's own words: "We need something to designate flows of translations," something that depicts how the relaying process is achieved. Such an account will show a "string of actions where each participant is treated as a full-blown mediator"; not as an intermediary, but as an agent of change.[2] A relay is an intersectional site that "induces two mediators into coexisting,"[3] a transaction in which something new or different has the potential to be carried over and actualized.

Intersectional nodes can be hard to describe: how are we supposed to *recognize* novelty? This is a problem Latour hardly tackles, but performance studies has been wrestling with it since its inception as a discipline. What else is the twice-behaved, but the return of something already done that is now being perceived as other? Nonetheless, for all our insistence on the vanishing nature of performance, or the ethnographic accumulation of data, our field has not yet developed a manageable discourse for the conceptualization of emerging cultures. It is at this juncture that Latour can be illuminating, since his main purpose is to analyze "the practical means necessary to delineate groups and keep them in existence."[4] Latour calls attention to the fact that we have to be open to finding figurations or narrative constructs that enable us to localize the multiple relays that are taking place at a given moment, and he warns us that "there exists many more figures than anthropomorphic ones."[5] Anything made by people, or anything that motivates people to do things can be proposed as a figure of relay: even "a hammer, a basket, a door closer, a cat, a rug, a mug, a list, or a tag could act."[6] For Latour, the boundaries between nature, technology, and society are extremely pliable.

Our capacity to discern how change *happens* is radically challenged by intercultural performance. Stumbling into situations, objects, or subjects that are not easy to categorize at first glance (or at first hearing) is without doubt a primordial intercultural experience, one the Jesuits became particularly adept at managing due to their worldwide interventions as Catholic preachers and ambassadors in the Americas, Japan, and China. Probing into the

Jesuits' emphasis on public spectacle during late sixteenth-century colonial Mexico (and working in tandem with ideas proposed much later by Alfred North Whitehead and Giorgio Agamben), I would like to explore and illustrate some of the figurations of intercultural performance. The fact that I am studying a religious festival has inflected my critical choices in several fundamental ways. First of all, the celebration of the relics was an example of enacted theology, a series of events designed to activate and confirm Catholic beliefs. Since the festivities were a communal enterprise, I am also interested in conceptualizing the festival in terms of social labor. What type of work did the participants in the festival think they were actually doing? In addition, I would like to interrogate the festival from the standpoint of its intercultural components. By combining Indian and European elements, the festival provided an opportunity for the emergence of semiotic and experiential alterations. Public rituals were, in this context, an invitation to expose the historical becoming of Mexico City, and to reenvision New Spain as an ongoing process. I will argue that, in situations of intensified intercultural exchanges, religious rituals tend to expand and emphasize their translational capabilities.

Fernando R. de la Flor suggests that public spectacles are in reality a sequence of translations. A funeral, a canonization, a shipment of relics is prone to motivate a series of symbolic transfers.[7] When analyzed as mediators, these fleeting and highly theatrical moments of translation can be seized as opportunities to retrace the advent of intercultural relays. How is cultural difference actually grasped and metabolized in media res, right at the moment when it is being performed and tentatively glimpsed? How is the glimmering of something unexpected or intriguing qualified, recognized, or discarded? How do we describe something that alters our understanding of others, and even ourselves? How can we account for the emergence of something *new*? For the historian of the performative, emergence posits an agonistic node. Restored behavior is, by definition, both the reenactment of something recognizable that was *there* before, and the transformation of those materials into something *else*. Similarity and difference are inextricably conjoined. The twice-behaved is only available to us in a re-singularized state, as an-Other. How do we notice the arrival of something divergent? How do we realize that something unusual is happening in front of us? If emergence takes place (and time) gradually, does that mean that it is a cumulative incident that could have been predicted or divided into smaller units? If, on the contrary, emergence is basically the shocking eruption of something new, does that imply that we would never be able to guess its outcome in advance?[8] In the first case, emergence will be understood deductively; in the second, by induction. I would like to introduce a third option, one in which translation becomes a model for emergent, intercultural relays.

Elizabeth Grosz reminds us of "the strange vectors of becoming that a concept of the new provokes . . . How to think of direction or trajectory without being able to anticipate a destination?"[9] Grosz's question underlines the difficulties faced by all intercultural historians: how can we isolate the impending signatures of an incipient culture without falling into predetermined enplotments, or excessive hindsight? I will claim here that, when dealing with intercultural practices, it is precisely this conundrum that entitles us to access the formation of what I call *alterative identities*. The logic of intercultural formations is retroactive: a new culture is noticed as an action before it receives a label. Emergent cultures are prone to activate doubts and irritations, semiotic instabilities and civil unrest. Frequently enough, alterative cultures are recorded as disturbances of feeling before they are accepted or resisted as structures of feeling.

While in chapter 1 I spotlighted how reassembled scenarios should be mapped, my task here will be slightly different. Assuming that scenarios and other events are articulated by a continuous replacement of mediators, during the rest of this book I will be more interested in figuring out how certain colonial networks have been affectively encoded. If, as we already saw in chapter 1, identities are networks re-performed through a series of relays and labors, how do these markers of self become modified and recirculated? I also would like to strategically suspend current polarizations between archives and repertoires in order to reenergize close readings of textual remains. To the extent that they provoke and illustrate their own relational articulations, written documents are also mediators, and quite often they are the only palpable relays through which the past can still be hailed into traceability. As Rebecca Schneider claims, the fact that a performance has disappeared does not necessarily imply that it has vanished: an embodied experience produces ripples of many kinds.[10] The public welcoming of the relics managed to replicate and reshape the becoming of the same community that hosted it. By producing a series of sacred objects, a literary contest, and a religious play, the Jesuits invested human labor with the power to address the presence of God as communal work; in some instances—a song in Nahuatl, and an allegorical costume—they also actualized transient moments of intercultural creativity.

Bones of Contention

By the time the Jesuits arrived in New Spain, most of the creative cultural adjustments made by the Franciscan, Dominican, and Augustinian missionaries had already been consolidated (and some were in peril of being discarded, too). As Samuel Y. Edgerton shows, Nahuatl plays fomenting conversion, open chapels for preaching, atrial *posas*, or small altars, stone crosses mixing Indian and European motives, and mural cycles in religious cloisters had become part of everyday life.[11] Since the 1530s, and originally under the astute supervision of Pedro de Gante, schools like San José de los Naturales and the Colegio de la Santa Cruz de Tlatelolco had been instructing the Indians in the skills of European architecture, painting, and music. A massive and frequently erratic process of translation had transformed the conquest into an anthropological laboratory. Unfortunately, only those things useful for Christian doctrine were intentionally preserved; the rest were severely censored, or destroyed. The friars promptly realized that Tenochtitlán was a ceremonial center,[12] and that Indian audiences reacted to theatrical productions with attention and enthusiasm.[13] After the 1550s, the friars started to suspect that Indian beliefs were not really forgotten: the gods of the past had not gone away, but underground, and David Tavárez has excavated the long history of the scrutiny indigenous devotions were subjected to all the way into the eighteenth century.[14] Philip II was particularly interested in strengthening Catholic orthodoxy and control.[15] The Jesuits had come to New Spain after the Council of Trent, and one of their aims was to educate the indigenous and European elites of the viceroyalty under the new tenets of the Counter-Reformation. Although the Jesuits' most important contributions to colonial architecture would have to wait until the eighteenth century,[16] the relics sent by the pope in 1578 were intended as a proclamation of the leading role the church expected the Jesuits to assume in the Americas.

A year after the festival that welcomed the bones, a detailed *relación* or *carta* describing that celebration was published in Mexico City by Pedro de Morales. Born in Spain in 1537, Morales studied at the University of Salamanca and worked as a lawyer for several years before joining the Society of Jesus. He sailed to New Spain in 1576, where he became a highly effective fund-raiser and a teacher of canon law. His devotion to relics was still intense in 1594, when he requested some samples of the veil of the Virgin and Saint Joseph's *palio*.[17] Morales was, in equal measures, a devout and a pragmatic Christian. *Relaciones* like the one written by Morales were expected to both validate and replicate an economy of semiotic excess and hyperbole.[18] The Horatian dictum—"ut pictura poesis"—found in the *relaciones* one of its most ambitious applications: visualized objects, scenes, places, and people were carefully re-encoded as language.[19] The rhetorical skills of *ekphrasis* convocated a verbal surrogate for material displays of consumption and expense. Implicitly and sometimes explicitly, a *relación* was a *paragone*, or competition, between the word and the eye. Morales's *carta* proves him to be an adept practitioner of the genre.

Festivals were a fundamental feature of what Stephanie Merrim has called "the spectacular city" of Mexico, a way of bringing together the vectors of urban life through the staging of agile and kinesthetic interactions.[20] A perusal of Chimalpahin's commentaries written during the first decades of the seventeenth century shows the extent to which processions were almost a weekly source of public gatherings.[21] In his letter, Morales emphasizes the highly competitive atmosphere spurred by the relics among the citizens of the viceregal capital. Motivated by the enthusiasm of the Indians, both Spanish and criollo believers felt a need to respond in kind, investing their money and their time in an effort to equal—and hopefully outdo—their fellow Christians. The Spaniards and their descendants had very good reasons to fear the theatrical acumen of the Indians. When Morales stated that, for the enhancement of the processions, it was necessary "to make some promenades of foliage, like those the Indians tend to create," he was alluding to indigenous practices that were admired by conquistadors and friars alike.[22] As early as 1538, Fray Toribio de Motolinía was able to see in Tlaxcala a performance in which the Garden of Eden was presented in full detail, including trees, flowers made of feathers and gold, and a sample of real animals and birds.[23] (As noted in chapter 1, a similar display was orchestrated for the baptism of Martín Cortés's twins in 1566.) The Spaniards knew that, in the realms of public spectacle, the Indians were not only collaborators, but also worthy rivals.

According to Morales, the adrenaline rush injected by the relics into the colonial life of New Spain inspired the Indians to compete among themselves, too. From the start, then, there were some bones of contention in the middle of a festival designed to honor the scattered pieces of multiple canonized skeletons. While the dismembered bodies of the saints, received as a gift from the pope himself, helped to reunite the members of that society within the miraculous solidarity of the church, the wedge of cultural differences among them was still very much at work, reassembling the communal fabric in subtle, deliberate ways. The loyal citizens of the capital loaned an impressive array of pearls, jewels, silk, and money that was used to create four luxurious reliquaries. The first one was dedicated to a thorn from Christ's crown. The second was a tribute to a small piece from the Holy Cross. The third included a bone from the head of Santa Ana, another was a bone from San José, and two pieces of wood from the home of the Virgin in Loreto. The fourth reliquary contained a bone from San Pablo's leg. A fifth *relicario*, already in existence before the festival, exhibited a bone of Saint Hippolytus, considered the patron saint of Mexico City, due to the fact that the Spaniards' triumph over the Aztecs coincided with his official day—August 13—on the Catholic calendar. The jewels loaned by individual citizens for the Mexican reliquaries re-encoded the divisive tracks of viceregal wealth circulation, turning a substantial amount of private goods—at least for a few days—into public capital. While still treated as marks of economic entitlement, the jewels were also utilized here to provoke a fragile neutralization of class and racialized distinctions.

Teasing out polarized meanings is to a certain extent one of the main semiotic characteristics of relics and reliquaries. Situated at the intersection of perishable matter and everlasting grace, relics create a link between corpses and souls that suspends the differences between the living and the dead. Replacing the ancient cult of heroes,[24] a Christian relic validates a highly personalized attachment to a superior individual who serves as a mediator between God and the rest of us. When Saint Hugh of Lincoln was criticized for his enthusiastic dismembering of a saint's arm, he justified his actions by claiming that he was just breaking the bones in the same manner that he broke the bread during the Eucharist.[25] Through his bones, a saint is absent and present simultaneously, actualizing our desire for God's proximity and our dependence on his blessings. A relic conflates all temporal vectors: it verifies in the present the sacrifices of the past and the promises of the future. Due to their portable numinosity, relics also modify space: if one is not able to go to the Holy Land, a splinter from the True Cross can bring Jerusalem to one's own parish.[26] Sacred bones were prone to be stolen, translated, and moved around quite frequently.[27] And relics were held responsible for their powers: if they failed to respond to the clamors of a community, they were sometimes thrown to the ground, and dishonored. The presence of bones in altars was not accepted without considerable discussions about the propriety of disturbing the original resting place of human bodies.[28] Neither Jewish nor Roman laws were ever welcoming to such a close proximity between living and dead people.

As a result of their apparent relation to miracles, and their iconic relevancy during times of turmoil, relics are paradigmatic performative objects: they *seem* to make things happen. (For a believer, they actually do.) Seeta Chaganti proposes a poetics of the reliquary in which certain dualistic notions—time and timelessness, interior and exterior, corporeal and spiritual—are forced to transcend their boundaries in order to address the problematic nature of their representation. To what extent is an object capable of expressing a devotional impulse that conflates the unseen with the visible? By perceiving the evident disproportion between a human-made artifact and the religious gifts that it contains, the believer has no choice but to ponder the supernatural quality of God's grace.[29] A reliquary is thus perceived as efficacious to the extent that it is recognized as a failed signifier, an inadequate analogy that enshrines its own contradictions.

Gathering the jewels and arranging them together so that everybody could see them, the Jesuits underlined the solidarity between rich and poor; but this allegorical move was potentially diluted by the necessary dismantling of the reliquaries at the end of the festivities.[30] Morales himself suggests that, even after being returned to their owners, the jewels would still preserve their power to transform the community.[31] Like in the Eucharist, the jewels had gained a different substance without changing their external appearance. But a major question remains: how are the invisible consequences of transformation accounted for? It is at this point that performance becomes relevant. The function of religious festivals and liturgical rituals is to translate theology into labor, to invest matter with a spiritual dimension. The jewels provided for the reliquaries were first assembled and then dismembered in order to instantiate how God *works*.

Ergonic Performatives

The feminist theologian Catherine Keller claims that "religious language meanders along the borders between proposition and invocation."[32] The performativity of the reliquaries hinged on a continuous oscillation between fragments and entireties, and this pendular gesture facilitated the emergence of some intriguing intercultural translations. Due to their temporal fluidity—they were past, present, and future simultaneously—the impacting force of the relics had to be constantly recalibrated, relocated, and pondered. The presence of the bones located all human activities in the in-between of their translational efficacy: once the relics were present, everything could be—and had to be—transcoded. During the festival, this enhancement of liminal conditions articulated a flow of *exposed becomings* in which objects and peoples acquired temporal and spatial elasticity. More than a representation of God's providence, the festival was a materialization of God's *ergon*, a disclosure of how God's will *acts*.

The Greek word *ergon* means, depending on the context, "work," "task," "product," and "deed." It was particularly important for Aristotle, who contrasted it to language or speech. *Ergon* is the opposite of *Logos*. In *The Kingdom and the Glory: For a Theological Genealogy of Economy and Government*, Giorgio Agamben studies the philosophical dynamics of "power as ceremonial and liturgical regality."[33] In Agamben's view, Catholicism was pressured to negotiate two different connotations of the word "kingdom." The church was both a terrestrial enterprise and a manifestation of God's providence. This co-belonging of the mundane and the otherworldly demanded a theology capable of addressing human and divine expectations simultaneously. The concept of *oikonomia*—a term that originally signified the administration of a household—became a common trope that facilitated a managerial system in which God and the church worked out their *doings* by means of a distribution of tasks and objectives. The organizational model introduced by the principle of *oikonomia* enabled theologians to reimagine God as a bureaucratic Being, a monistic ruler that expressed his authority through a tight cluster of coordinated functions.

Agamben claims that in the context of *oikonomia*, the Trinity became a description of God's labor. Father, Son, and Holy Ghost are not three separate entities, but different relays in an economy of production that actualizes God's will. The Trinity was "not an articulation of the divine being, but of its praxis."[34] The Trinity is not an assortment of persons, but an assortment of acts. The conflicted coexistence of tangible and mysterious qualities fostered by this economic template was only precariously reconciled by a recourse to the performative operations of the liturgy and an active praising of God's omnipotence. The Lord's "glory is precisely the place at which this bilateral (or bi-univocal) character of the relation between theology and politics clearly emerges into the light."[35] The material glorification of God's power was both a civil and a religious necessity. Heaven and earth came together in the evanescent sounds of hymns and amens, and the paradoxes of the Eucharist. For Agamben, this tendency "culminates in post-Tridentine and Baroque theology . . . [and] in the motto of Ignatius of Loyola, which became something similar to the insignia of the Society of Jesus: *Ad maiorem Dei Gloriam.*"[36] The Jesuits understood that, while the glory of God cannot be increased by human means, the glorification of God can be augmented through a commitment to comply with his sovereignty and by increasing the number of converted souls.

The glorification of God conflated a call for obedience with an aesthetic imperative. Since God's glory is unfathomable, no testimonial to its glorification can be considered excessive. Agamben's inquiry into the intersections of theology, politics, and *oikonomeia* posits a fruitful reframing of religious festivals as labor demonstrations. The reliquaries were not merely commemorations of spiritual gifts, but materializations of God's presence through a reassembled community. A glorified God is a God revealed in the multiplicity of his becomings, his doings, and his unfoldings. By putting together jewels for the *relicarios*, by ethnically dividing the city's population in order to describe it as a unified Christian community, the Jesuits were portraying the capital in the image of God's *oikonomia*.

As an example of *oikonomia*, the festival of the bones was certainly not as extreme as the Aztec practice of the god impersonation, or *teotl ixiptla*, where a victim is sacrificed after living as the god Tezcatlipoca for a full year.[37] By giving his or her body, the Aztec impersonator was nourishing Tezcatlipoca and paying a cosmic debt; for the Catholics, the relics were part of a soteriologic scheme in which the body of Christ had cleansed the sins of all humankind. The Christian equivalent of the Aztec impersonator was the rematerialized body of Christ during the Eucharist, and the fractured remnants of martyrs' and saints' bodies. What attracts me to Agamben's argument is its emphasis on religious performance as theological and social labor, a process that materializes God's *ergon* in the world. The priority of glorification is to restore certain behaviors in order to parcel out the becomings of God's grace. That was, after all, the function of the Mass. The labors of glorification are mostly transferential: the whole point of religious spectacles is to convey one signifier through another signifier, to authorize a translational machine.

In a city where Indian and European elements were inextricably linked, this urgency to translate was already quite prevalent, but the festival of the bones provided an additional opportunity to examine emerging cultural variations. Since the believer who attended the festival of the bones was constantly being asked to confront difference through the lens of analogy, the *ergon* of the relics was afforded by calling attention to a chain of translational operations. If the mystery at the core of the festival was the capacity of substances to change their effects without changing their appearance—jewels and bones still looked like jewels and bones, after all was said and done—each activity sponsored by the Jesuits was an invitation to recognize God's intervention in human affairs as a series of semantic adjustments. We already saw how the reliquaries actualized God's work during the festival. Now I would like to shift our attention to a play performed during the Jesuits' celebrations.

Figures of Relay

On the first and last Sundays of the festival of the bones (November 2 and 9) a dramatic text titled *Triumpho de los Santos* (*Triumph of the Saints*) was produced. The performance took place at a chapel located on the left nave of the Church of San Pedro and San Pablo. On November 2 the play started at eight in the morning and ended around noon. In his *carta*, Morales praises the excellent design of the stage or *tablado*, the attractiveness of the costumes, and the gestural skills of the students that embodied the roles ("el meneo y actión de cada uno y de todos juntos" ["the swinging and actions of each of them and all of them together"]).[38] The audience reacted to the performance with abundant tears—a quintessential sign of devotion revered by Saint Ignatius of Loyola himself. With this play the Jesuits added another piece to an extensive repertoire of evangelical plays created in New Spain since the arrival of the Franciscans in the early years of the conquest. The intercultural, linguistic, and theological features of this religious dramaturgy have been carefully studied by Fernando Horcasitas,[39] Othón Arróniz,[40] Louise M. Burkhart,[41] María Beatriz Aracil Varón,[42] and Michael K. Schuessler.[43] Nevertheless, it is important to keep in mind that *Triumpho de los Santos* is closer to classical models taught by the Jesuits in their schools (like the tragedies of Seneca) than to the catechistic experiments of the mendicant friars.

As Maya Ramos Smith recalls, Jesuit drama was primarily an academic enterprise.[44] *Triumpho de los Santos* was probably written for the occasion by Vicencio Linuci and Juan Sánchez Baquero, two professors of rhetoric and Latin from the Colegio de San Pedro y San Pablo. The bones of four of the characters in the play—San Doroteo, San Gorgonio, San Pedro, San Juan Mártir—were among the relics sent to Mexico by Gregory XIII. A quick summary of the play's plot should suffice. After realizing that Christian believers are not obeying his orders, Emperor Diocletian decides to persecute them. A violent campaign ensues; in spite of the cruelty of their torturers—described with lyrical precision by the playwrights—the Christians not only die enthusiastically, but their numbers seem to increase. The failure to destroy the Christians disappoints Diocletian to the point of making him sick, thus forcing him out of power. After his death, Constantine's father becomes emperor; at his death, Constantine himself is challenged by his enemies. Guided by a vision of the Cross, Constantine wins the war and becomes a protector of the Christians. After being miraculously cured of leprosy, Constantine pays his respects to the remains of the martyrs by having them excavated.

The nomadic destiny of these bones will take them, many centuries later, to the New World and the festival in which *their* play is being enacted. As the plot thickens, the spiritual resilience of the Christians is signified both by their dismemberment and by the reassembled victory of their recuperated bodies. *Triumpho de los Santos* is not a memorable piece, but the procession that preceded it and the play itself thrived in their capacity to dismantle the boundaries between spectators and performers. Public festivals are, by definition, activities that aim to transform their audiences into a fundamental part of the show. In this case the bones of four characters were attending their own hagiographic memorial; when, towards the end of the play, the actors worshiped their relics, everybody came to the realization that the saints had been already *there* with them from the beginning. The audience members were still Mexicans, but they had also become the equivalent of early Christians. Synchronized in space and time, the relics' past was thus compressed into a Mexican present that was just another step towards the future eschatological fulfillment of God's plan.

This dramatic telescoping of chronological vectors was sanctioned by the use of what Erich Auerbach calls a *figurative* mode of thinking. For Christianity, history is a cumulative sequence of types that gradually discloses a divine archetype, God's definitive plan for the world. Every individualized *figura* is a partial fulfillment of the future yet to come and a reflection of the past already attained.[45] To a certain extent, a *figure* channeled God's *ergon* forward—and backwards. Although Catholic history is irreversible (we are advancing towards the eventual return of Christ), the appearance of new figurative relations is always possible. Since history circulates in all directions at the same time, every singular event is a relay node in which multiple possibilities are articulated at once. It is in those relays that God's *ergon* can be experienced as a process that is both constative (it comes from the past) and proleptic (it opens itself to latent or potential affinities). If we consider that the relics were already sanctioning a fluid state between matter and spirit, the presence of figurative elements that permeated the festival as a whole added another transformative layer within which intercultural expressions had a chance to become detectable and tested.

In *Triumpho de los Santos*, the figurative conflation of historical coordinates into an enhanced dramatic experience was not afforded without risking a few potentially disturbing fractures. The predicament of the early Christians in the play frequently resembles another religious crisis: the relatively recent conversion of the Indians to that same faith. Since the play was written by two Europeans, this is not as much a question of digging out a hidden transcript but of pondering the inevitable ideological dangers of Auerbach's *figura* itself. It is possible—although we are unable to confirm it—that certain scenes of the play struck too close to home. When Chromacio suggests that, in order to eliminate the Christians, it will be necessary not only to inflict physical pain, but, even more importantly, to burn their temples and their books, those lines were prone to strike the chord of a different historical trauma. The Indians had seen too many of the material elements of their own culture torn down or turned into ashes not to find the parallel plausible. The carefully described torments inflicted upon Christian men, women, and children that open act 4 are not far from renditions of the massacre of Cholula—an episode ordered by Cortés during the conquest of Mexico—included by Fray Bartolomé de Las Casas in *A Short Account of the Destruction of the Indies*, published in 1552.[46] The mere possibility of this double reading of the play is already a sign of how permeable figurative encodings of history were to reversals and reinterpretations.

The staging of *Triumpho de los Santos* encouraged an intersectional force field. The figurative efficacy of the piece hinged on its audience's capability to entangle several historical vectors at once. But not all figures of relay were conveyed by means of characters or devotional relics. The festival of the bones was also deploying multiple acts of translation that implicitly exercised a similar function: to connect, to link, and to foster associations between heterogeneous materials. In the concluding scene of *Triumpho de los Santos*, an allegorical figure of the church ties up all the loose ends of the play, evoking the donation of languages given to the apostles at Pentecost.[47] The reference to Pentecost underlines the worldwide enterprise embraced by the church, and how much the preaching of the gospel depended on the translational talents of its missionaries. Practicing several languages was a fundamental aspect of the church's commitment to increase the Christian flock.

While the ornamental zest of the reliquaries tested the expressive limits of material representation, there were other aspects of the festival that introduced an explicit nod towards more literary endeavors. On October 2, 1578—a month before the actual transportation of the relics across the city took place at the beginning of November—the students of the Colegio de San Pedro y San Pablo organized their own ceremonial parade. A "cartel," or edict explaining the rules for seven literary contests (five in Latin, two in Castilian), was carried from the Colegio to the Plaza Mayor, where the viceroy himself saluted the enthusiastic members of this secular procession. The leader of the group was a student wearing clothes made of silk and gold and riding a white horse; he was followed by musicians and two hundred students among which some were disguised as Turks and English people.[48] As heretics, the English were enemies of Spain, and their own confrontation with the Spanish Armada was only a decade ahead (1588).[49] The so-called Turkish squadron, of course, stood for the Islamic forces that had been halted just a few years earlier in the Battle of Lepanto (1571).

The students' procession was nothing less than a jolly reminder of Spain's mission as a defender of the Catholic faith and the Colegio's commitment to the instruction of the sons of the Spanish and criollo elite that organized it. To educate these young subjects of European extraction was one of the main objectives of the Jesuits' work in New Spain. It was the concern of many citizens that the children of the Spaniards "críanse en el regalo y abundancia de las casas de sus padres y en la benignidad de este cielo y temperamento con mucha ociosidad" ("are being raised by their parents in the middle of complacency and abundance and the mildness of the climate that promotes laziness").[50] It was frequently observed that younger men in New Spain developed a facility to speak with wit and verve at a faster pace than their European counterparts; they also tended to be restless and melancholic. The misguided and inexperienced enthusiasm that in 1566 rallied young men like Alonso de Avila around the second Marquis del Valle—with the tragic consequences that we already know—was certainly seen as a confirmation of this. After the arrival of the Italian scholar Vincencio Lanuchi in 1574, the Colegio de San Pedro y San Pablo was able to provide a solid foundation in Latin grammar. Lanuchi was particularly fond of the pedagogical exercises—memorization, declamation, debates, and other theatrical activities—that supported the Ratio Studiourum Parisiensis, a methodology adopted by the Jesuits in emulation of the University of Paris.[51] Mastery of the Latin language allowed the students to read and imitate the literary models of antiquity. A rigorous understanding of the rules of Latin grammar—and the creative and persuasive uses of those rules in poetry and rhetoric—enabled the new generations to think and write with clarity, precision, and elegance.

In order to validate the fairness of the judging process, these literary contests called for the participation of the Audiencia, the church, and the university.[52] The instructions for the literary competitions held during the festival of the bones were written in Latin, and they specified not only the metric forms to be used, but also the topics to be developed and the prizes to be obtained by the winners. The themes included compositions praising the sacred thorn, the glorious deeds of all saints in general and all martyrs in particular, an exploration of potential symbolic links between Ezekiel's vision of the four animals and the four doctors of the church, an encomium of chastity, and a comparison between the tree of knowledge and the tree of the cross. The awards included food for thought—books by Thomas Aquinas—an intriguing array of objects made of silver (spoons, salt shakers, inkwells, a figurine of the Lamb of God) and a series of hats made of wool or taffeta. Silver utensils were precious possessions in New Spain, and in our first chapter we already saw how wearing—or not wearing—a hat in front of other people was a protocolary marker for the recognition of social rank and honor.

While these curious prizes acknowledged a link between mental work and the imperatives of the body, the award ceremony for the poetic contest at the end of the festivities replicated on a smaller scale the parameters of the complete event. After a sermon and a mass, a *coloquio* introduced two pairs—Poetry and Interest, Oratory and Honor—that tried in vain to convince each other until Religion and Justice requested them to place their skills at the service of the relics. A *villancico* was sung as part of this allegorical quid pro quo. Morales decided to include in his *carta* only a selective anthology of the poems submitted to the contest,[53] a choice we are grateful for if we take into account the perfunctory quality of many of the samples preserved.

The literary contests were probably the most predictable angle of the festival of the bones. Their emphasis on formal rules and genres precluded from the start almost any surprises—any stylistic derailment disqualified a poem immediately, thus keeping it out of the official records. The procession provided an excellent opportunity for the students' parents to display their wealth. The Jesuits' emphasis on the education of the European elite had also a more pragmatic side. Pedro Sánchez, the first provincial of the Jesuit order in Mexico, explained to Everardo Mercuriano that it was necessary to prioritize the education of Spaniards and criollos, since most of the monetary donations came from them. The Indians also needed well-educated masters.[54] Scouting donors was one of the main administrative tasks that the Jesuits focused on during their first decades in New Spain, and Pedro de Morales himself was a respected fund-raiser. Although the Colegio de San Pedro y San Pablo was technically founded in 1574, it was not until two years later that Alonso de Villaseca, owner of the mines of Ixmiquilpan, offered the necessary financial support to cover the costs of building it.[55] Due to his feeble state of health, Villaseca himself was unable to attend the festival, but the Jesuits sent him the relics of San Pablo and San Pedro, a piece of wood from the Cross, or *lignum Crucis*, and a thorn from Christ's crown.[56] The financial blessings brought by the interventions of sacred bones were never far from view: enhancing the traceability of cultural and economic networks is one of the primordial effects that organizers of public festivals tend to seek and produce. Writing compositions in several languages was another type of relay that accentuated that process. As I will show in the next section, one of the many poems performed during the festival also provoked the embodiment of an emerging intercultural subjectivity. No indigenous languages were included in the literary contest; in order to find them, we have to look elsewhere.

Translational Steps

During their first decade in New Spain, the Jesuits established a segregated educational system in which most of their Indian students—a substantial number of them members of the indigenous elite—attended their own school at the Colegio de San Gregorio. Morales's description of one of the monuments created for the festival gives us a glimpse of how some of these Indian students participated in the procession. Located in close proximity to the convent of Santo Domingo, this spot was the portal for the whole event, and it included an intriguing combination of emblematic encoding, public dancing, and dual translations. Built in three sections, an arch dedicated to San Hipólito, San Esteban, and San Laurencio was covered with Latin citations from the Bible and original *coplas* or short poems in Castilian. Morales pays careful attention to a performance that took place in front of it:

> En llegando la procesión a este arco, salió a recebir las Sanctas Reliquias un bayle de naturales indios niños, muy bien adereçados a su modo y hábito, con mucho ornato y plumería, los quales eran músicos; y assí, el son del baile era en canto de órgano concertado con quatro vozes diferentes que hazían consonancia al modo español, y juntamente con las vozes sonavan flautas y el instrumento proprio de ellos con que de hordinario tañen en sus bailes (a que llaman Teponaztli) de suerte que, sonando todos a una, resultava una muy buena consonancia. La letra que cantavan, aunque era en su lengua, yva en medida castellana, en alabança de todos los santos y particularmente de su patrón San Hyppólito.
>
> [When the procession arrived at this arch, a group of dancing Indian children welcomed the relics, dressed in their usual attire, with ornaments and feathers, and their music, and singing in polyphonic style while making consonance in the Spanish mode, and their voices were accompanied by flutes and their typical drum or *teponaztli*, and they were all well synchronized. The words they were singing, although in their own language, were measured and rhymed following Spanish models, and the song was in praise of San Hipólito, their patron saint.]

Morales preserved both the Nahuatl and the Spanish lyrics of this song. This is the poem in Nahuatl:

Tocniuane touian,
 Ti quin to namiquiliti
  In Dios vel ytlaçouan
 Matiquinto tlapaluiti.
  Xipapaqui, yuan xicuyca
 Quenmachtami intitochan:
 Yxachintin valmonica,
 Sant Hyppolito yuan
 Intomauiz Capitan,
 Maticto çiauhquechiliti,
 Auh in ylaço icniuan
 Matiquinto tlapaluiti.
  Y etopan omaxitico
 Intotecuio ypilhuan
  Otechmopaleuilico
  Inuicpa tayouan
  Mauel tipapaquican,
  Nimantiquin totiliti
   In Dios vel ytlaçouan
Matiquintotlapaluiti.

And this is the translation into Castilian in Morales's *carta*:

A compañeros salgamos
a recibir en presencia
a los que ama Dios, y vamos
a hazerles reverencia.
Alégrate, huelga y canta,
o dichosa tierra nuestra,
pues de sanctos copia tanta
te a dado la excelsa diestra.
Hyppólito se te muestra
capitán de tu creencia,
a él y a los otros vamos
a hazerles reverencia.
An venido estos amigos
y hijos de Dios a vernos,
y contra los enemigos
con su favor a valernos,
con gozo y affectos tiernos
y con grande complacencia;
a los que ama Dios, salgamos
a hazerles reverencia.[57]

I include here a translation into English made by Fernando Horcasitas:

Oh, our friends, let us go!
Let us go forth to meet them,
the precious things of God.
Let us go delight in them!
Be glad and sing
Blessed are they in our homes.
Many are coming
those of San Hipólito and
those of our glorious captain.
Let us go receive them
and his revered women
Let us go delight in them!
Now they have come to us
against our enemies.
The Children of our Lord
Have come to aid us
Let us rejoice greatly,
Then we will go to dance
to the precious things of God
Let us go delight in them![58]

According to Morales, the translation into Spanish was made by a Jesuit father, and the poem "aunque era en su lengua, yva en medida y consonancia castellana . . . no van declaradas por los mismos vocablos, por ser tan diferentes los de la una lengua y la otra en medida de sílabas, pero van conforme al sentido como por ellas consta" ("although it was in their Indian language, the poem was presented in Castilian metrics . . . but it was not possible to use the same exact words, because the words and the syllabic count in one language are so different from the other that only their sense has been conveyed."[59] If I understand Morales correctly, he is basically saying that sense and metrics are slightly at odds in this translation, and that something about the song cannot be entirely accounted for in Spanish. This is not necessarily unusual, as any translator of poetry certainly knows. But Morales had already explained earlier that the Nahuatl version was molded by Spanish forms. If that was the case, the Nahuatl song was not *just* in Nahuatl, and the Spanish version was not *just* its Spanish equivalent. A former act of translation was already *embedded* into the original Nahuatl song. The translation here was not from source culture to target culture, but a *sharing* between both, an interweaving, a blending. Morales realized the song was mobilizing both languages in mutual alteration of each other: they were entangled from the start.

What exactly was going on—and going *through*—during the performance of this song? Or, to say it differently, how many relays are taking place while the young Indians dance? First of all, like James Joyce's *Finnegans Wake*, the poem is perhaps untranslatable due to the fact that it was, from the beginning, an exercise in translation. The poem is not exactly based on code switching, but on a structural compromise that I prefer to qualify as code *merging*. Morales recognizes the singularities of the Indian language, and the incapacity of his own Spanish to effectively surmount them. It is his recognition of this inadequacy that signals for us an emergent cultural alteration. The poem is not just a combination of Nahuatl and Castilian, but an object that resents and dislodges that dualism. The poem—although a minor one—implicitly questions the stability of Nahuatl and Castilian as linguistic constructs; it de-essentializes them both by pushing them into a semiotic co-belonging that inflects their expressive range.

It was not incidental that the Indians were dancing as a tribute to San Hipólito, the patron saint of the Spanish conquest of Tenochtitlán. As I will explain in more detail in chapter 3, dancing was one of the aspects of Mexica culture the Spaniards dreaded the most. Cortés and his soldiers associated Indian dancing with war and human sacrifice, and the friars saw it as the *ergon* of the devil. The missionaries adapted it to Christian practices, but Motolinía, Durán, and Sahagún acknowledged their incapacity to fully grasp the meanings of Indian songs. As for the dance steps, surviving descriptions are vague. This one was made by Francisco Cervantes de Salazar in his *Crónica de la Nueva España*, written in the 1560s:

> Indians of several ages joined these dances, after getting drunk together in order to stimulate their devotion; they organized themselves in circles of four or six people, and at the center of each circle they placed their drums . . . they lowered their heads, they combed their bodies while rising their right arm, holding up on it some of their sacred objects . . . they looked like intoxicated men that are falling apart . . . They can spend the whole day dancing without getting tired. Since it is hard for us to understand what they are saying, they trick us by moving their heads saying "god" very loudly at the beginning and the end of their songs, and then mumbling everything else they say in between.[60]

It is thus evident the Indians were merging Nahuatl and Spanish codes in their danced translations very early.

Nahuatl has two different verbs for dancing, and they are both associated with specific types of songs: *itotia* is the source for *netotiliztli*, or songs of entertainment and historical stories; and *macehua* is the source for *macehualiztli*, or songs dedicated to the gods. The song used during the festival was, then, a Christian version of *macehualiztli*. It is possible that the flutes mentioned by Morales were examples of the *tlapitzalli*, a recorder-like instrument "made of either clay, reed, or bone," but flutes of other kinds were also popular. The drum is, without doubt, a *teponaztli*; similar to a xylophone, it was made from a hollowed piece of wood, with an incision on top with two tongues that produced two different pitches. A *teponaztli* was ornamented with "carvings representing birds, beasts, or grotesque human heads,"[61] and it was played on top of a pedestal, while the drummer used mallets covered with rubber. (See figure 2.1.)

As James Lockhart explains, it was only after the 1550s that Nahuatl speakers started to borrow Spanish nouns with increased frequency, actively coining neologisms in order to describe the extensive list of new objects and animals brought by the Europeans. Musical instruments were no exception. The Spaniards classified their musical instruments into three main groups: winds, strings, and percussion. The Indians only recognized two groups: winds and percussion; for them, string instruments like the *vihuela*, the harp, or the lute were called *mecahuehuetl*, or "cord drums." The organ was particularly difficult to assimilate, since it was "a wind instrument not blown by a human being, and struck with the hands in a percussive manner. Drawing on both typological analogies, the Nahuas came up with the mixed term *ehhuatlapitzalhuehuetl*, 'hide wind-instrument drum,' 'hide' referring to the bellows."[62] Artifacts like the organ were an incentive for translation and the emergence of mixed tropes.

Many new categories of self are rehearsed for the first time through an effort to describe objects and unprecedented practices. W. V. Quine explains how translations between non-kindred languages advance by means of

Figure 2.1. Indian drummers. We can see another drum called *huehuetl* (left) and the *teponaztli* (right). *Florentine Codex*, Biblioteca Medicea Laurenziana, Florence. (Med. Pal. 218, c.313r)

a cumulative process of sedimentation that slowly combines gestural and analogical approximations. Quine believes that, under most circumstances, an "indeterminacy of correlation" accompanies all bilingual exchanges: languages are never completely equivalent to each other.[63] If translation was the *ergon* of the festival of the bones, Morales's exposure of the Nahuatl song as a problematic bilingual artifact shows that translations also produced alterative discourses in which the emergence of a different culture acquires visibility. Using the words of Roland Faber, it is feasible to say that this song conveys "the relationship between experience and reality as one that is conditioned in such a way so as to be able to account for novelty."[64] The doings of singing and dancing actualized the labors of this particular translation in a way that transitorily suspended the boundaries between archive and repertoire. Places like colonial New Spain, in which intercultural exchanges had been intensified by a violent redistribution of semiotic materials, are prone to be traversed by translations that crystallize the becoming-other of two or more preexisting languages. Samuel Weber reminds us that "translation always involves not merely the movement from one *language* to another, but from one *instance*—a text already existing in one language—to another instance, that does not previously exist, but that is brought into being in the other language."[65] These translations are, in the end, more metamorphic than transferential: their result is not an equivalent message, but a potential alteration of the referents of the message itself.

The Appreciation of Novelty

As we stated at the beginning of this chapter, Bruno Latour thinks that a translation involves the co-participation of two or more mediators, an encounter in which things are not only being carried on, but transformed. The festival of the bones was organized around a series of overlapping transferential moments, and it is in this sense that our Nahuatl-Castilian poem stands for a figure of relay as relevant as the sacred relics, a literary competition, and the allegorical inductions of *Triumpho de los Santos*. In the poem, two languages inflect each other into mutual alteration. This verbal jointness was only partially actualized by the text; the poem was just one of the many traces left behind by a productive network that included the embodied interventions of Indian dancers, singers, and musicians. What we call a network in this case is this holding together of words, motions, and labors, the material and affective energies that made this intercultural togetherness performable in the first place.

Morales explains that the song was arranged for four voices, "in the Spanish mode." Starting as early as the 1520s with the initiatives of Pedro de Gante, the Indians became quite attached to European vocal and instrumental music, and their fondness for dancing before and after the Mass was closely monitored by the church authorities. Musicians were greatly admired and respected among the Mexicas, and the Indians embraced their role as players and singers under the Spaniards with an enthusiasm that by the late 1550s was alarming Archbishop Alonso de Montúfar. Although Indian musicians were far from being well paid, they considered themselves eligible for tribute exemptions and were also able to spend a substantial amount of time practicing and, to the dismay of the friars, even enjoying it. By 1561, Philip II—always willing to intervene in all aspects of his subjects' lives—was requesting the royal Audiencia to address this issue. Hymns in Nahuatl were often composed, and at least two dedicated to the Virgin Mary and attributed to Hernando Franco have been preserved in a manuscript collection that includes several masses by Palestrina.[66] The song heard—and seen—by Morales was thus far from being unusual.

As an exercise in code merging, our song was also a minor moment in a long series of efforts to master aboriginal languages initiated by the mendicant friars many decades earlier. Nothing in Castilian prepared the friars for the realization that in Nahuatl, neither nouns nor adjectives have gender.[67] Joseph Errington observes how Horatio Carochi, in his *Arte de la lengua mexicana* (1645), complains that Spanish speakers were unable to replicate a glottal sound made by the Indians—known as *saltillo*—and that Nahuatl was on occasion closer to Hebrew than to Latin.[68] In his *Vocabulario Nahuatl-Castellano, Castellano-Nahuatl* (1571), Fray Antonio de Molina declares that he learned Nahuatl very slowly because there were noticeable variants from one province to another, and the lack of certain ideas either in Nahuatl or Spanish created "largos circunloquios y rodeos" ("long meanderings and hesitations"). He recognized that in some cases it was necessary to create new words and locutions,[69] and that the Indians merged the two languages themselves very often.

Although the Council of Trent prohibited the translation of the Bible into vulgar languages, preachers and evangelizing friars were allowed to use translations authorized by a priest. The decrees of the Counter-Reformation probably came as a shock to a land in which translation was nothing less than a lifestyle systematically arranged around the education of the sons of the caciques. Founded by the Franciscans in 1536, the Colegio de la Santa Cruz de Santiago de Tlatelolco taught Latin to its Indian students so successfully that Bernardino de Sahagún promoted a vast ethnographic exchange based on trilingual informants who spoke Nahuatl, Latin, and Castilian. The administration of the Colegio de Tlatelolco was later transferred to the Indians themselves, but after the provincial councils of 1555 and 1565 the Franciscans abandoned their original plan to produce a native clergy. At least until 1558, quickly trained adolescents recruited from indigenous elites—like the ones dancing in the festival of the bones—were used to convey the good news in villages and local churches, and Indian assistants were allowed to administer certain sacraments, including baptism and the rituals for the dying.

Nevertheless, to classify our song mainly as an example of hybridity somehow simplifies its effect. The poem is not an additive act, but a process that interpellates a positionality that has not been named yet, a new subjectivity that Morales vaguely adumbrates. Who *exactly* is the addressee of a Nahuatl song danced by Indians and written following Castilian rhymes? Is this poem an incidental example of colonial transactions, as transient as the arches built for a religious festival? Or is this bilingual song a moment of semantic experimentation, a glimpse of alterative modalities and structures of feeling? Like in the Trinity, the different components of the song are *moments* in a process that is working out God's management of New Spain. The text of the poem is neither Indian nor Spanish, but something else that both cultures are deploying during the performance itself. In the poem, both Nahuatl and Castilian face the fact that they are languages in the making, constantly reworking themselves into multiplicities than can only be contained by God's glory.

Neither Agamben nor Latour facilitates a conceptual figuration for the emerging quality of relays, the alterative nature of the translational *ergon*. We still need a category that comes to grips with cultural *novelty*. I will argue that we can categorize these figurative relays more effectively if we take into consideration some arguments proposed by Alfred North Whitehead. I am aware the British philosopher is an unusual choice when it comes to the unpacking of a religious festival, but he pioneered an epistemic understanding of becoming that can be quite enlightening for the historian of the performative. In *Process and Reality*, published in 1929, Whitehead ambitiously proposed a series of rationalizations conducive to a discourse capable of describing the emergence of novelty. Whitehead was invested in showing that "process is nothing else than the experiencing subject itself," and that "an experiencing subject is one occasion of sensitive reaction to an actual world."[70] Out of the disjointed diversity of phenomena we are constantly confronting, we manage to emphasize certain features in order to turn that multiplicity into something intelligible. Concrescence—the patching together of our perceptions into a provisional unity—takes place only when we intensify some elements over others, when we "elicit into relevance" a particular set of objects.[71] To localize an event is to interrupt, to abstract, to isolate a portion of our experience from the continuity of its becoming. In Whitehead's speculations, our awareness of self is the outcome (not the precedent) of an experiential process: we are "conditioned, though not determined"[72] by our exposures to action and change.

Interestingly enough, Whitehead seems to suggest that becoming is a frictional process in which teleology and contingency are equally at work. A world fully constricted by a predetermined goal will be inaccessible to anything new; but a world made of pure potentiality, devoid of any vectorial leanings, will disperse itself into something incomprehensible. Philosophy aims to capture the world as it unfolds, in between these polarized strictures. According to Whitehead, only the notion of God can conceptually reconcile this fundamental rift between constancy and mutability. In *Process and Reality*, Whitehead claims that becoming is apprehended as a "clutch at vivid immediacy."[73] Becoming is at its most actual when it is qualified by emergence, when it is tackled in terms of its performability.

By holding a view of God as *ergon*, a divinity at work in the world—a performative God—Catholic theologians revealed an understanding of becoming very similar, *grosso modo*, to Whitehead's. Liturgical occasions and public festivals were intensifiers of becoming, displays of God's labor actualized by means of human mobilizations. While Agamben helps us to reframe the festival of the bones as theological labor, Whitehead provides us with an epistemic elaboration that facilitates a critique of figurative relays in terms of the degrees of process they disclose. By casting process as "the rush of immediate transitions," Whitehead focuses on how concrescence actualizes a sense of otherness, the eclosion of something new.[74] For Whitehead, novelty is both an effect (it has causal determinations) and a moment of creativity (it posits something that cannot be fully explained by causality alone).

For the intercultural scholar, Whitehead's approach comes as nothing less than a welcomed compromise, a dispensation authorizing us to live with our essentialist guilt. Since cultural innovations can only be measured against an antecedent, we tend to conceptualize intercultural constructs as in-betweens, hyphens, and hybrids, but these categories only facilitate our arguments at the cost of abstracting the constitutive heterogeneity of each anterior culture. Essence is always a *situated* concept; when we talk about Mexican *mestizaje*, we provisionally forget that neither "Indian" nor "Spaniard" were ever fixed or stable quantities. Postcolonial identities are not only derivative constructs or perpetual spin-offs of their traumatic history: both before and after colonialism, multiplicity was the norm, not the exception. What has to be convened is how and why moments of cultural concrescence end up being occluded, selectively reduced, and even lost.

My reading of Morales's *carta* utilizes it as an archival remnant of certain relays, a textual recording of vectors that helps me retrace intercultural emergences. The Nahuatl-Spanish song analyzed earlier is an instantiation of concrescence, and it rejects any attempt to be reduced into one culture or another, since the act of translation has been etched within the text itself. While participating in two languages simultaneously, the song also denotes the emergence of a potential substitute for each of them, an innovation. The element missing from the *carta* is, of course, the dancing, the embodiment that compressed these two languages into the nonverbal registers of gesture and motion. The dance steps reformulated the textual tensions of the poem in terms of somatic prescience. The dancing Indians were able to experience as becoming what the poem preserved for us only as script, and the emerging identity channeled through the dance enjoyed—for only a few minutes—the always fragile advantage of movement over any standard modes of notation. But those bodies are still here, somehow, in the affective aftermath of our reading.

Wearable Becomings

Up to this point, I have been stressing how Morales's *carta* scans the celebration of the relics as a sequence of relays: Indians and Spaniards compete with each other and among themselves; jewels are gathered, turned into reliquaries, and then returned to their owners; a religious play conflates past, present, and future providential convocations; a literary contest in Latin enables students and parents to show off their wealth; and a group of young Indians dance to the tune of a bilingual song. I am proposing we should understand the festival as a deliberate networking of theological labors: the sacred bones were encoded as agents of God's *ergon*, and as such they had the power—the *performativity*—to reassemble the material resources of Mexico City in order to advertise the spiritual investments of the Jesuits. The function of the festival was to replay and redirect an ongoing affective economy in which expenditures and beliefs were densely intertwined. For the Jesuits, the festival was more a matter of ideological gains than a matter of financial profits, although fund-raising was not excluded from the picture. (Later on, the Jesuits were also highly regarded as business administrators.) I have also been arguing that certain relays are productive sites for the phasing out of intercultural formations. By focusing on a minor Nahuatl-Spanish text, I underlined the capacity of some relays to actualize alterative practices in which emerging cultural variations become traceable. Merging two languages and the physical exertions of indigenous dancers and musicians, the song articulated a double bind in which causality and innovation moderated each other into an intensified disclosure of New Spain's intercultural everyday life.

To acknowledge an admixture is to insinuate that things are still being worked out: mediators tend to foreground their own becoming. Emergence is the contrary of suture. Another example from the *carta* is a case in point. Towards the final days of the festival or *octavario*, the Colegio de San Pablo y San Pedro—to which Morales is evidently partial—outdid itself by staging another play. After a sermon, eight children wearing rich costumes danced, and then an allegorical *coloquio* followed in which sinful Mexico, reprehended by Truth, was advised to request the relics from Rome. Although Envy and Malice tried to distract Virtue, the bones arrived at their destination and Peace gave Mexico a victorious embrace. Morales reserves his praise for the visual representation of Mexico itself:

> El vestido y aparato con que salió Mexico (por ser particular de esta tierra) creo dará contento . . . porque sacó en su acompañamiento algunos al trage indiano con sus tilmas (que acá llaman) de damasco azul, que son unas ropas largas desde el hombro hasta el suelo, y Mexico con un vestido mezclado de Español y de Indio (denotando la variedad y mezcla de gentes que en sí tiene) llevaba el cabello cogido al modo de acá con muchas joyas de oro y perlería. Su vestido interior era a la española y encima un huypil (que es una sobre ropa cerrada y sin mangas que las indias usan) la qual rematava en la cortapisa con una orla de oro y seda, y en la mano sacó las armas de la ciudad.
>
> [The garments wore by Mexico (since they are particular to these lands) will provide joy to the reader . . . The accompanying figures appeared wearing an indigenous *tilma* of blue damask pending from their shoulders all the way to their feet as they usually do, and Mexico itself entered with a garment mixing Spanish and Indian elements (in order to express the variety of peoples living here), and Mexico had a headdress arranged in the local manner with jewels and pearls.

Figure 2.2. Indian women wearing *huipiles*. *Florentine Codex*, Biblioteca Medicea Laurenziana, Florence. (Med. Pal. 219, c.281r)

> Mexico's inside clothes were Spanish and they were covered on the outside by a *huipil* (which is like a blouse without sleeves used by the women here) and the borders of the *huipil* were ornamented with gold and silk, and Mexico was holding the symbols of the city.][75]

In her succinct study of the festival of the bones, Solange Alberro[76] notices the mestizo quality of Mexico's dress while calling attention to how the Jesuits utilized the welcoming of the relics as an opportunity to rehearse a new image of the viceroyalty. The costume admired by Morales is neither entirely Spanish nor Indian, but an assortment of elements from both cultures: a Spanish dress ("vestido interior") and an Indian garment ("y encima un huypil"). Patricia Rieff Anawalt has summarized the complex assortment of clothes and accessories circulating in Mexico before the conquest, and how carefully the Aztecs regulated sumptuary displays.[77] Among the Aztecs, costumes were carriers of a diverse array of social discourses: rank, group affiliations, and places of origin were associated with specific designs and textures. Garment pieces were prominently displayed in the tribute listings of the *Codex Mendoza*. A *huipil* (from *huipilli*, "shirt") is a squared blouse or sack-like piece with openings for head and arms.[78] (See figure 2.2.) *Huipiles* were adorned with a variety of colors (orange, yellow, blue), and coyote and rabbit furs.

It seems that after the conquest, the *huipil* started to have short sleeves, and that rectangular collars were replaced in some cases by round ones.[79] Fray Diego Durán admired their colors and how roses and eagles made of feathers were placed in their front and back.[80] Chloë Sayer observes that in the illustrations for Sahagún's *Codex Florentino*, prostitutes are shown wearing excessively ornamented skirts and *huipiles*,[81] but even more modest *huipiles* had decorative motifs in their lower borders, below the neck, and in the back (animals, birds, and plants).[82] On special occasions, *huipiles* were covered with shoulder shawls, or *quechquemitl.*

Going back now to the performance, in Morales's description we can see that Mexico was escorted by some males wearing *tilmatli*, mantles or capes made of blue damask. Since the students from the Colegio de San Pablo y San Pedro were of European extraction, I suggest that this can be—like Avila's masquerade in chapter 1—another example of Spaniards playing Indians. (There is a strong possibility the personification of Mexico was performed by a male, too.)[83] A *tilma* was a rectangular cloak-like piece (called a *manta* in Spanish); a loincloth was worn under it. Commoner males were not allowed to wear them below their knees, and they were punished by death if their *tilma* reached their ankles. (Warriors were permitted to do so if their legs were wounded in battle, a sign of prestige and courage.) More often than not, the knot was tied over the right shoulder, but males of high status—like nobles and priests—tied the knot in the front. Some maguey *tilmatli* were given an application of maize dough that once dried provided them with the tones and the sounds of pottery; turkey and other types of feathers were also added. Yellow, red, white, black, and purple capes were widely appreciated by the Spaniards, and Sahagún counted at least ten different prints or designs.[84] Morales ignored the designs of the *tilmas* he saw but emphasized their color (blue) and their fabric (damask). Blue was one of the sacred colors of Aztec cosmology: it denoted both sky and water. (The Franciscans replaced the original dark brown [*pardo*] color of their habits with blue—a color associated both with the kings of Texcoco and the god Huitzilopochtli.) Damask was an Islamic fabric Spaniards knew well since the Middle Ages due to their long territorial *convivencia* with Arabic cultures.

While indigenous males—especially caciques and other functionaries—started using European clothing quite early, many Indian females kept their pre-conquest appearance, adapting it to new materials and prints without discarding local styles. Spinning and weaving were considered fundamental skills for Aztec women.[85] (The gradual replacement of the traditional Indian backstrap loom by the European treadle loom induced an increasing number of males to seek work in textile factories organized by guilds, thus introducing a radical change in Mesoamerican gender mores.)[86] Although Indian female attire usually included a skirt, or *cueitl*, Morales is quite sure that Mexico was wearing a Spanish dress under her *huipil*. The "vestido interior" he alludes to could have been either a *basquiña* (a black skirt), or a combination of such a skirt with a *jubón*, or doublet (a tight shirt that covered the torso down to the waist). A *basquiña* was normally creased, and under it women carried a *verdugón*, a bell-like armature. Morales says Mexico's hair was "arranged in the fashion used *over here*," which I interpret as meaning in the Indian style. Aztec women accessorized their hair with jewels and flowers for important rituals, and Indian females combed their hair in several ways: in long tresses; wrapped or twined on the top of the head with cords; and even colored with red or yellow.

In her analysis of Corpus Christi celebrations in seventeenth-century Peru, Carolyn Dean suggests that Inca caciques wore highly elaborated costumes that intentionally showcased their role as mediators between the Spanish authorities and their Indian subjects,[87] but the students of the Jesuit *colegio* were doing something slightly different. The *colegiales* were performing as Indians in front of Indians; they were actively embracing an act of intercultural drag the Jesuits were particularly fond of. Following the routes of the Portuguese merchant ships that spotted in Asia a lucrative trade based on spices, silk, and silver, the Jesuits had established missions in India and Japan before coming to New Spain. A few years after the publication of Morales's *carta*, Michele Ruggieri and Matteo Ricci initiated their evangelical campaign among the Chinese of the Ming Empire.[88] Ricci's efforts in the celestial kingdom were based on a flexible doctrine of semiotic accommodation that motivated him to exchange the Buddhists robes he wore at the beginning of his mission for the hairstyle and the costumes of the mandarins. Gauvin Alexander Bailey has demonstrated how the Jesuit missions encouraged a blending of local and foreign artistic traditions in Asia and Latin America.[89] Attempting to convert the Chinese was worth a change of clothes and manners.

Morales read Mexico's costume both as a composite (some parts are Indian, some parts are Spanish) and as a blending (this particular performer was a figuration of New Spain and its demographic diversity). The garments were treated both as distinctive and unified: the Indian *huipil* and the European dress accessorized each other into the actualization of something that superseded their singularity. Since the Spanish costume was placed beneath the *huipil*, how much of it was actually seen by the audience? At what exact moment does a piece of garment become a signature of self? At what point does an accrual of details and colors become the index of a nascent object? This epistemic jolt from metonymy to emergence is a fundamental transition in the concrescence of new cultures. In all intercultural settings, a qualitative leap marks the passing from cultural coexistence to cultural innovation. The numerous synthetic instants that gradually naturalize such changes cannot be avocated by simply adding up their vectorial forces. In the festival, Mexico's clothes indicated an altered perception of identity; affectively speaking, they exceeded their materiality. A polymorphic reality that Morales could barely encompass with his imagination was suddenly compressed into his experiencing of a costume. And then he moved on.

Catching the Mediators

Two figures of relay gave Morales an affective opportunity to grasp the processing of history: a song merging languages, and a body mixing clothes. He found the first one perplexing; the second, dashing. As I previously stated, Latour's actor-network-theory provides an efficacious template for a critique of public events, but it lacks an explanation for their affective payoff. Through this discussion I have been able to supplement and expand Latour's concepts by combining Agamben's and Whitehead's ideas. Each of these thinkers was preoccupied with issues of potentiality and becoming,[90] and both of them proposed philosophical discourses in which teleology was avoided by an inclination to a nondeterministic (but still conditioned) understanding of the historical, a commitment to immediacy over *thelos*. I am trying to catch up with intercultural concrescence, those intersections in time and space where something *other* breaks into the surface. Agamben claims that "a critique of the instant is the logical condition for a new experience of time."[91] I have intentionally selected two minor moments (a song, a costume) in order to crystallize the notion that intercultural exchanges should be illustrated at the molecular level, and that identitary alterations can be retraced as translational relays, emerging gradients of change that oscillate between the recursive and the unprecedented. Translation is a performative practice that iterates by recognizing its incapacity to repeat. If restored behavior is a *never for the first time* (a retroactive, conservative move), translation is a *never for the last time* (a recourse to replacements and retrials).

Alterative instants—like a dance or a costume—are easy to overlook, and highly provisional; their function is to reveal the vectors of a particular network as they move along, transforming themselves and their environment. I am studying these almost imperceptible relays as figurations of possibility, not as attempts at closure. Our language hits its limits as soon as we decide to convey immediacy, the flash of awareness that disrupts our continuity while still facilitating our flow. Some words are, of course, more promising than others: I am thinking of expressions like the Latin *hic et nunc* (here and now), the Nahuatl *nepantla* (between this and that), or the Chinese *bian-tong* (modification and continuation) and *zhong-shi* (end-beginning).[92] But the jolt between our perceptions and our conceptual classifications of them is not easy to quantify—language can tell us about it, but language cannot stand for it. Ergonic activities like the festival of the bones—a purposeful unfolding of God's labors—are frequently organized in order to track their own process: they are engineered reactualizations of networks that cannot be experienced otherwise. Cultures are *staged* because we can only encompass their complexity by simulating them.

What we call essentialism is an attempt to focus on the endurance of things, and it is a necessary tool in our critical interventions. Nevertheless, once we are dealing with the performative process, the concept of essence has to be qualified by the alterative. Performance is precisely the suspension bridge that links being to becoming—it is the relay in which space inflects time, the event that reenergizes predictability into concrescence. As *restored* behavior, the genealogy of performatives is not reversible, but as affective leaps, performatives are radically elastic and have the potential to alter history. Intercultural encounters are at their most traceable when they are envisaged as relays, sites in which—according to Whitehead—"the weight of repetition" meets "the intensity of contrast." Whitehead defines emergence as "an enhanced intensity of feeling arising from contrast between inheritance and novel effect."[93] Morales confronted such intensities in a doubly translated song and an attractive costume. Those two moments included dance and motion, the elements of rhythm and pulsation that according to Whitehead convey "the realization of contrast under identity."[94] Morales's observations about these instants are discreet, maybe even marginal or incidental to the overall intentions of the *carta*. But it is their casualness that accounts for their documentary value: for a few seconds, we share with Morales an epistemic shifting from habit to commentary.

As historians of the intercultural, we uncover certain patterns—nothing is recorded in a vacuum—but we also see how those patterns fluctuate and slip away. When confronting the song and the costume, Morales knew that something was evidently familiar (there is no re-cognition without repetition), but he also knew that something was not exactly the same. Morales himself seems to have a guiding pattern in his *carta*: for him, New Spain is primarily a contract between Indian and Spanish codes. The pedestrians that followed the processions were caught in a serial re-disclosure of their city: they were being asked to walk around, to stop and look and listen, to read textual citations imprinted on walls and porticos, to immerse themselves in the refashioning of the capital as a Jesuit place. Michel de Certeau observes that moving across a city is a fragmented operation that can only coalesce into a whole—Mexico, Madrid, Rome—when we transform the experience of passing-by "into points that draw a totalizing and reversible line on the map." Cities are summoned, evoked: "The memorable is that which can be dreamed about a place." Certeau postulates a split between how the city is lived and how the city is imagined; for him, "to walk is to lack a place."[95] But the purpose of the festival of the bones was to *make place* by walking; the Jesuits were able to generate a sequence of physical encounters that marked those locations with their imprint. This mapping was done by feet, not by lines. In this case, the memorable was, from the beginning, site-specific and planned in advance.

The Jesuits were—literally—*figuring out* their new city. We have emphasized two instantiations of that desire that caught Morales's eye. The bilingual song danced by Indian bodies was a verbal relay in which two languages courted and distracted each other. Morales was cunning enough to notice that the poem was not just transporting ideas from Spanish to Nahuatl, but that somehow it contained elements from both. Paul Ricoeur has described translation as the process of finding "a correspondence without adequacy."[96] By perceiving the translation of the song as an inadequate relay, Morales was signaling his encounter with an intercultural mediator he was not entirely able to classify yet. Mexico's costume—probably worn by a Spanish or creole boy—was a visual relay in which the contiguity of Indian and European cultures was presented as a layering of garments and textures. The co-presence of these elements as part of the same body signaled the creation of a third element that integrated them both into a picture of New Spain. The costume was an invitation to *jump* into conclusions, to imagine the emergence of unity out of difference.

There were other places in the festival in which this invitation was also extended. The third arch described by Morales included a section that presented the lagoon of Mexico City with Indian rowers crossing the waters and allegorical representations of pagan sirens and satyrs dancing under the orders of the god Pan.[97] Since "Pan" in Greek means "all," the god was associated with the sun (a source of all life) and Christ. Like Jesus, Pan had a double nature (half human and half ram). Pan was considered a protector of shepherds (a tendering labor assigned to bishops and other members of the clergy, too). Plutarch mentions a mysterious voice that, during the rule of Emperor Tiberius, announced that Pan was dead. This remark was interpreted either as a proclamation of the defeat of paganism by Christianity, or as an acknowledgment of Christ's sacrifice. Last but not least, the serendipitous coincidence in Spanish of the god's name with the name for bread (*pan*) was easily connected to the miracle of the Eucharist. The third arch introduced references to Italy, Spain, China, and Japan side by side with the provinces of Campeche and Guatemala holding samples of cacao and *achiote*. Peru was a man in ancient clothing and New Spain was a modest woman crushing heretic heads under her feet. This third arch was built—it should not come as a surprise—by the Colegio de San Pedro y San Pablo. The arch had the semiotic and analogical density that we are expected to disentangle when reading baroque *relaciones de sucesos* (chronicles of events), but in this chapter I looked in a different direction. Festivals are deployed, among other incentives, to emphasize the present tense, to enhance the relays of a community. While the arch was implicitly asking the crowds to process its allegorical patterns, the Indian dancers and the *colegiales* were figuring out their lives for themselves and for others. They were *doing* something that was still not entirely recognized as *being*. What we have learned from the festival of the bones is that alterative cultures are detected as a verb before they receive a noun.

Chapter 3

✦

Indian Weddings and Translocalized Drums: Mobilizing the Intercultural in the *Cantares Mexicanos*

On June 4, 1564, Don Luis de Santa María Cipactzin married Doña Magdalena Chichimecaçihuatl. The groom was the governor of the Indian *república* of Tenochtitlán. He was also the grandson of Ahuitzotl, the ruler or *tlatoani* who had commanded the Aztecs from 1486 to 1502, leaving his unlucky successor Motezuma II an expanded empire and an extensively rebuilt religious center, or *templo mayor*, the remains of which still mesmerize us when we visit the archeological excavations at the main square or Zócalo in Mexico City. The bride was a descendant of the indigenous rulers of Tlatelolco. The ceremony was vibrantly celebrated with blessings, music and dance:

> Por ellos se predicó y los bendijeron dos veces . . . Al traer a la señora le tocaron música de viento en el templo y en el camino, al llegar le venían tocando música de viento. Y al llegar al palacio, al pie de las escaleras se colocaron la gente de la iglesia, los cantores, allí le cantaron. Y una vez que entró, luego empezaron a danzar, primero se interpretó el chichimecayotl y luego se empezó el atequilizcuicatl y el señor en persona danzó. Y en ese entonces se pintó su tambor (ihuehueuh), se doró.
>
> [For them there was preaching and they were blessed twice . . . They played wind music for the señora at the church and on the road while she arrived they played wind music too. And when they arrived at the palace, at the bottom of the steps the singers from the church stood there and they sang for her. And once she went in they started to dance, first they did the chichimecayotl and after that they did the atequilizcuicatl and the lord himself joined the dance. And at that point his drum (ihuhueuh) was gilded.][1]

Don Luis's wedding was a regal display in everything but name, and the fact that a drum was specially gilded for such an occasion will be my point of departure for an inquiry into the links between everyday objects and the social practices they shape and motivate.

Bruno Latour claims that networks are in a constant state of performation—a continuous, nonstop process of reassembling, re-collecting, and recomposing their relays. Since relays are multidirectional, any attempt at narrowing them down into neat protocols of causality is (albeit not entirely arbitrary) always partial. "Mediators are not causes," says Latour; they act more like plug-ins or clamps that can be provisionally localized: "without transformations or translations no vehicles can transport any effect."[2] I have already suggested two different modes of accounting for actors: *prepositional* and *figurative*. Prepositional analysis is primarily vectorial, and it aims at reconstructing, as much as possible, the relations that enabled a particular event or scenario to be reassembled and re-encoded. Figurative interpretation focuses on finding the relays in which concrescent cultural adjustments and innovations become legible. While the prepositional approach emphasizes labor components and investments, the figurative slant tends to underline semiotic and aesthetic calibrations. In both cases I am spotlighting how flows of activity (the ergonic operations that keep networks going and receding) are moved around and passed on.

It should also be evident by now that my goal is to intersect a materialist critique with a poiesis of emergence. It is my position that only a deliberate merging of these two lenses can compensate for one of Latour's most serious shortcomings: his general overlooking of how affective attractions and dismissals can motivate certain forms of relay over others. Latour's mobilization—following Michel Serres—of the prefix "*quasi*-" marks his efforts at reminding us that networks are facilitated by a sequence of transactions through which objects and persons, human and nonhuman elements, inflect and reposition each other. For Latour, hybridity is not merely a by-product of networking, but one of its fundamental structuring features. What has to be explained, more often than not, is how and why that hybridity becomes occluded or ignored—how the *quasi*- or partial functions enabling the flows of *performation* become the apparently stable or fixed positions assumed and studied as *performances*.

My insistence on the category of emergence is a direct response to this situation. I realize that emergence is nothing less than a troubled and at times disconcerting concept. As Isabelle Stengers states, emergence forces us to "recognize the powerlessness of analytic thought."[3] To think process accurately is difficult enough; to write about it without veering into the coruscations of baroque, dialectic, or rhizomatic prose is even harder. Nonetheless, I still want—like Stengers—to localize that "interlink [of] heritage and novelty, the coherence of previously stabilized meanings and unforeseen possibilities" that only emergence can bring to the picture.[4] On the one hand, neither vectors nor relays can be described outside of an axiological field in which at least some relational patterns are already readable. Contingencies are only relevant in opposition to a minimal degree of predictability. On the other hand, identities are primarily circulatory constructs, functional operations that are constantly shifting and morphing. Identities can be mapped (they have a history, a retraceable itinerary) but they cannot be entirely pre-encoded or anticipated.

A network cannot be grappled without tackling a paradox: its labors and translations are recognizable because they are constantly being *newly* reassembled. Each scenario is a repetition that instantiates its own alterity. It is due to this tensional conditioning that performance acquires its power to unpack and mobilize the intricacies of becoming: scenarios are empirical forms of a thinking and grasping process. As we have seen, scenarios tend to emphasize and profit from a densified convergence between aims (vectors) and means (relays). In an environment where intercultural relations are particularly intensified—by conquest, by conversion, by trade, by theater—scenarios are prone to catalyze the emergence of alterative expressions of self that are open to be provisionally figured out, tested, and contested. In this chapter, I will discuss Aztec drums not primarily as props or musical instruments, but as material relays in a network of relations that produced them and was inflected by their circulation.

An analysis of Mexica drums as vectors or directional markers can refine and expand our grasp of how modes of doing and being are interlaced. I am less concerned with imagining objects as agents with a will of their own than I am with exploring how they contribute to setting the parameters and the flows of our social environments. Tapping into the work of David Graeber and Brian Massumi, I envision indigenous drums in terms of their axiological capabilities and complications. Both Graeber and Massumi emphasize the affective dimensions of matter, the capacity of objects and bodies to facilitate ideological and communal formations. Graeber claims that certain objects acquire a "power to enchant and attract" because "they represent frozen processes." As a result, "the objects that are the ultimate stakes of some field of human endeavor are, in fact, symbolic templates which compress into themselves those patterns of human action which create them."[5] Massumi, meanwhile, reminds us that we make the body thinkable by fixing or positioning it at a particular moment, thus canceling from the start its phenomenological complexity: "After all is signified and sited, there is the nagging problem of how to add movement back to the picture."[6] Massumi points out that the body has to be "theorized [as] a nature-culture continuum."[7] To accomplish this, we have to understand the body as a sensorial switchboard: "Rhythm, relay, arrival and departure. These are the relations of motion and rest: affect."[8] In passing, transforming, or discarding information, the body acts as the locus wherein process qualifies our perceptions: affect is the somatic experiencing of emergence. The challenge here is to analyze the body both in its trajectory (something that passes from one point to another) and its transformations (something that is being modified while it travels). In this book, emergence refers to any circumstance in which being is reexperienced as becoming, the deployment of affective environments in which bodies and objects are reactualized as process.

In one of his few incursions into the affective dimensions of our experience, Bruno Latour explains how each body "leaves a dynamic trajectory by which we learn to register and become sensitive to what the world is made of."[9] I propose that human bodies cannot be fully grasped without considering some of the objects that contribute to their affective impact. Aztec drums were part of a translocalizing ethos that permeated Aztec culture; one of their main functions was to delineate a space where social labor was reexperienced as dance. I will also show how in the specific case of the *Cantares Mexicanos* or song-dances, drums enabled a convergence of overlapping practices that included movement, words, sounds, and a potential to redirect collective energies into unexpected intercultural configurations. To explore these claims, we have to attend—as uninvited guests—Don Luis's and Doña Magdalena's wedding.

Crashing an Indian Wedding

The *Codex Mendoza* includes a detailed account of how most Aztec marriages were celebrated. When a man wanted to get married, a *cihuatlanque* or matchmaker contacted the family of the prospective wife and stayed with them while the parents studied the petition. If the response was positive, the families consulted a soothsayer to find a favorable date for the marriage ceremony. On the wedding day, both bride and groom received extensive advice from their parents, and

> as sunset approached, the bride was bathed by the women in her family . . . they washed her with soap, perfumed her, decorated her with red feathers, and sprinkled her face with red or yellow colors. She was covered with a huipilli and a head cloth [and] she was lifted on the back of a woman that carried her, amid a procession of two rows of people carrying torches, to the groom's house.[10]

Notice how both the torches—fire was associated with the fifth sun of creation—and the body of the bride are *carried* to the wedding: the future wife is visibly relocated by another female in a tangible relaying of communal energies and duties. The couple sat on a reed mat and a corner of the man's cape was tied to the bride's clothes; then the newlyweds retired to a chamber for the next four days; on the fifth day they came out and joined another round of gift exchanges, dancing, and eating.[11] The ceremonies also included specific events for the groom: if the couple was—literally—tying the knot, the husband also had to cut his links to the past by sponsoring a feast for his school friends in which he gave an axe to his teacher as a farewell present signifying the severance of their pedagogical ties.

The wedding between Don Luis and Doña Magdalena reinforced pre-conquest political ties between two cities (Tenochtitlán and Tlatelolco) but it was also part of a process intended to transform Indian polygamous practices into Christian monogamous standards. Before the conquest, and for many years after it, Aztec males—especially merchants and nobles—married one wife but supported several concubines. The friars were particularly invested in promoting Catholic marital bliss: one of the reasons they gradually abandoned their plans to create an indigenous clergy was their perception that the Indians did not have a penchant for celibacy.

At her wedding, Doña Magdalena was escorted from church to palace by a group of singers and a wind ensemble that probably included flutes, cornets, trumpets, and *chirimías*, a double-reed instrument resembling an oboe that was introduced in Spain by the Moors. By 1564, Indian musicians were well versed in playing and assembling European instruments; they also handled quite well basic Western compositional techniques. The Aztecs lacked a generic noun for "music"; Nahuatl had no words for "playing music," either. Musical practices were described in terms of means (types of voice) or intentions (songs of praise or offense), and musicians were defined by their instruments (something along the lines of "the-person-using-the-drum" or "the-person-using-the-flute").[12] In some narratives, Quetzacoatl restarted the cycles of life and death by playing a conch or snail shell. Pedro de Gante's decision to integrate indigenous dance and vocal music with Catholic worship had been, without doubt, one of the most successful incentives for Indian conversions, although not everybody agreed.[13] The same Indian musicians that served Aztec rituals before the conquest ended up playing for the masses organized by the friars,[14] and by 1576 there were approximately one thousand choirs singing in the churches of New Spain.

Two song-dances were also performed at Don Luis's and Doña Magdalena's wedding. The *chichimecayotl* was a piece about "the chichimecs," the legendary ancestors of the Aztecs who migrated from the lands in the north to the lakes of central Mexico. The *atequilizcuicatl* was a "water-pouring" song-dance. Traditionally, families blessed wedded couples with water, and this choice of song-dance might have referenced that practice. On this occasion, Don Luis himself joined the dancers, thus linking remembrances of the Aztecs' historical past with a nod to the sacraments of their new Christian faith. Among the Aztecs, priests were responsible for celebratory music, but the *tlatoani* was occasionally involved in sponsoring the song-dances, too.

Most religious festivals included dancing and singing, and the Aztecs' educational curriculum attests to their relevance. There were two main schools: the *calmecac*, dedicated to the formation of priests and civil servants from the nobility or *pipiltzin*, and the *telpochcalli*, which was focused on military skills. In both cases, learning the songs that recalled the past and the dances required by the different deities and commemorations was paramount. At sunset, students gathered at the *cuicacalli,* the "house of song." Attended by male and female adolescents chaperoned by elders, the *cuicacalli* included a courtyard where students danced into the night. As the mendicant friars slowly discovered, dancing in front of a temple and dancing in front of a church were, for the Indians, equivalent actions: they both implied a kinesthetic entanglement between god and world.

In his study of Aztec dances and their role during and after the conquest, Paul A. Scolieri summarizes Bernardino de Sahagún's listing of the multiple choreographic arrangements utilized by the Mexicas in their ceremonies. Scolieri focuses on the massacre in which Pedro de Alvarado attacked the Indians while they were celebrating the festival of Toxcatl.[15] Apparently, one of the Spanish soldiers' first actions was to cut off the hands of the drummers in order to stop their playing and disband the dancers. The conquistadors grasped quickly how closely intertwined objects and social actions were among the Mexica, a situation directly linked to a worldview in which an original, common substance was constantly adopting new forms and uses.

The Aztecs believed that the world was sustained by a series of dualistic contrasts: male and female, life and death, light and dark, dry and wet. Humans had the responsibility to nurture the interplay of these forces through deliberate acts of consumption and reciprocity. As illustrated by Lourdes Turrent[16] and Ross Hassig,[17] the calendric dexterity of the Aztecs was directly related to this imperative to pay their debts to the gods. Paying a debt was equivalent to making an investment. What we call sacrifice was for the Aztecs *nextlahualtin*, a recharging of the system by giving something back. Captured enemies were treated as fuel, their hearts and blood destined to replenish the engine of nature. The god's substance was constantly flowing through the material objects of everyday existence, and every member of the community was expected to participate in a continuous refilling of their *ergonic* capabilities. The song-dances rendered at Don Luis's and Doña Magdalena's wedding—in tandem with the drum painted for him that day—were sources of merriment and expressions of religious fervor, but they also implied an affective mobilization of social labor.

Affective Translocations

The *huehuetl* gilded at the wedding was probably "a cylindrical wooden drum sitting on three legs, the top of the drum stretched with animal hide, the bottom open." As we already saw in chapter 2, another drum commonly used—the *teponaztli*—was "a hollowed-out wooden cylinder laid sideways" with two tongue-like incisions that were stroked with mallets.[18] David Graeber believes that a materialist analysis must include a mapping of how relations between objects and subjects are fostered, idealized, abstracted, managed, or eclipsed. For Graeber, materialism is a holistic exploration of human creativity; labors and values are inseparable; and explicit demonstrations of networking—rituals, contests, weddings, or theater—reconcile "social structure and individual desire."[19] What kind of networks were these Mexica drums propelling and sustaining?[20] We should not imagine Tenochtitlán as if it were a series of scenographic backdrops made of stone. The city was less a copy of the Aztec world than a vehicle for the transportation of that world's substance. The ethnomusicologist Mark Pedelty suggests that under those circumstances the "ritual spectator did not have to function in the world of simile but rather experienced myth as material metaphor . . . the Great Temple was not *like* Coatepec, it *was* Coatepec."[21] This translocalizing *ethos* was directly tied to the historical conditionings of the Mexica.

Forced by other cities in the late thirteenth century to live as vassals and inhabit a small set of islands, the Mexicas confronted their ecological shortcomings by building mud gardens or *chinampas* and eating salamanders and snakes. By the mid-fourteenth-century, Tenochtitlán became a rising empire. Still, a basic vulnerability remained: the city only supplied 5 percent of the Aztecs' foodstuffs, and famines were frequent and floods could be devastating. Aztec policy was determined by a need to demand from others what they themselves were unable to produce. As Alan Knight explains, "the Aztec state has, with justice, been termed a gigantic 'potlatch state,' a state predicated on the collection, redistribution, and conspicuous consumption of a vast quantity of diverse goods. Sacrifice represented a hypertrophied form of potlatch, with humans playing the part elsewhere reserved for pigs."[22] We have to turn off our notions of free-market trading in order to appreciate the extent into which the Aztec economy was based on an ideology of reimbursements; their priority was to give back what had been borrowed or stolen from nature, to keep all partial goods moving as a way to preserve the flows of the whole. The profit was measured in terms of conservation and—for the elites—the amount of control exercised over luxurious items that had the power to enhance and qualify performation paybacks: feathers, jade, gold, fine textiles, cacao, blood. The rest of the population bartered agricultural surpluses in weekly markets, and even the *pochtecah*, or traveling merchants, were less interested in increasing their revenues than in scouting attractive objects and spying for the *tlatoani*; their capital was made of accumulated prestige and their capacity to acquire their own slaves for sacrifice.

This was the ideological environment in which Aztec children were trained to sing and dance to the beats of drums, a schooling process that only ended when they married. The Aztecs saw themselves as conduits in a distributive enterprise that connected everybody—from the *macehuales*, or commoners, to Motezuma II—in a highly concerted and extremely hierarchized effort to retrofit the *momentum* of their existence. Animals, objects, and people were the transitory containers of a borrowed energy, an energy that traveled through matter by traversing the *malinalli*, double-helixed portals that allowed the substance of the gods to circulate among all things. Aztec imagery tended to emphasize this constant transit of a shared substance, or *teotl*, from one form or shape into another. James Maffie recommends that we "gloss *teotl* as a verb denoting a process rather than as a noun denoting a static being."[23] In Mesoamerica, contrasting forces were metabolically attached to each other. In Tlatilco and Oaxaca, we can find split-faced masks (one half-alive, one half-dead), and the Olmecs were fond of half-man, half-jaguar carvings and figurines.[24] The Nahuatl expression for poetry—*in xochitl in cuicatl*—merges songs and flowers into a cluster of supplementary denotations. When the Aztecs thought at the beginning of the conquest that horses and Spaniards were somehow entangled—so that they sacrificed the animals, too—they were being consistent, not confused (as many conquistadors assumed).

In the context of Aztec religious festivals, then, mimesis was a form of operational feedback, a reassembling of the inputs and outputs of a cosmic élan; it was less a copying of something than a *redirecting* of existing vectors and relays. The ambulatory character of certain rituals confirms this. The person selected to be the living image of Tezcatlipoca for a complete year moved about the streets of the city greeting people and playing the flute. The defeated warriors offered to Xipe Totec were paraded through the city; after dying in a gladiatorial-like fight, their bodies were flayed and dismembered for a meal. Since the victims were ritually adopted by their captors (they called each other son and father), the captors declined to eat the flesh of the dead soldiers, but several males took turns wearing their detached skins, running around while provoking skirmishes with other males and going from home to home asking for food. These localized co-embodiments of gods and ritual victims—so marvelously depicted by Molly H. Bassett[25]—illustrate how Aztec sacrifice was an opportunity for reassimilation and recycling, something enacted to ensure the nourishment of an ongoing network.

If possible, the Aztecs avoided war during the harvest season. The impressive number of ritualized activities embraced by the Aztecs was a concerted effort to keep things going, to promote an uninterrupted sequence of restitutions, tensions, releases, and adjustments. Few cultures have embodied the intensities of their networks as literally as the Mexicas did. What we read mainly as metaphors, songs, and dances were for the Aztecs templates of affective engagement that ensured the continuity of their material existence. In Aztec public rituals, signifier and signified were prone to collapse into each other. Signs and actions were not just symbolic representations of ideas or objects, but actualized reproductions of them. This explains why drummers and dancers who lost their timing were seriously penalized, if not sentenced to death.

A sharp distinction between *performation* (the supporting networks that articulate a community) and *performance* (reassembled behavior intended as imitation in the Aristotelian sense, or as restoration, à la Schechner) was not exactly what the Aztecs had in mind. When it comes to Mexica singing-dancing, such a distinction can be distracting. The Aztecs would not have described their religious festivals—like we tend to do today—as manifestations of theatricality. If there is any notion that approximates how the Aztecs reassembled many of their rituals it would have to be choreography, not drama. But even choreography is not entirely accurate: the task assigned to prisoners of war, singers, and dancers was to sustain everybody's becoming, to *personate*—not only to impersonate—the *ergon* that both made and unmade them. A foreign warrior standing for a god was not merely a surrogate: he was actually inhabited by the substance of that god while simultaneously recharging it. Inga Clendinnen spotlights the fact that god-images or *ixiptlas* were not only human; they could be also made of stone or seed-dough:

> I suspect the words between which we strive to choose—"representation," "substitute," "impersonator," "image," "representative"—are equally misleading and equally useful: sometimes appropriate, sometimes not. But given that to a modern ear the notion of "representation" can carry the suggestion that that which represents is quite distinct from that which is represented, and given that "impersonation" and "representation" imply presence rather than "the rendering present by simulation," which is closer to the Mexica view, perhaps "god-presenter," "that which enables the god to present aspects of himself," best approximates the Nahuatl term.[26]

To a certain extent, mineral and vegetal materials were as acceptable as flesh, but only a human *ixiptla* could dance—and he or she also had a beating heart.

Some readers might find my insistence on the regenerative elements of Aztec dancing either excessive or reductionist, but I am committed to avoid recolonizing the Mexicas with a dramaturgical trope that Westernizes their practices too comfortably. It is undeniable that the Aztecs had a sense of the mimetic. Miguel León-Portilla mentions, among several other practices, the *tlaquetzque* or "those who made things stand out," public reciters of songs and stories that frequented the markets. He also describes a farce in which a buffoon acted "in different costumes, rapidly and skillfully putting on different masks [portraying] a human being, then a deer, a rabbit, a thrush with a red breast, a quetzal bird, a parrot, and finally the same funny man again."[27] Nevertheless, I still feel that seeing all Aztec ceremonies as larvarian dramatic forms—forms that were moving *towards* theater as we know it—somehow limits our grasp of what those ceremonies meant for them. We know there was an understanding among the Aztecs of the persuasive powers of spectacle. Guests and enemies alike were invited to watch ritual sacrifices, and it seems that scenes from their migratory stories were actually reenacted.[28] It is tempting to compare some of the profuse ceremonial deployments of the Mexica with the totalitarian schemes of everyday performance studied by Suk-Young Kim in contemporary North Korea,[29] but in Tenochtitlán, the threatening and carefully orchestrated offerings of blood and drummers and dancing bodies were also perceived as a *continuation* of the world's becoming by other means. More than a theater-state, I prefer to call Tenochtitlán a *performation-state*, a rigorously planned mechanism that reproduced the rules of its own materialization. While it is true that most societies tend to perform themselves with variable gradients of intensity, in the Aztecs' case a focusing on auto-poiesis was dominant. To the extent many Aztec celebrations reproduced the original immolation of their gods or the dismemberment of Coyolxauhqui's body,[30] they were certainly mimetic; but the thing being reassembled was the vectorial redistribution of a common substance or *teotl*. As we will see, it was the deictic import of drums—their power to affectively relocalize that substance—that made them so central to the Mexica's understanding of life and death.

If theatrical or dramatic are not exactly the best labelings for Aztec song-dances, how should we name them? How can we theorize the performative impetus of the Mexicas, their sumptuous and frequently violent pursuit of morphing deeds and *ergonic* restorations? Might we approach Mexica song-dances from a perspective that is not exclusively rooted in para-theatrical discriminations? I propose that an affective analysis of performance may at least restrain us from our obdurate inclination—inherited from Victor Turner—to impose a dramaturgical model over social changes and interactions. Trained by Augusto Boal to be suspicious of neo-Aristotelian and post-Brechtian poetics, I find this prospect attractive. I believe an affective approach to Aztec singing-dancing can prevent us from falling too quickly into the comforts of analogical historiography that have pervaded the study of intercultural events.

What exactly were those dancers *doing* at Don Luis's and Doña Magdalena's wedding? The Mexicas had what Susan Leigh Foster denominates a "standardized regime of bodily training." Leigh Foster comments that "where bodily endeavors assume the status of forms of articulation and representation, their movements acquire a status and function equal to the words that describe them," and that "the idiosyncrasies of a given physique, the smallest inclination of the head or gesture of the hand—all form part of a corporeal discourse whose power and intelligibility elude translation into words."[31] The Aztecs were kinesthetically entrained to see themselves as translocalizing entities, bodies that contained and passed forward the substance of their existence. Among them, dance intensified affectability, the body's potential to foster a state in which somatic perceptions are reexperienced as processual matter.

The uses of affect have been conceptually unloaded by Silvan Tomkins[32] and Eve Kosofsky Sedgwick.[33] Both believe drives and affects are the foundational building blocks of our emotional states; their affect theories lead to the analysis of feelings. Teresa Brennan has made an enticing distinction between affects ("the physiological shift accompanying a judgment") and feelings ("sensations that have found the right match into words").[34] For Brennan, affect is a somatic reaction accompanied by an act, while feelings are emotions that have been already assimilated, at least partially, into the realm of language. Sianne Ngai goes as far as suggesting the existence of affective ideologemes, areas of experience in which certain values and expressions become tightly intertwined and even related to specific literary tropes and practices.[35] For Brian Massumi, the affective realm is mainly physical and kinesthetic, a cluster of intensified sensations that sooner or later trigger certain reactions over others. Gradually isolated from the flows of perception, these qualified responses build up the emotional gradients of our experience.

The Mexicas understood what Massumi calls the difference between "being-in-the-middle" and the "being-of-the-middle": intervals and thresholds had for them an *in-itself* quality that our categories of mediation tend to overlook.[36] In his *Memoriales*, Fray Toribio de Benavente—better known as Motolinía—offers us a glimpse of how Aztec dancers carried themselves into an *ergonic* trance, a purposeful sponsoring of coordinated bodies that were fully participant in their own becoming.[37] Motolinía describes how several groups of people reassembled themselves around the drums; some of them whistled loudly while others guided the rest into forming an expanding series of concentric ripples. The friar observed two basic vectors at work within these dances: a vertical one (from low to high: arms and hands were alternatively moved up and down, while drums and voices slowly increased their speed and volume); and a horizontal one (the interlocked dancers looked at each other in order to keep the steps regular and systematic). The dancers coordinated two other sets of affective intensities: speed (faster at the outer margins, slower towards the center) and alternation (sometimes the singing stopped while the dancers continued until a new song started). Following Susan Leigh Foster again, the dances described by Motolinía produced a visceral collaboration between kinesthesia and empathy: Aztec mirror neurons were certainly being entrained and stimulated in radical, sophisticated ways.[38] These dancers were—like a *malinalli*—a translocalizing mechanism that supported a basic discharging and recharging of energy from one body into another. The rest of this chapter will ponder the possibility of interpreting Aztec drums and the songs performed beside them as axiological ideologemes, expressive relays in which affects became feelings.

Beside the Drums: The *Cantares Mexicanos*

The Mexicas were resistant to see nature as the opposite of culture. Most Mesoamerican groups envisioned their existence as something made of one substance dualistically engineered but still unified by *ergonic* restitutions.

(Playing with an analogy, alas, we can say the Aztecs were in the end closer to Spinoza than to Descartes). Paraphrasing Massumi, I think that *adding movement back to their picture* was probably the signature enterprise of Aztec social life. It should not come as a surprise that, according to Diego Durán,

> I heard something about the existence of the god of dance, of whom the people asked permission before beginning the dance. First, they adorned the idol in the native way, bringing out its costume and placing flowers in its hands and around its neck and feathers down its back like those the natives wore in their dances. Occasionally they pretended that the idol was angry and that he did not wish them to dance. To placate him, they composed new chants in his praise, glory, and honor, making sacrifices and offerings to him. This idol was made of stone, with its arms open like a man who dances. In his hands were holes in which flowers or feathers were placed. He was kept in a chamber in front of the courtyard where the usual dances were held. It is said that during some feasts he was brought out into the courtyard and was set down next to the drum which is called *teponaztli*. In Mexico, in Tetzcoco, and in many other places of the land [the *teponaztli*] was honored as god, given offerings and made ceremonies as a divine thing. And it does not surprise me that this instrument was honored thus since even the bark of resinous trees was revered so that it would create a good fire. The ancient blindness was such that even large and small animals, fish, and tadpoles were adored and revered.[39]

Durán conveys an almost paratactic accumulation of flowers, feathers, sacrifices, offerings, and an honored drum or *teponaztli*. We encounter in Durán's description of the god of dance something Mark Pedelty has described as the "ritual sensorium" of the Mexica, their commitment to produce ceremonial enclaves in which architecture, incense, costumes, accessories, and physical exertions were tightly coordinated in order to ensure the material transportation of a sacred substance across objects, locations, and people.[40] When envisioned in terms of their affective efficacy, the sounds of Mexica drumming are prone to acquire a deeper meaning.

Mexica song-dances re-performed the relation between time and space, opening up the moving bodies to their own histories. As in some African and Afro-Caribbean religions, drums among the Aztecs had a privileged role as markers of transportation. (See figure 3.1.) The activities involved in ornamenting a drum were particularly cherished. As we have seen, at Don Luis's and Doña Magdalena's wedding, a *huehuetl* was gilded. Bernal Díaz del Castillo never misses a chance to mention how Mexica drums both fascinated and terrified the Spaniards. Díaz del Castillo associated indigenous drums with war and sacrifice. At the *templo mayor* he admired a big drum made

Figure 3.1. Indian dancers and drum players. *Florentine Codex*, Biblioteca Medicea Laurenziana, Florence. (Med. Pal. 218, c.262v)

with serpent skins that could be heard two leagues away, and he noticed that Motezuma sent a gilded drum to the Cholulans when asking them to attack Cortés and his men. During the siege of Tenochtitlán the loud beatings of the drums announced the sacrifice of Spanish men: captured European soldiers were being treated as if they were also *indigenous* enemies, forced to join the Mexica's translocalizing dance. Absorbing the other, assimilating the invader into their common substance and affective entrainments, the Aztecs showed an intercultural disposition both violent and extremely elastic. Díaz del Castillo himself confronted this disposition when the Indians presented the Spaniards with a living imago of Cortés, a cacique so similar to their own leader that they ended up calling him "Cortés," too.[41] This cacique was not exactly a copy, or an impersonator of Cortés: in my opinion, the similarity between the Indian leader and the Spanish conquistador was the sign of a shared *ergon*, an embodied statement of cosmic continuity. Taking the other *in* was an affective mechanism the Aztecs were indisputably good at, and their songs-dances were no exception.

Although the song-dances performed at Don Luis and Doña Magdalena's wedding have not been preserved, the manuscript of the *Cantares Mexicanos* includes two compositions that seem to share a similar focus or topic. This collection of alphabetized Nahuatl texts was probably completed by the

1590s, and together with the *Romances de los Señores de la Nueva España* it is the most important depository of what today we call Aztec poetry.[42] To enter the world of the *Cantares* is to access a veritable hermeneutic labyrinth, one I do not intend to replicate here.[43] The functions and meanings of the collection are still being passionately investigated, and those controversies will not be abated soon. The *Cantares* reveal a complex imaginary: it hails and reveres the memory of past Mexica leaders while mentioning more recent figures; resistance to Spanish local authorities appears alongside Christian references; and it criticizes those Indians who collaborated with Hernán Cortés (like the Tlaxcalans). This is, in fact, the Tenochtitlán in which Don Luis de Santa María Cipactzin lived, a city in which the Aztec aristocracy was starting to fathom the irreversibility of European intervention.

The *Cantares* are the remnants of an Aztec practice inflected by post-conquest adjustments.[44] Independently of their precise goal—either as expressions of specific authors, as Garibay suggests, or as convocations of dead soldiers or ghosts, as Bierhorst claims—the songs-dances deploy a series of prepositional features that deserve closer attention.[45] The manuscript also contains one of the few hints available in relation to how Mexica drums were played. Many of the pieces utilize different arrangements of the syllables *ti*, *to*, *co*, and *qui* in order to mark drum cadences; it has been speculated that "i" and "o" stood for two different pitches while "t" and "q" (or "k") indicated moderate and faster dynamics.[46] During the seventeenth century, a combination of these syllables (*titocoti tocoti tocoti*) became synonymous with a particular musical practice called the *tocotín* or *tocontín*.

Gary Tomlinson has tried to reconstruct the presence of the human voice in these texts. His analysis emphasizes the figurative density of the song-dances, their tendency to overlap multiple connotations metonymically.[47] By stressing relations of contiguity between objects and attributes, the *Cantares* constantly interpellate warriors, flowers, cacao drinks, lords, jewels, precious metals and feathers, butterflies, and birds. They summon all these parts to join a whirling whole—asking them to come closer, to arrive or to rain down, connecting paradise to earth, the dead and the living. While I find Tomlinson's foray into the semiotic articulations of the *Cantares Mexicanos* extremely persuasive, his recourse to metonymy underlines proximity at the expense of movement, thus occluding the anaphoric *ergon* that linked words to gestures, songs to dancers. What happened around the drummers was the reenactment of the *becoming-next* of performation, the *passing-from-one-form-into-another* of existence and annihilation.

A *huehuetl* always redirected an ongoing relaying chain, a network. John Bierhorst points out how "stationed beside the drum, the . . . singer reshapes the world around him and envisions a world beyond."[48] The first song-dance mentioned at Don Luis and Doña Magdalena's wedding was a *chichimecayotl* that told "things about the Chichimecs," and song 83 of the *Cantares* wears a similar title. According to Bierhorst, this particular song-dance recalls

Motezuma II and the attacks of the Tlaxcalans while demanding Aztec dead warriors to return and fight again. The text explicitly establishes a contrast between Aztec songs that rematerialize the Mexica's past and other songs that might enforce Spanish power: "A multitude of flowers! In a pack basket! Dance, lords and rulers! And make acquaintance where the drum lies! But Jesucristo is the only redstone bird that's here. Don't sing for Him!" Still, both Indians and Spaniards are described as dancing "in the new land."[49] Exposing a conflicted adjustment from pre-conquest to post-conquest identities, the song addresses some Spaniards (like viceroys Antonio de Mendoza and Francisco Velasco, and Martín Cortés)[50] and some Indian lords that joined the conquistadors (like Diego de Alvarado Huanitl).

The second dance alluded to in the *Anales of Juan Bautista* is a "water-pouring" song, or *atequilizcuicatl.* Song 68 of the *Cantares* is also a "water-pouring" piece,[51] although this coincidence does not imply that it was the same song-dance performed at the wedding. Nevertheless, I want to make a case for its potential chronological proximity to that event. The song starts by telescoping two scenarios: the Mexica's final migration to the shores of Chapultepec, and the first encounter between Motezuma and Cortés, after which the Tlaxcalans are nothing less than amazed by the unexpected surrendering of the *tlatoani* and his city. In the song, it is only when Malitzin conveys Cortés's demands for food and water for his soldiers that the Aztecs decide to fight back. This bellicose response signals one of the recurrent themes of Song 68: the nobles' reluctance to pay tributes to the conquistadors, an issue that became particularly acute for the caciques during the fiscal reforms spearheaded by *visitador* Valderrama in 1564.

The *Anales de Juan Bautista* provides an account of several occasions in which the painters of Tenochtitlán—a brother of Don Luis among them—adamantly protested against Valderrama's reforms. (In Nahuatl, painting and writing are denoted by the same word, and many of these painters were indigenous males from the Aztec nobility trained in the skills of pictographic communication; after the conquest, some of them learned to paint in the traditional Western manner, too.) On August 18, 1564, a friar notified the painters that some fathers were willing to travel to Castille to intercede for them, and on September 29 of the same year, Fray Antonio de Molina told the painters that those fathers were already on their way to meet the emperor and even the pope if necessary.[52] I suspect song 68 mirrors some of these discussions (although by 1564 the "emperor" has to be King Philip II, not Charles V). The proxemic triangulation of Molina's admonition to the painters—from Tenochtitlán to Castille and then to Rome—is a prominent feature of song 68, one that will facilitate an intercultural figuration of radical conceptual consequences.

The text of song-dance 68 explicitly manifests a correlation between the Indians' discomfort caused by paying tribute to the Spaniards and their remembrance of dead military heroes. Those in paradise (like the dead warriors) are being called back to earth, and those living in the city (like the Indian lords in distress) are hoping to enter paradise. While in the past the deeds of heroes were pictographically registered, now the things that are being written down are mostly tributary lists (like those in the *Codex Mendoza* or the *Codex Osuna* we can still read today):

> Ynic onemacoc tlacochihcuiliuhtoc yn huel conitto capitan teuctli ma xocõxioamoxyhcuilocã amoxtli ypanon ha in intequiuh Mexicame O anqui nohuian in altepepãhuic oncuihuac tequitl aya ayahaya Et.
>
> Can in ya chocaque in tlaocoxque teteuctin tlatoque, auh otomacehualtic otopã mochiuh in conxioahamoxihcuiloque.
>
> So it is that they who were swallowed are painted as spears. Indeed, the lord Captain has said it: "Paint them as turquoise pictures: the Mexicans' labors in pictures!" And oh it would seem that this labor's been taken from everywhere to the city.
>
> Now they who've wept in sadness are the lords and rulers. It's our destiny and circumstance: they've painted them as turquoise pictures![53]
>
> Los que así fueron tomados
> fueron pintados como dardos.
> Lo dijo el Capitán, el señor:
> pintadlos en el libro precioso,
> en el libro,
> lo que ha sido el tributo de los mexicas.
> De todas partes, de las ciudades,
> fue tomado el tributo.
>
> Donde lloraron,
> se aflijieron los señores, los que gobiernan.
> Ah, es nuestro merecimiento,
> sobre nosotros ocurrió,
> fueron pintados en el libro precioso.[54]

The "lord Captain" is Hernán Cortés, and the shift from Aztec domination to the caciques' subordination is being described in terms of a spear that stands for tribute, not for battle (a situation the song aspires to reverse, bringing the spears back to their military use by recalling Cuauhtemoc and other lords and by pouring more water, or blood, or songs, or all of the above).[55]

Both Bierhorst's and León-Portilla's renderings of the Nahuatl text are nothing less than a dazzling—and dizzying—exercise in prepositional cartography. The city (here, but also there) and paradise (there, but also here) are tightly interlaced in a simultaneous movement toward and from each other. This type of vectorial and semiotic mobility is exactly what the drums intended to both unleash and guide: Aztec song-dances were relaying rites in which the incorporation of heterogeneous materials, different spatial referents, and multiple chronological frames were not only possible, but expected. In song 68, some European scenarios—a visit to the emperor, an audition with the pope—are utilized as figurations for the translocalizing ethos that grounded all song-dances. What we find in song 68 is the inclusion, within an indigenous practice, of a circum-Atlantic network. First, Tenochtitlán: "There were plume willows at the turquoise-green waters in Chapolco. We Mexicans had reached jade water's flowing-out place . . . It resembles that time of our utmost eagerness when we Mexicans set out from Acocolco to reach *this place that is* here." Then, Spain: "The bells have sounded, brother. Haul away your jade-water jars, your sky-water carried ones. And you've have made them dance in Castille! Don't go in vain." Next, Rome: "Who is this reclining on a golden chair? Look! It's the pope. He has his turquoise blowgun and he's shooting in the world . . . it seems he has his cross and golden staff, and these are shining in the world . . . It seems the pope's home lies painted in golden butterflies. It's beaming."[56] Blowguns were used in ceremonies honoring the goddess of flowers, Xochiquetzal: dressed as other gods, men and women aimed their shots at artificial branches where boys dressed as birds (there were others disguised as butterflies) fluttered their green, blue, red, and yellow feathers.[57] Butterflies were also a coded word for dead warriors.

In song 68, a pope, a blowgun, butterflies, a cross, and a staff—and all the other objects that accompanied them—twist and blend into a powerful intercultural figuration. Occasionally it feels as if the Indians were discussing their travel preparations and arriving at their destination at the same time. While studying the *Cantares*, we must brace ourselves for vertiginous and agile juxtapositions that are certainly harder to read than to *move* along with. The zapping impression frequently produced by the *Cantares*—the quickly paced jolts from one register to another—is the closest these texts come to the kinetic skills that actualized these songs in performance, skills the Aztecs were affectively entrained to display and that their own language—with its capacity for lexical agglutinations—expressively fomented. The song-dances are extremely malleable in terms of their spatial and temporal coordinates; they seem to be here and there simultaneously, to move backwards and forwards within the same lines, to recount history by bringing the past into the present (and vice versa), to merge the synchronic with the diachronic. These translocalizing feats are not separable from the drumming, the dancing, and the singing. The beats and the steps and the voices were the vehicles that carried and bundled all those vectors into and through each other. Embodied in the Mexica past by dancers, singers, and the objects that expanded and supplemented them; now partially preserved in the dazzling words of a colonial manuscript; and still echoed today by postcolonial drummers in Mexican festivals—the *Cantares Mexicanos* were, by all means, affective spectacles of prepositional transportation.

Geochronic Rhythms

As we have proven, the merging of warriors, birds, flowers, stirred waters, winds, Tenochtitlán, Rome, Castille, and paradise that traverses song 68 is the kind of figurative networking that gets actualized when we situate ourselves *huehuetitlan* or "beside the drum." The song-dances activated something I describe as a *geochronic* mechanism, an embodied historiography in which singing and dancing become modes of traveling, an opportunity to re-encode time and space through the manipulation of affect. When Don Luis joined the singer-dancers around the recently (or soon to be) gilded *huehuetl* at his wedding, he was tapping into a kinesthetic chance to repurpose his own destiny.

"The network," says Brian Massumi, "is the relationality of that which it distributes. It is the being of collective becoming. Communicational technologies give body to the relationality as such and as set in motion—as the passing-on of the event."[58] Aztec song-dances were a translocalizing technology that kept in motion the relations between objects, animals, geographies, peoples—and adversaries. Due to their almost uncanny capability to conflate memories and references, drummers mobilized several scenarios at once, compressing into their sphere a full process of social concrescence. Arrivals and departures collapsed into each other; verbal storms replicated the whistling and billowing of dancing bodies; paradise was falling upon earth while revenants ascended to it; and the pope was seen while surrounded by sparkling butterflies.

An intriguing scene from song 68 seems to underline the potential effects of crossing the ocean:

> Çan moquetza in ehecatl cocomocan tetecuicaya yc poçonia yn ilhuicaatl huiya nanatzcatihuaya yn acallia. ohuaya ohuaya
>
> Yn huel totech onquiquiçaya ymahuiçon Tiox, toconyaittay atetepepeyotl ye xochipixahui nanatzcatihuaya yn acalliya ohuaya ohuaya
>
> Yyo ho huaya tocnihuane ma xõtlatlamahuiçocã atliyaytiqui çan ye ticonchaloa ça ye titon Maltini hualxaxamacatimani a yn ilhuicaatl ya ohuaya Et.
>
> Y mahuizpan tontlachia o ypalnemohuani acueyotl hõ totlã moteteca y man tipopolihuiti a xictli a y malacachihuiya ohuaya Et.
>
> Ho ayac tlaçotli yn acalli ytiqui yn antocnihuã y cuix nel oc tilotizque mã tipopohuiti a xictla y malacachihuiya ohuaya Et.
>
> Yyoyahue yahue huixahue yahue nihualicnotlamati topã moquetza nican quetzalitzahuachtli canpanel toyazque ohuaya ohuaya

Teicnotlamachti in quichihua nican ypalnemoani y tlanel nocniuh y tlanel tonehuan in tiyolque yeehuaya ayocac teca y acalla ytica ohuaya ohuaya

Acala ytiqui huel mahuiçocan çan ye topã onquiça çan ca chalchiuhatl in yeic poçonia y mecatl yhcoyocaya cã michin patlania ma xicyaithuacã ohuaya Et.

Wind arises, roaring, hissing. The ocean seethes, and the boat goes creaking along.

We see great waves flowing over us, wonderful things of God. It's raining flowers, and the boat goes creaking along.

Friends, rejoice in these waters. You're splitting it open, O Don Martín! It's broken to pieces here in the ocean.

O Life Giver, you're alive in this place of fear. The waves are rolling over us. Let's go perish at the navel, at the roundel.

"No one in this boat is precious, friends. Can we return?" Let's go be counted at the navel, at the roundel!

Alas, I grieve. The emerald dew is on us. And where are we to go?

Life Giver causes grief. If only He were my friend, if only He were kinsman. No one cares anymore about anyone here in the boat.

Inside this boat, this place of fear, jade waters are flowing over us, seething. Ah, these garlands roar, these fish are flying. See them!

Ah, and yonder stands the tree of sustenance, stands our palace. And these garlands roar, these fish are flying. See them![59]

Sólo se levanta el viento,
truena, retumba,
espumea el mar,
va crujiendo la barca.

Junto a nosotros sale la gloria de Dios,
vemos una gran ola,
hay lluvia de flores,
va crujiendo la barca.

Amigos nuestros, admiraos,
en el interior del agua te reñimos
sólo a ti don Martín.
Se agita el mar.

Contemplamos en la gloria del Dador de la vida,
las olas del mar junto a nosotros se extienden,

que no vayamos a perdernos en el ombligo del agua,
donde ella hace giros.

He venido a entristecerme,
sobre nosotros se posan
gotas de rocío que punzan.
¿Adónde en verdad iremos?

Aflige a la gente lo que hace aquí el Dador de la vida,
si en verdad fuera mi amigo,
si en verdad estuviera junto a nosotros
los que vivimos.
Nadie se ocupa de los demás en el interior de la barca.

El interior de la barca es lugar de temor,
sobre nosotros sale el agua de jade,
la que espumea.
La cuerda hace ruido,
vuela el pez,
vedlo.

Allá se levanta el árbol de nuestro sustento,
se yergue en nuestro lugar del mando,
la cuerda hace estruendo,
vuela el pez,
contempladlo.[60]

In his perceptive reading of song 68, Serge Gruzinski tallies many of the Indian and Christian reverberations of this passage, the amalgamation of Aztec and European materials that makes some of its images so haunting.[61] I am more interested, though, in exploring how the affective predispositions inherent to Mexica singing-dancing provided in this case a prepositional engine that was entrained, from the beginning, to conflate disparate elements, times, and locations.

According to Bierhorst—and in this case, I feel inclined to agree with him—the tempest that assaults the Indian vessel reminds its passengers of the Aztec lord Martín Ecatl's trip to Europe in 1525, during which he was received by Charles V. Ecatl returned to New Spain five years later, but during his sojourn in the Old World, a troupe of Mexica performers went there with Hernán Cortés in 1527 while Charles V was residing in Valladolid. The emperor enjoyed those thirty-nine dancers and musicians so much that he sent them to Rome for the entertainment of Pope Clement VII. That song 68 recalls these precedents should not come as a surprise: sponsoring such chronological recoils is one of the stylistic features of the *Cantares*. But there is more. Ecatl—also known as Ehecatl—was the god of wind, and cocreator of the world with Tezcalipoca; he wore an *ehecailacacozcatl*, a pectoral made of conch shells. One of the accessories associated with Mexica dancing was the *ehcatehuaztli*, a feather fan. Towards the conclusion of song 68, the emperor advises the travelers to visit the pope and the text compares the holy father's dwelling with a "cavern house of colors." One of Ehecatl's temples resembled a cave: it was circular, with a conical roof and a serpent's mouth at the entrance. Wind was supposed to come from the underworld, not from the sky.

This cluster of references to the wind—from Martín Ecatl to the cavern-like site where the pope welcomes the travelers—suggests that the boat carrying the Indians to Europe is emerging within (and from) the actual whirling of the dance itself.[62] Flowers fall, garlands roar, waves roll, fish fly—the language we are reading in song 68 was affectively intertwined with somatic exertions, bodies incited to dance together, creaking, breaking, and splitting while encircling the drums. This skirmish with the waves describes not only a trip across a perilous ocean but the power of the song-dances to translocalize substance, to physicalize concrescence: things are falling together, in, out, and apart simultaneously. This is a storm made of mixed metaphors, a nodal accumulation of bundled relays and allusions.

My reading of this passage from song 68 might seem at first too self-referential—even slightly analogical—but among the Aztecs and their neighbors, moving over waters was, after all, directly linked to the attractions of singing and the origins of some percussive instruments. Gruzinski feels that the maritime perils experienced by the Indian voyagers reflect previous trans-Atlantic crossings, but there are indigenous narratives in which crossing the waves had a central role, too. In his *Historia Eclesiástica Indiana*, Fray Jerónimo de Mendieta documents a story about Tezcatlipoca that explains the provenance of the *huehuetl* and the *teponaztli*.[63] Standing in front of the sea, a worshipper of Tezcatlipoca was commanded by the god to call a whale, a siren, and a turtle in order to build a bridge over the waters and reach the house of the sun. Texcatlipoca wanted his follower to gather some musical instruments and singers for him. When the sun heard Tezcatlipoca's messenger singing and coming to his palace, he told his entourage to ignore the allure of his voice—whoever answered would have to go back to earth with Tezcatlipoca's envoy. Fascinated by his song, Huehuetl and Tepoznatli responded to the messenger and were thus tricked into descending to land.

It is interesting to observe that song 68 is also invested in the power of music:

> Çan quiquiztica tlamimilintoc aya ye ompiedo ycaca ytlatol Tiox y tzinitzca quentica a ontzaucticacon techonyaithuitia ohuaya ohuaya
>
> Y ma xicaquican in antepilhuan I tonahuac onoque can i ma iuhcã ohua ca ye iuhcan yn ychan Tiox in Loma aya oncan ontlapiya õ ce yehua ya Papayan ohuaya ohuaya

A oncan ya onoqui ca yehua y tenan yn itoca yn Santa sellaya a y Loma aya oncan ontlapia on çã yehuaya papaya ohuaya ohuaya.

On account of trumpets there's a stirring. Aya! And they're honored where it stands; God's words, these trogons! They're ensconced in war capes. Ah, they give us life.

Bring them in, you princes. They're our comrades. Where? With God in Rome! Aya, there the pope is paying honor.

There in Rome she dwells, she the mother called Santa Cecelia! Aya, there the pope is paying honor.[64]

Con música de caracoles está brotando,
con esto es aguardada la palabra de Dios,
engalanada cual ave tzinitzcan,
custodiada nos alumbra.

Escuchad, vosotros príncipes,
los que junto a nosotros estáis,
porque así sea,
así en la casa de Dios,
en Roma,
allá vigila el Papa.

Allá está ella,
la madre de los hombres,
la llamada Santa Cecilia,
en Roma,
allá vigila el Papa.[65]

The same effect of vectorial bundling produced by the boat and the storm reappears here in response to trumpets: birds (trogons) and God's words conflate into warriors (war capes) that are being brought in—while Santa Cecelia (the patroness of musicians) accompanies them.[66] As we already know, this merging of warriors, birds, flowers, stirred waters, winds, Tenochtitlán, Rome, Castille, and paradise has been happening through the entire song. Dancing was for the Aztecs an act that involved cosmic dimensions. A Mexica body was made of the interaction of three forces: the *tonalli*, or fundamental heat that resided in the head and came from the sun; the *teyolía*, or the emotional tendencies that resided in the heart; and the *ihíyotl*, or the gaseous emanations that resided in the liver.[67] Sacrifice, dancing, and singing phased these three forces into affective recirculation.

Within this constant reinvestment of *ergonic* energies, drums were among those objects that—as David Graeber argues—are able to attract into their

Figure 3.2. Objects and instruments associated with singing and dancing. *Florentine Codex*, Biblioteca Medicea Laurenziana, Florence. (Med. Pal. 219, c. 281r)

sphere a full process of social invention. In Nahuatl, the *huehuetl* belongs to a lexical chain that includes the *huehue*, or venerable elder, and the highly sophisticated speeches known as *huehuetlahtolli*, or advisory pieces. *Huehuetitlan*—being beside the drum—was also the name of any gathering of singers and musicians. A *huehuetl* could be the size of a man, and sometimes bigger than that—like the *tlalpanhuehuetl* or war drum admired by Díaz del Castillo at the *templo mayor*. Some singers accompanied themselves with smaller drums (like the *teponazcuicanime*, or teponaztli-singers). Many texts of the *Cantares* seem to imply the participation of more than one speaker-singer, and some songs are quite specific about the number of drums involved: some of them request as much as ten, adding them incrementally in order to expand sound volume and enforce the solemnity of the performance. (See figure 3.2.)

Following Robin Bernstein's distinction between object and thing can be, at first sight, a convenient way of accessing the dynamic relevance of Mexica drums. For Bernstein, while an object is basically unthought matter (something we use), a thing is matter we interact with (something we are aware of): "An object becomes a thing when it invites a person to dance."[68] Things acquire or intensify their performativity when they are experienced as if they were scripts, implied sets of instructions that suggest potential forms of behavior and reaction. But among the Aztecs, a sharp separation of object and thing—a clear segregation between *assumed* and *addressed* shapes or utensils—was less important than their translocalizing value. This systematic appreciation of matter as a conductor of substance made drums central to Mexica networking, and explains why the affective entrainments of dance were so carefully transmitted and counted upon. Beside the drum, time and space traveled, morphed, agglutinated, and *became-next*. Mexica drums were conveners of interlaced bodies, but their cultural impact was also measured in terms of the pliabilities they enabled, their convocation of multiple relays of signification. Eleanor Wake extrapolates that some of the imagery of the *Cantares* was transposed into early colonial church architecture.[69] It is certainly easy to find flowers and birds spinning on many façades and ceilings of colonial Catholic temples across Mexico. Wake goes as far as to compare the sculpted and painted syncopations of these ornamental images with the drumming pulsations of the song-dances themselves.

The affective reverberations of Aztec drums and dancers traversed both walls and words, but they were not only enacted at weddings and church-sponsored processions. According to Sahagún, the *huehuetl* and the *tepoznatli* were also prominent in more private environments, especially those inhabited by the itinerant merchants or *pochtecah*. These ambulatory merchants were expected to travel to other regions in search of items of high quality like feathers, precious stones, obsidian knives, or textiles. Some merchants entered alien territories in disguise, wearing local clothing and speaking the area's language; if discovered, their audacious combination of espionage and intercultural transvestitism would have led them to their death. The merchants returned home late at night, hiding their goods so as to increase the curiosity of their customers and their own reputation. In times of war, the long-distance merchants were in charge of assessing the enemies' spoils and their tributary worth. Merchants were able to acquire their own slaves for sacrifice. Their celebratory banquets were costly: soothsayers were consulted, tamales and cacao beverages were plentifully made, flowers and gifts were shared, and the best dancers and singers were recruited. In some *pochtecah* celebrations, after rendering homage to Huitzilipochtli, drums received at midnight their own offerings of copal incense and flowers. People started whistling and in some cases they touched the earth and then tasted it, while saying: "Our Lord is sounding." Quails were killed in front of the drums to divine the future, and the four corners of the earth were blessed.[70] While the merchants observed, several Aztec warriors usually joined the dance.

It is revealing to find that so many elements present at the *pochtecah* rituals were also prominent at Don Luis's wedding or in the manuscript of the *Cantares*. The "metaphors" at work in the song-dances frequently have a direct referent in some kind of social labor. Flowers, in particular, are a fundamental feature both in the *pochtecah* banquets (where they are presented in homage to the drums) and in the imagery of the song-dances themselves (where they ascend, blossom, and rain down—like they do over the boat in song 68—in magnificent profusion).[71] As Berenice Alcántara Rojas explains, flowers were "the primary materials of apparel and insignia worn and held by nobles, rulers, warriors, priests, god-impersonators, singers, and many other Nahua during the song-dance rituals." Flower-inspired attires and ornamentations were produced by three highly specialized groups: the women that weaved the clothes; the *amanteca*, or feather artists; and the *xochichiuhque*, or flower makers "in charge of cutting, handling, and interlacing flowers and otherwise turning them into ritual settings, bouquets, mosaics, and garlands."[72] That flowers, feathers, and drums were equally central to public rituals and private feasts illustrates how much of their relevance was based in their faculty to ignite and realign the doings and undoings of the community as a whole.

According to Mark Franko, dance "calls social space into being."[73] When the guests at Don Luis's and Doña Magdalena's wedding gathered around a drum, they reentered an unfurling affective transportation of voice, muscle, rhythm, and history. The somatic tweaking of space and time; the accretions of past, present, and future; the interface of forwardness and reversals authorized by the drums were the result of kinesthetic templates or ideologemes that both preceded and survived the conquest. By reproducing emergence and reimagining the archives of collective memory (time) through embodied interventions (space), the *Cantares* deploy what I have called here a *geochronic* historiography, one in which transportation becomes self. In such a context, Aztec drums exhibited the *quasi*-qualities of mediators: they translated the substance of their community from one form to another. The most important function of these drums was to make boundaries available, to reactualize and restart the narratives and the scenarios of collective networking.

Intercultural exchanges are oriented by affective availabilities that can only be retraced effectively by scrutinizing the objects that signaled and provoked them. Taking a cue from Lorraine Daston, I have analyzed Mexica drums as translocalizers, trying as much as possible "to make things eloquent without resorting to ventriloquism or projection."[74] The Aztecs kept performation and performance tightly connected, and in Tenochtitlán many mimetic acts were relays that stood *with* the flow, not *for* the flow. Before the trauma of the conquest, Mexica imitative practices were both *constative* and *reproductive*, not only representational. Tzvetan Todorov described the conquest of Mexico as a tragic process of semiotic misreadings, but here I prefer to see it as a confrontation between different ways of *absorbing and redirecting* the Other.[75] In song 68, the ability to redirect the ongoing becoming and unbecoming of matter actualizes a *geochronic* transaction, an affective resetting of space and time. Song 68 was an embodied act of historiography, one in which kinesthetic entrainments provided a field for a redoing of Aztec vectors and stories. This was a potential implicit in the structuring of the *Cantares* from their inception, and I believe one of the functions of the song-dances was to reorganize the ongoing process of becoming, to make becoming incipient again, emergent, and (as a result) re-doable. In such a processual ecology, song 68 embraced a circum-Atlantic, intercultural network and turned it into a remapping of indigenous desire beside—and *through*—the beating exertions of Mexica drummers.

In Tenochtitlán, the singing and dancing that accompanied many Aztec ceremonies were part of what Lawrence Grossberg defines as a "mattering map," a distribution of labors that articulated specific ceremonial and gestural *relays* for the benefit of the community. According to Grossberg, "Affect . . . is the plane on which any individual . . . is empowered to act in particular ways at particular places," and as such, "it demands that we speak of the body and of discursive practices in their materiality."[76] The texts included in the *Cantares Mexicanos* are surviving traces of a collective becoming, one that was articulated by the action of dancing bodies invested with the affective power to recharge and remobilize the meanings of their time and their space. Aztec drums were at the center of a deliberate resetting of scenarios, vectors, and figures that today are only accessible to us through one surviving form of translation: poetry.

A Death after the Wedding

The Aztecs' understanding of substance as plasticity—the world as an *ergonic* continuum that perpetuated itself by constantly changing its shapes and circulations—was not entirely indifferent to contingency: after all, as David Graeber reminds us, Motezuma was quite adept at gambling, a skill that implies a recognition of uncontrollable serendipities—like luck. Motezuma was extremely tolerant of how Hernán Cortés and Pedro de Alvarado cheated him when they played together; according to Graeber, by following the rules of the game in spite of the Spaniards' dishonesty, the *tlatoani* was waiting for his opportunity to gain everything back.[77] I wonder if song-dances became, especially after the conquest, a highly regulated form of embodied gambling—an affective game in which the world was reexperienced as a chance for time and space to inflect each other again and—maybe—to alter history itself.

At the end of his life, Don Luis de Santa María Cipactzin confronted the limits of his affective entrainments. On May 24, 1565, while the sun was sinking below the horizon, the Aztec lord appeared on the roof of his house in Mexico City. Once there, he "anduvo gritando golpeándose la boca, llevaba puesto su escudo, en la azotea con su espada andaba escaramuceando." ("He moved on top of the roof shrieking and hitting his mouth, he was carrying his shield, on the roof with his sword he was making fighting gestures.")[78] This behavior continued for several hours. According to the account preserved in the *Anales de Juan Bautista*, at some point Don Luis fell into the street and seriously hurt himself. When the morning arrived, the neighborhood was extremely silent and worried. Don Luis's actions troubled civil authorities as well: after all, Don Luis was a cacique, a member of the Aztec ruling minority that now served as mediators between the Spaniards and the rest of their indigenous subjects.

What was Don Luis trying to accomplish, almost a year after his wedding, when he started his crepuscular display of bravura? It is almost certain that his nocturnal intervention was an act of protest against the fiscal reforms promoted by Jerónimo de Valderrama, the same *visitador* that (in chapter 1) was sent by Philip II to New Spain in response to escalating frictions between the second Marqués del Valle Martín Cortés and the ailing Viceroy Luis de Velasco. As we already explained, in his zeal to increase the revenues of the monarchy, Valderrama requested monetary contributions from Indian towns that were already paying tributes through forms of manual labor like agricultural produce, construction works, weaving, and painting. (Since Don Luis's brother Martín Momauhti was a painter, these new tributary exertions struck quite close to home.) When Don Luis failed to stop Valderrama's reforms, the Indians turned against him.

On July 13, 1564—just a few weeks after his wedding—an angry crowd attacked Don Luis, shouting insults and throwing stones at him. The turmoil only ended when Martín Cortés (the marquis's half-brother, son of Malinche) and other *encomenderos* intervened.[79] The tributes exacted by Valderrama were supposed to be delivered on September 26 of that year, but the following day Don Luis was imprisoned for his reluctance to comply with them. Although he was freed from jail on September 30, the emotional and political wounds inflicted by these events were still fresh in everybody's memory when Don Luis enacted his rooftop, dancelike exhibits nine months later.

When Don Luis deployed his weapons on the roof of his house, he was counting on ritualistic implications that relied more on indigenous referents for movement and fighting than on any Catholic sacraments. The chronicler of the *Anales de Juan Bautista* says that during all the ruckus Don Luis behaved like someone possessed by the devil, a remark that sounds more Christian than Aztec only if we forget that "demons" was also the name given to Indian deities after the conquest. Don Luis was being possessed by his own Mesoamerican past—a *defeated* past he was evidently trying to reassemble and transform. There were some precedents to Don Luis's accident (or attempted suicide). Moquihuix, the ruler of Tlatelolco, threw himself from a temple after losing a battle against Axayacatl, and one version of Motezuma's death has him falling from a roof or parapet while addressing his subjects. In Don Luis's case, the same community that a year earlier had joined him and Doña Magdalena for their wedding now decided to ignore his twilight rumbling. It seems that Don Luis attempted to recover his power—but he was out of luck. On December 28, 1565—only a few months after his skyline vigil—Don Luis de Santa María Cipactzin died. He was not immediately replaced, and his posthumous reputation was far from heroic: he was remembered by some as "he who sold out the homeland."[80] A leader who was initially respected and celebrated with gilded drums at his wedding ended being poignantly isolated, falling to the ground from his roof under the starry desolation of his colonial night.

Chapter 4

✦

Geochronic Scripts: Sor Juana Inés de la Cruz and *The Divine Narcissus*

In 1690 Sor Juana Inés de la Cruz published a Corpus Christi play or *auto sacramental* titled *El divino Narciso* (*The Divine Narcissus*). The piece appeared again, now as part of the nun's collected works, in Barcelona (1691) and Seville (1692). It has not been possible to document any performance of the play around those years either in New Spain or on the Spanish peninsula. After Sor Juana's death in 1695, her works were reissued on several occasions through the eighteenth century, but we have no way of knowing how widely read the *auto* truly was. My decision to conclude this exploration of intercultural encounters with a dramatic text might come as a surprise. Up to this point, I have focused on describing specific events (a rebellion, a festival) or Aztec practices that predated the arrival of the Spaniards and managed to survive the shocking aftermaths of military conquest and enforced conversion (like singing-dancing entrainments). While Sor Juana's *auto* contains quite a familiar scenario—the first meeting between Mexicas and Europeans—we don't have enough information to retrace its prepositional investments, and any attempt at puzzling out its figurative articulations would have to rely more on an understanding of its rhetorical underpinnings than on the excavation of any specific production details.

The Divine Narcissus is precisely the kind of *literary* object that performance theory has done so much to deemphasize and even discard in its quest to disclose the theatrical mechanisms of everyday life. Nevertheless, I will pursue a different task here. Dramatic scripts are also conveyers of translocalized energy, written relays participating in the vectorial currents that inflect the material reassemblings of our experience. Sor Juana's *auto* will provide me with an opportunity to combine the expectations of philological accuracy with some of the lessons learned from the affective historiography deployed in the pages of this book. Looking at the intricacies of Catholic theology through the lens of Amerindian accomplishments, my reading will also elucidate the concept of *geochrony* introduced in the previous chapter as part of my unpacking of the proxemic and temporal elasticities found in the *Cantares Mexicanos*.

The Aztecs' commitment to merging performation with performance, their vocation for structuring a community and a pedagogic system in which dancing was a channel for the transportation of a common substance from one shape to another, challenges and refines our engagements with the boundaries between spectacle and self. Among the Mexicas, the body was constantly exposed to the demands of its becoming, ready to serve the translocalizing imperatives of the world's ergonic flows. To a certain extent, Nahuatl songs were *phatic* utterances, enacted statements that pointed at their own function as communicators and enablers of emerging recirculations. As we have seen, some of those song-dances were capable of opening themselves up to an intercultural field that confronted, in words and motions, the presence of a circum-Atlantic network.

The Aztecs' interpretation of life and death as a sequential transportation of energy through matter led them to instantiate a poiesis of compulsory violence. For the Mexicas, pragmatics and aesthetics were drastically intertwined: human sacrifice, enforced war cycles, and the intentional reutilization of objects and bodies (stones, buildings, feathers, ritual offerings, tributes, or the flawed skins of defeated warriors and ceremonial *personators*) were closely tied to each other. Both the Indians and the friars manipulated the potential similarities between certain indigenous and Christian narratives in order to tackle the intercultural clashes provoked by the victory of the invaders. The voluntary immolation of the gods at the beginning of the fifth sun and the eating of a figure of Huitzilopochtli made of seeds and blood were compared to and superseded by the image of Jesus sacrificed on the cross, his resurrection, and the ingestion of his glorified body during the Mass under the appearance of bread. *The Divine Narcissus* takes for granted the validity of these analogical efforts, but it also relocates them as a way of addressing the intensities of its own emergence.

I would like to argue that Sor Juana's *auto* deserves a place in an affective regime that, as we already saw, was very much active at least a hundred years before *The Divine Narcissus* was created. My reading of the *auto* can be seen as an exercise in what W. B. Worthen defines as an investigation of dramatic performativity, the "dynamic interplay between the specific identity of a text and the practices of its embodiment."[1] There is, nonetheless, a fundamental difference between his project and mine. Worthen is interested in monitoring how a text from the past is *ergonized*—so to speak—in contemporary settings, but I am trying to tease out how the force of past embodiments was reinscribed in Sor Juana's text. Guided by Bruno Latour, I have been presenting the return of some specific scenarios—a *mitote* replicating the first encounter between Indians and Europeans, young Indians dancing to the beat of a *tepoznatli*, actors staging the death of martyrs in front of their blessed bones—as an opportunity to retrace the occurrence of certain intercultural networks and to navigate them as identities in the making, not identities ready-made. By making intercultural entanglements affectively available, aesthetic productions and their reception facilitate the emergence of new identities as objects of inquiry and modes of living. In the notion of *geochronicity*—extracted from my study of the *Cantares Mexicanos*—I have forged a concept tightly related to the process of intercultural adaptation and innovation.

Bruno Latour explicitly claims that networks can only be mapped effectively if we follow their traces: "action is dislocal, it does not pertain to any specific site; it is distributed, variegated, multiple, dislocated, and remains a puzzle for the analysts as well as for the actors."[2] Charting the flowing assemblages of relations that maintain a network is extremely difficult; the intensities and the variances involved are constantly shifting, and any attempt at studying them comes at the cost of slicing them down into selective set pieces. I have suggested that—although for very different reasons—the Aztecs were particularly invested in confronting a similar problem. To translocate (to follow the flow) was for the Mexicas a mode of existence. In the *Cantares Mexicanos* the spatiality of dancing (the motions organized beside the drums) provided an opportunity to rearticulate history (the song-dances recasted substance as temporality). This explains the figurative density of the *Cantares*, the vertiginous ways in which the songs juggle as many potential scenarios as possible in an effort to embody *through* the dancers multiple, emergent options. Boundaries were not only crossed or passed through, but *carried along* and inhabited. The song-dances were somatic acts of translation.

This process of experiencing identity as transportation is what I have called *geochronicity*, and I believe that intercultural scenarios tend to both facilitate and thrive on its production. It would be easier to define scenarios as chronotopes or heterotopias, but neither of these well-established critical categories will do. For Bakhtin, time is the most relevant aspect of a chronotope; space is shaped by it.[3] Foucault combines his heterotopias (the coexistence in one place of several, incompatible spatial dimensions) with his heterochronias (temporal discontinuities or *découpages*).[4] For these influential authors, time is either the dominant vector (Bakhtin), or something conceptually separated from space (Foucault). Scenarios present highly specific challenges to both chronotopes and heterotopias. Many scenarios evoke an original *moment-place* that can be reproduced elsewhere in response to diasporic or local variations; in such instances—think of Avila's *mitote* in chapter 1, or the martyred Christians in the Jesuit play studied in chapter 2—it is probably inadequate to *think* of time and space as different entities. As I have shown in previous chapters of this book, it is the portability of scenarios that has to be accounted for—the fact that they *travel* and reassemble the networks they intersect. What is needed for intercultural scenarios is a category—like *geochronicity*—that conflates time and space without creating a hierarchical distribution of their value. I have already shown in chapter 3 how the Aztecs managed to forge an environment in which space and time were radically entangled; the rest of this last chapter will *figure out* how a Mexican nun managed to arrive, in her own fashion, at intriguingly similar conclusions. In order to accomplish this goal, I will start by addressing philosophical discussions about process and geography introduced by Gilles Deleuze and Félix Guattari. While these recent geophilosophical discussions are incredibly fruitful, I think we have to be cautious when we use them to explain baroque sacramental plays like *The Divine Narcissus*. The conceptual tenets of the Eucharist dramatized by Sor Juana offer a philosophical and lyrical poiesis of emergence that I plan to unpack by considering both the critical challenges faced by the doctrine of transubstantiation and the affective entrainments mobilized within her *auto*. Guattari (without Deleuze) will prove to be very helpful again once we allow Sor Juana to speak as what she certainly was: an intercultural Catholic subject living in a circum-Atlantic capital.

The Question of Geophilosophy

The work of Sor Juana Inés de la Cruz (1648/51–1695) has become a pivotal piece in our understanding of the circum-Atlantic baroque. From the groundbreaking and still influential portrait of a voracious learner confronting ecclesiastic authorities presented by Octavio Paz,[5] to the enlightening comparison of her literary endeavors with other early modern women writers offered by Stephanie Merrim,[6] Sor Juana has become a key figure whose impact intersects contemporary discussions in—among other fields—cultural, postcolonial, gender, and feminist studies. As Frederick Luciani has shown, Sor Juana herself was quite dexterous at exploring multiple facets of her own self.[7] The philosophical force of her thought and the iridescent quality of her poetry are united with singular success in *The Divine Narcissus*, the sacramental play I will focus on here. I will argue that Sor Juana's *auto* is one of the few colonial productions from New Spain that matches the *geochronic* skills shown by the *Cantares Mexicanos*. Both the *Cantares* and *The Divine Narcissus* share an investment in affective mechanisms associated with indigenous forms of dancing, but I am not suggesting the *Cantares* were a direct source for the play, nor that Sor Juana was deliberately trying to imitate them. Still, I find that the Nahuatl song-dances and the Catholic liturgical drama—as utilized by Sor Juana—coincide in paying inordinate attention to how moving bodies re-encode time and space. What attracts me the most in this case is how Sor Juana's *auto* recognizes the connection between location and self, the ways in which geography molds the itineraries of identity.

Since my *geochronic* assessment of Sor Juana's sacramental play will tap into some issues associated with recent discussions of geophilosophy as introduced by Gilles Deleuze and Félix Guattari, I feel this is the right place to address their ideas in a general way. Their focus on describing how assemblages coordinate multiple ramifications and resistances will prove to be particularly helpful—and equally problematic—for my elucidation of the *auto*'s wrestlings with issues of time, space, and change. Bruno Latour's actor-network theory already allowed me to investigate intercultural scenarios as deliberate *performances* or replayings of previous events that are also segments of an ongoing process of *performation* that traverses, shapes, and disperses them. I believe Deleuze and Guattari (and Guattari *without* Deleuze) can help us to supplement Latour's model.

Geophilosophy is committed to theorizing how the earth and our becoming are closely linked, and it offers a revamping of thought from the perspective of territorialized conceptualizations of labor.[8] One of Deleuze and Guattari's goals is to provoke a critical apparatus in which becoming is exposed as simultaneity, not as succession. According to them, "every becoming is a block of co-existence [and] one can only get it by the middle."[9] To think from the middle we need to sabotage all dualistic constructs and abandon, as much as possible, the predetermined patterns of dialectical narratives. Cartesian dualisms (like subject and object) and Hegelian steps (like sublation) are exactly the opposite of the middle: in the first case, we face an either-or construction; in the second case, the middle is exactly what is being surpassed. Becoming is either overlooked entirely by Descartes or only grasped by Hegel as it passes *forward* into something else. Deleuze and Guattari move away from these insufficient options by persistently adapting and accumulating decentralized qualifications of movement like the rhizome, the assemblage, or the minoritarian. Instead of occupying a preexisting space or consuming a preestablished time, these new concepts mark the emergence of their *own* immanent sense of time and space.[10] (As we have seen, in *Reassembling the Social*, Latour is not willing to drop subject-object distinctions entirely, but he stretches their fluidity by making them partial as *quasi*-objects and *quasi*-subjects.)

Deleuze and Guattari's interlacing of becoming and geography articulates a cartography of thought based on a *spatialization* of concepts and figures. In their last work together—*What Is Philosophy?* (1991)—they suggest that philosophy is not an activity that happens in isolation from water and soil. The sharp Cartesian division between *res cogitans* and *res extensa* has to be set aside in order to elaborate a philosophical discourse in which "thinking takes place in the relationship of territory and the earth."[11] In their opinion, concepts are tested by their capacity to facilitate vicinities to and for other concepts. As opposed to symbols or metaphors, concepts can facilitate transportation but are not available for transference.[12] Concepts are immanent zonings that garner their own proximities and contiguities because they cannot be replaced—they stand for themselves, not for something else. Figures, on the other hand, are transcendental markers of proportions—they can represent something else or can be exchanged for other referents if a *comparable* signification is still preserved.[13] Contrary to concepts, transference is a figure's main mode of transportation: figures can be borrowed, bartered, and carried around.

Concepts and figures (like adjacent or vicinal territories, lands, or neighborhoods) are constantly flowing into each other; what truly matters here are the types of thinking they precipitate. Concepts promote a philosophical emphasis on the uniqueness of every event. Figures—being prone to substitutions and displacements—serve the purpose of introducing analogies and allegorical constructs. Empires and proselytizing religions (invested in covering as much territory as possible) will create a wealth of figurative alternatives. A city (enclosed by a perimeter, a wall, a river) might lean towards a robust conceptualization of its own singularity. Concepts facilitate multiplicity: every situation acquires its own template, its own irreducible individuality. Figures encourage diversity: instead of fostering highly specific determinations, they translate one particular determination into a series of equivalent alternatives.

Concepts tend to work horizontally: they adapt or recoil as they contact each other (or not). Figures are organized vertically: they emanate from a dominant location that reproduces itself through a cascade of correspondences and similitudes. Deleuze and Guattari suggest that while the Greeks *almost* accessed the radical domain of the concept, other regions ended gaining a mastery of the figure. Germany and England owe their philosophical influence to "their break with Catholicism," and France to its passionate "Gallicanism." Italy and Spain were "the two Western countries capable of a powerful development of *concettism*, that is to say, of that Catholic compromise of concept and figure which had great aesthetic value but which masked philosophy, diverted it towards a rhetoric and prevented a full possession of the concept."[14] In Deleuze and Guattari's assessment, in Spain and Italy philosophers were exceptional and solitary, like burning comets traversing a darkened sky.

Roberto Esposito has justly rejected Deleuze and Guattari's anemic description of Italy's role in the history of philosophy,[15] and I myself find their summation of Spain's philosophical contributions rather shallow. I feel that in this case the French collaborators are guilty of a serious blunder. First of all, Deleuze and Guattari's description of the Spanish situation wrongly assumes that philosophizing—the production and circulation of concepts, as they define it—was an incidental practice in a country saturated by scholastic controversies. If anything, on the Iberian peninsula—and in Sor Juana's New Spain, too, as Mauricio Beuchot attests[16]—there was an excessive dependence on Thomistic concepts and subtleties, one that through the *Disputationes metaphysicae* (1597) of Francisco Suárez had a profound impact on the minds of Descartes and Leibniz (and, later on, Martin Heidegger). If rhetorical dexterity—verbal games, hair-splitting nuances, and lexical density—ultimately *masks* philosophy, then Deleuze and Guattari are shooting at their own feet, and their remarks are nothing less than an egregious instance of the kettle calling the pot black.

For Deleuze and Guattari, baroque *concettism* signals a preference for the skills of persuasion (rhetoric) over the skills of the concept (philosophy).

In their opinion, an abundance of figures privileges an aesthetic experiencing of thought that fails to attain conceptual immanence. The fact that both authors are missing here is that this vacillation between concept and figure also enabled the baroque to experience the aesthetic as a philosophical domain. It is not serendipitous that the baroque utilized theater as a trope for the understanding of everyday life. As William Egginton has shown,[17] from public spectacles to *comedia* offerings and political propaganda, the Spanish baroque developed a magisterial awareness of how the aesthetic compromise between concept and figure sets the stage for an interrogation of the boundaries between reality and illusion, internal self and external persona. As early as Machiavelli's *Il Principe* and Castiglione's *Il Cortegiano*, social interaction was defined as a performance of the self, and plays like Shakespeare's *Hamlet*, Calderón's *La vida es sueño*, Lope de Vega's *Lo fingido verdadero*, or Corneille's *L'Illusion comique* are based on an understanding of theatricality as a protocol of affective behavior that we all inhabit, respond to, and learn from.

Concettism was philosophical because it forced concepts to manifest themselves through figures (which is precisely what a *geochronic* practice also does). Theater is a field in which this epistemic operation is not incidental, but almost strictly necessary. The immanent quality of theater—its singularity as a conceptual construct—consists in its capacity to be serially *figured out*, repeated, cited, twice-behaved, or (like in Sor Juana's *The Divine Narcissus*) reinterpreted as refrain and echo. During the baroque, no other form of theater was so consistently dedicated to thread the interplays of concept and figure as the *auto sacramental*, and it is to that practice that we now turn.

Dramaturgies of Substance: The *Autos Sacramentales*

Sor Juana Inés de la Cruz wrote at least three *autos sacramentales*, and the prologues or *loas* for all of them are imbued with a strong awareness of her American origins. The prologue for *El cetro de José* describes the arrival of Christianity in the New World.[18] Catholicism wants to eliminate human sacrifice and polygamy, but Idolatry (presented as an Indian woman) wrestles back, arguing that certain indigenous practices—like sacrificing some Tlaxcalans—are still valid. Idolatry prefers the tangibility of Aztec rituals to the invisible transformations of the Eucharist. The *auto* itself, then, proposes a compromise: by *materializing* as drama the mysteries of transubstantiation through an allegorical reading of Joseph's story, Sor Juana will replicate the same intellectual leap—from naked eye to religious faith—that Idolatry is expected to take in order to complete her conversion.

Another *auto*—*El mártir del Sacramento, San Hermenegildo*—develops this idea even further. In the *loa*, two interpretations of Christ's sacrifice are debated.[19] While one student thinks Christ's major *fineza*, or gift to us was his physical death, another student feels that his presence in the consecrated host is the most important manifestation of Christ's love. In the middle of this scholastic debate, an older student intervenes and tries to placate the confrontation by magically bringing in two different visions or scenes.[20] In the first scene, Hercules and his soldiers build the famous columns that marked the end of the world as they knew it with the words *Non plus ultra* ("Nothing beyond this place"). In the second scene, Columbus defies those words by landing in the New World. It is only then that the third student reveals that these visions are not magical, but theatrical: since he has been writing an *auto* dedicated to San Hermenegildo, he decided to use the actors of a theater company waiting nearby in order to teach a lesson to his younger classmates. Sor Juana's argument seems to be that Christ's bodily death was not the end of his life, but an extension of that life into unexplored shores and peoples that can now memorialize it through the Eucharist.

In these two *loas,* Sor Juana praises the power of theater to materially evoke the abstractions of thought. Each ensuing *auto* reproduces as embodiment the conceptual workings of reason and our efforts to visualize—*theorize*—the challenges of religious belief. Sor Juana's *fineza* lies in her understanding of theatricality as an opportunity to reexperience the emergence of a particular type of knowledge. By utilizing America as a trope for this realization, Sor Juana places herself at the intersection between geography and epistemology. Deleuze and Guattari emphasize the fact that we are not merely thinking within the earth—as if we were looking at things from the insides of a container—but as part of the earth itself. And the earth is not just our ground either: what we experience as earth is a presence in process, a process that is also our own becoming, a milieu in which vectors and relays are continuously appearing (territorializations) or vanishing (deterritorializations). We are always in the middle of things; these flows are coterminous, not sequential. Emergence and dissolution are simultaneous, not successive: they don't follow each other like the words you are reading in this sentence. In these two *loas*—and, even more, in the prologue to *The Divine Narcissus*—Sor Juana reaches an envisioning of geography in which lands and peoples clash and mutually enplace and displace each other.

While local elements appear in other areas of Sor Juana's work—she replicated Nahuatl and Afro-Mexican voices in some of her poems—the *loas* to her *autos* demonstrate a sustained commitment to emphasize her position as a circum-Atlantic writer. Sor Juana is able to access her own Mexican location conceptually by turning it into a figure that connects geography and Catholic faith, a figure that expands and amends the European logos. America is, after all, a landmass *beyond* the waters that proves the *non plus ultra* of antiquity wrong. But philosophy has also something to learn from these *loas*. By introducing the figures of theater into a scholastic controversy modeled on arguments taken from Augustine's and Aquinas's works, the older student in the prologue to *El mártir del sacramento* quite bluntly *aestheticizes* and redirects a *conceptual* unpacking of Christ's gifts. The figurative capability of theater has become in Sor Juana's hands a conceptual category in its own right.

That Sor Juana's most consistent exploration of her geographic singularity is directly connected to her interest in the transformative dispositions of the Eucharist should not surprise us. Sor Juana found in the symbolic architectonics of the *autos* what the song-dances had given to the Mexicas a hundred years earlier: a practice with the potential to refashion the spatial and temporal vectors of her milieu. Caught between Aristotelian categories and their Thomistic adaptations, the Eucharist was both a philosophical aporia and a numinous miracle. Like Aztec sacrifice—although for very different reasons—the Catholic Mass was closely linked to theorizations of substance. Transubstantiation is a change that meets the soul but not the eye. In its zeal to oppose Martin Luther's fierce denunciations against the Mass, the Council of Trent consolidated transubstantiation as the key concept that explained the spiritual power of the Eucharist.

In his detailed survey of how this doctrine acquired its Tridentine shape, Edward Schillebeeckx[21] suggests that transubstantiation was the only possible way of confronting—and in the end, setting aside—evident frictions with prevalent understandings of change. In Aristotle's *Physics*, substance is defined as something that underlies everything while not depending on anything else; any changes observed in matter are only affecting the accidental aspects of substance—its predicates—but not its core. In this treatise, Aristotle also associates change with either visible or divisible qualities (space, motion, time). For Aristotle, change is always oriented towards a goal; growth, for example, is the actualization of an organism's inherent tendencies.[22] The Eucharist challenges all these principles: the accidents of the bread remain while its substance is replaced; the body of the Son of God is not exactly increasing or diminishing the bread, but it still occupies that bread entirely; and the body of Christ stays in heaven while being touched locally through the bread, thus sharing two places at the same time (something Aristotle would have denied as impossible).

Aquinas, in his *Summa Theologiae*, tried to tackle some of these challenges by claiming that the *species* (appearances) of bread and wine are preserved because the body of Christ is now conflated with them: neither their matter nor their form has to be destroyed in order to make room for God's presence. After all, Aristotle himself occasionally seemed to support the notion that matter and substance were difficult to distinguish from each other, so this issue was far from clear. Aquinas felt the conundrums of the Eucharist were a manifestation of God's wisdom. Since the body of Christ was in the host in its entirety (including nerves and bones), the preservation of the visible characteristics of the bread protects the believer from any potential fears of cannibalism.[23] And transubstantiation takes place instantaneously; the becoming-Christ of the bread is not a sequential process (and, therefore, not divisible in terms of Aristotelian space or time).

Francisco Suárez followed Aquinas's ideas closely. For him, transubstantiation implies a change of substance from one thing (*a quo*) to another (*ad quem*). Suárez suggested that the body of Christ is produced in the bread by the consecration, instead of being transferred there from another location.[24] But after Descartes, this scholastic version of the Eucharist became harder to sustain.[25] As Ronald Laymon has argued, Descartes's emphasis on a sharp division between a corporeal or extended reality and an incorporeal, thinking realm guided him into explaining transubstantiation not as the actualization of Christ's flesh, but as the presence of Christ's mind in the bread.[26] Leibniz—never afraid of grappling the most polemical topics—even attempted to find a conceptual solution that would have allowed Catholics and Protestants to settle their differences. According to Leibniz, a body needs a mind if we expect it to be able to move by itself (instead of being always moved by other objects). For Leibniz, the substance of a body actually lies in this linking of matter and thought. Another way of phrasing this would be to say that the extension of a body is not exclusively material—which means that Christ can actually be in two places at the same time. The visible surface of the bread can still be sustained while a different force acts *through* it without annihilating its former appearance.

In his epistolary exchange with Des Bosses, Leibniz proposed that all manifestations of matter are somehow connected by a *vinculum substantiale*, or substantial bond. This bond functions like a line traced over a series of dots (or monads). Such a connective line can be traversed by something else without altering any of the dots involved: "Multipresence does not require the expansion or replication of dimensions. Rather, it should be explained through a kind of presence having no relation to dimensions, just as if God should bring it about that something operates immediately at a distance."[27] Leibniz felt that his *vinculum substantiale* could be used to explain both the paradoxes of Catholic transubstantiation and the tenets of Protestant communion, but nobody (including the philosopher himself) was entirely convinced by it.

It is necessary to keep these philosophical densities at hand if we want to consider the complexities that lurk behind the verbal and visual splendors of Corpus Christi plays. As Sarah Beckwith points out, of all the rituals of the church, the Eucharist was probably the closest one to theater in terms of a fundamental realization: empirical appearances can be—and in some cases *should* be—deceiving.[28] Aquinas himself gave a rationale for this approach when he stated in his *Summa* that "our faith is not in opposition to what our senses tell us, but is concerned with something to which our senses do not reach."[29] The *auto sacramental* was dedicated to negotiate this gap between the sensorial and the metaphysical by means of actors and special effects. The *autos* thrived as theater by tapping into the tensions of a doctrine that depended—like the reliquaries discussed in chapter 2—on a devoted embracing of the limits of representation.

By positing an ergonic process that transforms substance while preserving accidental characteristics, transubstantiation both territorializes and deterritorializes the earthly components of bread in order to reenact a narrative of salvation. Christ's crucifixion was supposed to take place only once, but the redemptive effects of that exceptional sacrifice can be reiterated through the periodic commemoration of the Mass. As a miracle, the Eucharist canceled the split between concept and figure: the bread became Christ himself. As a topic for thought or contemplation, the Catholic Church relied on that same split to articulate the tantalizing mysteries of the sacrament. With their recourse to allegorical expositions and their affective call for an embodied figuration of theological intricacies, the *autos sacramentales* actualized a spatialization of reason that Deleuze and Guattari ignored too easily and to the detriment of their own geophilosophical critique.

The Prologue to *The Divine Narcissus*

As Max Harris explains, "the theatre would appear to exist . . . at a point of tension, blessed or handicapped, depending on your point of view, by two limitations: the impossibility of precision copying and the impossibility of pure abstraction."[30] Few forms of theater have embraced this conundrum so radically as the *autos sacramentales*. These plays inhabit, quite intentionally and even jubilantly, a conflicted zone between replication and failure, and they thrive on it to a degree that many theatrical practices—especially those committed to a realistic or psychological agenda—always tend to resent. The *autos* rejected verisimilitude for the sake of a theological truth that can only be appreciated—if not fully understood—through the intervention of an *affective* mode of thinking. The *autos* extended an invitation to ponder the perplexities of Catholic belief while still acknowledging that our capacity to analyze life is a fundamental part of our humanity. Between reason and faith there was always a recourse to theater, that liminal and agonistic *ergon* in which space and time can be manipulated, producing an aesthetic chance for figure and concept to coexist and collaborate as embodiment.

The sacramental plays became particularly relevant as part of the Counter-Reformation's campaigning against Lutheranism, one Spain was proud of championing even at the cost of financial and demographic disarray. As Francis Clark documents, the paradoxes of the Eucharist were central to theological controversies between Catholics and Protestants. While Catholics insisted on the incarnational dimensions of the Mass—the fact that something was actually *happening* to the bread through the mediation of the priest—Lutherans rejected the need for a sacerdotal intercession and saw communion as an intrinsic reaffirmation of God's pledge to humans.[31] In his detailed account of Catholic efforts to explain and control the *mysterium fidei* of the Eucharist, James T. O'Connor leaves no doubt that transubstantiation was an idea fraught with the potential to provoke both passionate and perilous exaltations.[32] On the one hand, the Eucharist is the quintessential leap of faith: the believer has to accept as true something that his or her senses are not able to observe. On the other hand, from priests who claimed finding themselves with a piece of flesh in their hands instead of the host, to women who starved themselves into trance by not eating anything else, the question of the real presence of Christ in the consecrated bread was prone to fuse and confuse the boundaries between emotion and reality.

The bull by Urban IV that in 1264 instituted the Feast of Corpus Christi was, in part, inspired by a desire to underline the miraculous implications of the Mass as a performative act, an *ergonic* recall of Jesus's flesh and blood that made his body available to be ingested and digested and—due to some unfortunate, physiological consequences—even accidentally chewed or exposed to excremental travails. We have to keep in mind that it is due to the Eucharist—a commitment to the materiality of Christ—that the church found itself obliged to tolerate what Jonathan Bishop calls a sense of *bodiliness*, the tangible consequences of the incarnation of God as human.[33] In her magnificent investigation of the medieval invention of Corpus Christi, Miri Rubin calls attention to the fact that this feast was also one of the few holidays of the church that can be directly connected to the initiative of women (a detail Sor Juana was surely appreciative of).[34] I wonder if Sor Juana was also aware how the original liturgy of the feast placed a strong focus on the wisdom or *sapientia* delivered by the sacred food to the believers.[35] *Sapientia* was usually portrayed as a female, but later versions of this liturgy attributed to none other than Thomas Aquinas emphasized the mediatory role of the *sacerdos* or priest instead.

When Sor Juana wrote her sacramental plays, the genre's most important author, Pedro Calderón de la Barca, had been dead for a decade.[36]After his ordination to the priesthood in 1651, Calderón monopolized the production of *autos* at the Spanish court. Alexander Parker[37] and Ignacio Arellano[38] have studied Calderón's masterful ability to interlace theology, allegory, music, and spectacle into a seamless synthesis that was widely admired later by the German romantics and even influenced Wagner's *Parsifal*.[39] As Barbara Kurtz has shown, Calderón utilized mythological, biblical, and historical narratives to create a dazzling tapestry of analogical references to the Eucharist and its redemptory power.[40] An *auto* by Calderón—*El divino Orfeo*, published in 1677—has been considered by some a potential model for *The Divine Narcissus*.[41] Christian reinterpretations of classical mythology were a popular humanistic exercise, and the *Ovide Moralisé* (written towards the end of the thirteenth or the beginning of the fourteenth centuries) was particularly influential in this regard. In Calderón's *auto*, Orpheus's skills as a singer are used to present an allegorical description of the creation of the world through the powers of voice, harmony, and language.

In Madrid and other Spanish cities the feast of Corpus Christi motivated an increasingly complex *performational* network made of processions, festivals, plays, sermons, and fraternities responsible for the annual preparations and fund-raising activities that paid for the expensive displays of embodied concepts involved. When she created *The Divine Narcissus*, Sor Juana was counting, at least nominally, on the luxurious resources normally assembled for this type of celebration in Mexico City and the Spanish court.[42] The prologue to *The Divine Narcissus* starts when two figures dressed as Indians (Occidente, a man with a crown) and America (a woman wearing *huipiles*) enter the scene to the sounds of a *tocotín* and accompanied by a group of dancers "con plumas y sonajas en las manos" ("with feathers and rattles in their hands").[43] The Indians are praising Huitzilopochtli, a god linked both to war and the productive power of the sun. An effigy of Huitzilopochtli—made of seeds mixed with human blood and turned into a paste—was honored by the Aztecs during one of their festivals each December, carefully dismembered into smaller pieces, and then ingested by a selected group of attendants. In her *auto*, Sor Juana profits from an analogy, skillfully developed by the mendicant friars, between the Aztec feast of the *Teocualo* ("god is eaten," in Nahuatl) and the Eucharist.

In the first segment of the *loa*, the Indians describe the nourishing resources of their lands, and their need to periodically reenergize them through offerings of human sacrifice:

> Y pues la abundancia
> de nuestras provincias,
> se le debe a él, que es
> quien las fertiliza,
> ofreced devotos,
> pues les son debidas,
> de los nuevos frutos
> todas las primicias.
> ¡Dad de vuestras venas
> la sangre más fina,
> para que mezclada,
> a su culto sirva;
> y en pompa festiva,
> celebrad al gran Dios de las semillas!
>
> [And since we owe
> the abundance of our lands
> to Him, the one
> that fertilizes them,
> let's devoutly offer
> —'cause they come from Him—

the initial productions
of this new harvest.
Give from your veins
the best, finest blood,
so it can be mixed
and used to praise Him;
and with festive exuberance
let's celebrate the God of seeds!][44]

The second section of the prologue brings in a new set of characters: Religión (a Spanish lady) and Celo (or Zeal, a Spanish soldier), followed by a military regiment. These figures represent the goals of the Spanish conquest of Mexico: the conversion and domination of the Indians. The rest of the prologue will oppose these two couples along gender lines: while Occidente and Celo stand for physical strength and pragmatic justifications of violence, América and Religión will build a more intellectual compromise between Aztec and Christian beliefs.

The most notable aspect of this *loa* is that the foundational scenario of the first encounter between Indians and Europeans is at the beginning presented from the indigenous point of view, and that by the end of the prologue both positions had become a third one (the Viceroyalty of New Spain). Religión and Celo are evidently interrupting an Indian ritual when they arrive, and the Aztecs are both surprised and annoyed by their intrusion. When the Indians decide to ignore the Spaniards, Zeal attacks and defeats them. Once the battle has ended, it is Religión's turn to persuade the mind of the Indians. It is at this juncture that the aesthetic alliance between figure and concept leads to a dramatized sermon in which Religión tries to persuade the Indians by using three strategic arguments: after recalling Paul's preaching of the unknown god during his sojourn in Athens, Religión ensures América that the Christian god is responsible for the maintenance of the world, and that certain concepts are better understood through visualized metaphors than through spoken words alone. Asked by América how such metaphors can reach the eye and the ear at the same time, Religión announces the allegorical content of the *auto*: a Christian retelling of the story of Narcissus from Ovid's *Metamorphoses*. The prologue then concludes with a final *coup*: this *auto* will be staged in Spain, not in Mexico. When Zeal expresses his discomfort with this idea, Religión says: "¿Pues es cosa nunca vista / que se haga una cosa en una / parte, porque en otra sirva?" ("Is this by chance the first time / that something done in one place / ends being utilized in another?"). Since Zeal is not willing to change his mind yet, Religión adds: "No habrá cosa que desdiga, aunque las lleve a Madrid: / que a especies intelectivas / ni habrá distancias que estorben / ni mares que les impidan" ("Nothing will disqualify my ideas / even if I take them to Madrid: / intellectual concepts are not hindered by distances / or oceans").[45] And now all the characters join in one more reprise of the *tocotín* before they exit together.

Sor Juana herself had written two *tocotines* before: one (in Nahuatl) for a cycle of *villancicos*, or sacred carols in 1676, and another for a similar cycle in 1677 (in which she combined Nahuatl and Castilian lines).[46] As we saw in chapter 3, the *tocotín* was an indigenous dance named after the markings for Aztec drumbeats, some of which have been preserved in the manuscript of the *Cantares Mexicanos*. Sor Juana commences her *auto* by probing into an indigenous form of affective entrainment that was already assimilated into viceregal culture. More than a touch of local custom, this *tocotín* is fully embedded with the forces of nature. Both América and Religión emphasize the role played by Aztec and Christian deities in the *ergonic* process of the earth: fields, rain, heat, plants, and agriculture. Sor Juana is not activating nature here as a mere backdrop for her prologue, but as an enabling milieu. The New World is a lived and living space within which a particular becoming is taking (and remaking) its place. It is through a shared respect for the cycles of nature and the participation of god in their maintenance that Religión and América find common ground. (Sor Juana's investment in the presence of nature in the prologue is also preparing us for the ecological props of Narcissus's myth: trees, rocks, fountains, water.)

In the *loa*, we find an example of what Enrique Dussel calls a "theological economy." Dussel argues that the bread of the Eucharist—and, I might add, the dough prepared by the Aztecs to make an edible image of Huitzilopochtli—implies a "subject-nature relationship . . . the bread prepared for the sacrifice, is *real* bread; it is really the product of someone's work, in time, specific human work."[47] In the Eucharistic liturgy bread is not only nature, but nature as reshaped by human labor and then transformed by transubstantiation. In Sor Juana's scenario, the initial subject-nature condition of the Aztecs is destroyed by the conquest and then restored through the Eucharist as bread, as food extracted from the earth, that realm of the god of seeds the refrain of the *tocotín* recalls at least twelve times during the prologue.

For Sor Juana, the conversion of the New World marks a moment when location demands to be thought historically, as a material enclave for the next becoming of salvation. Theology is entangled with the confluences of geography. But there is also a dramatic precedent for Sor Juana's *tocotín*. In 1620, Francisco Bramón included a laudatory *auto* in honor of the Immaculate Conception in the third part of his novel *Los sirgueros de la Virgen sin original pecado*, a pastoral narrative invested with religious symbolism.[48] In this *auto*, Mexico ("Reino Mexicano") appears seated in the middle of a garden while the voice of Time describes the portents of the Mother of God, and in the last scene the Reino celebrates the arrival of the Virgin to the New World.

Bramón's piece is hard to find and deserves to be better known; its wealth of detail justifies a full quotation. In his *auto*, he describes the following pageant:

Sacaron diversidad de instrumentos que usan en esta danza, entre los cuales aquel que es más necesario se llama teponaztle, que es de palo, y todo de una pieza, muy bien labrado, hueco, y sin cuero ni pergamino por de fuera, con cierta hendedura o muesca por lo alto; tócase con palillos, aunque son los extremos delicados, por ser de algodón; de otro instrumento usan, que es mayor que éste, alto más que hasta la cinta, redondo, hueco, entallado por de fuera y pintado, en su boca tiene un ancho parche de cuero de venado, bien curtido y estirado, que, apretado, sube, y, flojo, abaja el tono: tócase con las manos, aunque con trabajo . . . dieron los siete [el Reino y los caciques] principio a una vistosa danza, que llaman, los mexicanos, netotiliztle, y en nuestro vulgar, mitote o tocotín: es danza que para relación o escrita no tiene gracia y donaire [es decir, pierde la gracia y el donaire cuando se escribe sin verla], que le comunican aquellos que diestramente deleitan en ella con sus agradables vueltas, reverencias, entradas, cruzados y paseos, como lo hicieron maravillosamente estos siete mexicanos, que excendiendo y dejando atrás el arte, dieron sufiencientes muestras que solo los movía y animaba el celo de su gozo y triunfo sacrosanto de la sin culpa Concebida. Al paso que danzaban, unos diestros músicos cantaron, al son de los instrumentos, así:

Bailad, mexicanos
suene el tocotín,
pues triunfa María
con dicha feliz.

[They brought a diversity of instruments for this dance, among which the most important is called the *teponaztle*, [a drum] made of a single piece of wood, well carved, hollowed, and without any leather or skin around it, and with an incision on top; they play on it with sticks delicately covered with cotton. They also use another instrument that stands slightly higher than a man's waist, [this drum] is round and hollowed too, carved and painted; on its mouth it has a deerskin patch quite terse and tightened so when the skin is relaxed the tone is lower and when the skin is tense the tone is higher; this one was played with their bare hands, and was quite demanding . . . the performers started an opulent dance, called by the Mexican, *netotiliztle*, and in our language, *mitote* or *tocotín*; no verbal description can convey the grace and elegance of the dancers, the pleasant rounds, the reverential gestures, the entrances, and intersecting motions . . . while they danced some dexterous musicians sang, accompanied by all these instruments, the following song:

Dance with joy, Mexicans!
Listen to the *tocotín*!
Mary is now triumphant,
Jubilant and happy!][49]

Bramón's *auto* shows that by 1620 many indigenous performative practices and objects—drums, dances, and songs—were already fully integrated into the service of Catholic doctrines.[50] In this particular case, Indian dancers and singers were being summoned to defend a theological proposition the church was far from admitting as dogma yet (the Immaculate Conception was not made an official tenet of Catholicism until 1854). Bramón's *auto* also allows us to realize how ambitious Sor Juana's *loa* truly is. The nun starts where Bramón ended—with the *tocotín*—and her Indians are not only willing providers of spectacle, but subjects that express their own opinion of things. There is an implicit geopolitical dimension to Bramón's scenes (after all, Mexico is welcoming the arrival of the Virgin to its lands), but Sor Juana's *tocotín* in *The Divine Narcissus* is structurally relevant to her complete *auto*: it sets the pace for an increasing accumulation of motions, relocations, leaps, and re-encodings that facilitate an almost vertiginous sequence of emerging identities. I will argue that it is this figurative commitment to the concept of change through repetition that enables Sor Juana to turn her geography into a *geochrony*, a reassembling of history through the deployment of embodied thought. When Sor Juana combined the *tocotín* with the Eucharist, two different understandings of substance (one Mexica, one Catholic) encountered each other. In spite of their differences, both theories of substance produced—in the *Cantares* and in *The Divine Narcissus*—textual remnants that manage to perform verbally the same ergonic investments that human bodies were expected to express kinesthetically. Nahuatl poetry and Christian drama are bodies that reemerge by other means, scripted entrainments in which philosophy thinks itself through aesthetic figuration.

Anaphoric Networks: Refrains, Mirrors, Echoes

More often than not, a written play is a verbal construct intended to be made flesh, a template for the production of certain bodies and circumstances. Every dramatic text occupies a threshold position between its incarnation and its virtuality. The idea that a script remains incomplete unless performed sounds less convincing once we see that text as another relay in the transportation of the *quasi*-objects and *quasi*-subjects that articulate the flows of our performations. Since all cultural vectors are by definition partial—they need other vectors to stay in circulation—a dramatic text is not morphologically that different from other forms of networking. A play produced and a play read are certainly two distinct objects, but there is no reason to consider one more efficacious than the other. A script channels and moves along its own networks, emerges from them and with them; it is a response to them as much as an effort to influence them. Metaphoric bodies are not imagined ex nihilo, and archival bodies are part of the gestural repertoire of a community. A dramatic text contributes to the history of our bodies in its own, irreplaceable manner—and it should count as a performance in its own right. Trained as philologists, Leopardi, Nietzsche, and Gramsci—although quite different from each other—never lost sight of how relevant textual formations are for the grasping of social and somatic genealogies. For a historian of colonial Mexico, those genealogies—when available—are still indispensable and quite rewarding if analyzed with an affective slant.

In Sor Juana's prologue, dancing and singing bodies have the responsibility of conveying a close connection between earth and belief, matter and self. By selecting a *tocotín*, Sor Juana leaves no doubt that her *auto* is firmly rooted in a somatic syntax directly associated with indigenous practices that had been adapted for Catholic purposes. The *loa* recapitulates the history of the *tocotín* itself, from its existence as part of an Aztec ritual to its preservation as part of the Corpus Christi celebrations. Sor Juana's translocalizing device in the *loa* is a refrain first introduced by the Indians and then adopted by the Spaniards. Mimicking transubstantiation, an *estribillo* alluding to the god of seeds gradually acquires new meaning—a different semantic substance—while still maintaining most of its original wording. If in the opening of the prologue the Indians are honoring an Aztec god, then by the closing scene both Indians and Europeans seem glad to have made the acquaintance of their Christian Father. Although all the characters speak Castilian, the refrain is originally an Aztec figuration that gets re-encoded *conceptually*—not lexically—into a mixing of indigenous discourse and Catholic hermeneutics. Transporting us from Mexico City to Madrid, the refrain has become New Spain, an expression of intercultural concrescence.

There is nothing particularly unusual about Sor Juana's use of a refrain: from popular medieval ballads to lyrical imitations of Petrarch's *Canzoniere*, refrains were a common stylistic tool in Renaissance and baroque literatures. But the refrain in *The Divine Narcissus* does something unexpected: it translates one culture into another without changing its language. In *Schizoanalytic Cartographies* (1989) and *Chaosmosis* (1992), Félix Guattari investigates the theoretical ramifications of the *retournelle*. A refrain creates what he calls "a system of repetition," an area of "intensive existence" that localizes the enunciation of new referents.[51] By coming back to itself—moving forwards by moving backwards—the refrain indicates an itinerary, a mapping of energies, a bundle of vectors. For Guattari, assemblages are patterned by refrains, pulsating sequences that crystallize into zones of intensity perceived as states of self or existential territories. In the vicinity of these intensities, affects emerge, collide, and produce subjective positions experienced as "the crossing of a threshold . . . the locus of a labor, of a potential praxis."[52] A refrain—like anaphors—*spatializes* and *temporalizes* language; reiteration becomes orientation and measurement.

Like the drums in the *Cantares Mexicanos*, the *tocotín* in Sor Juana's *loa* has a *geochronic* function: it signals a re-encoding of bodies and locations as entities in process that are being translated, like the refrain itself, while they are moving. As we have seen, the Aztecs wanted their dancers and singers to manifest the perpetual translocations of substance from one form to another. As a Catholic writer, Sor Juana intersects a different comprehension of spatiotemporal relays. Edward S. Casey notices how Renaissance and baroque thinkers oscillated between two proxemic notions—space and place—until the former superseded the latter during the Enlightenment. If space was associated with unlimited extension, place was linked to limiting containment. "Is it accidental," Casey asks, "that the obsession with space as something infinite and ubiquitous coincided with the spread of Christianity, a religion with universalist aspirations?" Casey adds that once "the age of exploration had begun . . . the domination of native peoples was accomplished by their deplacialization: the systematic destruction of regional landscapes that served as the concrete settings for local culture."[53] In her prologue, Sor Juana balances both concepts: Mexico is disclosed as a place originally self-contained, then disrupted by the conquest, and—after its conversion to Catholicism—dutifully transported to Madrid. Old and New worlds meet and pass through each other across the vast expanses of the ocean.

In *The Divine Narcissus*, water is the element in which bodies are *decontained* into otherness, fluidity, and change. In the proximity of the fountain the contours of place melt down into the pliable spaces of metamorphosis.[54] The traumatized relation between voice and echo complicates this scheme by introducing the transversal capacity of sound to travel through *space* and from one *place* to another. But the entire *auto* constitutes a sustained effort to figure out—as literally as possible—the transactions between space and place. "In archaic societies," argues Guattari, "it is through rhythms, chants, dances, masks, marks on the body, ground and totems, on ritual occasions and with mythical references, that other kinds of collective existential Territories are circumscribed."[55] Setting aside Guattari's clumsy reference to "archaic societies"—the fact is that contemporary cultures are no less prone to relying on embodied transactions than earlier ones—this observation is confirmed by Sor Juana's play. The *tocotín* brings a particular territorialization to the picture—one that becomes deterritorialized and readjusted through the iterations of the song-dance, too. In *The Divine Narcissus*, nothing stays the same for a long time: metamorphosis is here etched into the plotting and the diction of the text itself.

As if it were a second prologue, the first scene of the *auto* confronts two nymphs and their cohorts: Gentilidad (Gentility, representing the legacy of classical antiquity) and Sinagoga (Synagogue, standing for the Judaic law). They are dutifully followed by Naturaleza Humana (Human Nature), and each of them has its own refrain: "¡Alabad al Señor todos los hombres!" ("The Lord be praised by all!") (Synagogue) and "¡Alabad a Narciso, Fuentes y flores!" ("Praise Narcissus, flowers and fountains!") (Gentility). Human Nature explains that she is taking from the Old Testament the body of its precepts, while adopting her covering garments from Gentility (Hebrew wisdom will provide the concept or *sentido*, while mythology will add the rhetorical figurations or *voces*). Human Nature has been created in God's image, but in spite of the blessings available through baptism, her imperfections are keeping her away from God's love. Sin—compared here to opaque, contaminated waters—is not allowing Human Nature to reflect God's grace properly. A clear, pristine fountain can reverse this state of deprivation if Human Nature manages to be seen by Narcissus on its surface while the shepherd is looking at himself—two overlapping faces merging, for an instant, into a single image.

Sor Juana daringly rewrites the quintessential story of obsessive self-love gone astray into a narrative of Christian forgiveness and reconciliation. The disturbed emotional conditions suffered by Human Nature are staged in the *auto* by three characters: Eco (Echo), Soberbia (Arrogance), and Amor Propio (Self-Love). This comic trio—their exaggerated, quarrelsome manners are quite entertaining—is both annoyed and mesmerized by the musical declarations of Gentility and Synagogue. Lucifer-Echo decides to follow suit—if Human Nature is pursuing Narcissus, he or she will become a nymph, too:

> Os referiré mi historia
> con la metáfora mesma,
> para ver si la de Eco
> conviene con mi tragedia.
> Desde aquí el curioso
> mire si concuerdan
> verdad y ficción,
> el sentido y letra.
>
> [I will tell you my story
> through this same metaphor,
> and see if Echo's predicament
> corresponds to my tragedy.
> From this point, everybody
> will have now to decide how truth and fiction coincide
> with this meaning and this sign.][56]

Since Echo has been rejected by Narcissus in the past, she is enviously committed to keeping Human Nature's eyes averted from his gaze as much as possible. A lesson in sacred history ensues: in quick succession the flood, the tower of Babel, Cain and Abel, Enoch, Abraham, and Moses cross the page—and the Corpus Christi carts—illustrating the figurative precedents for the allegorical actions included in the *auto*. Only Christ, as a merging of the human and the divine, can heal the severe disjunctions between creature and maker fostered by the resentments of the reprobated angel (Lucifer-Echo). The vengeful nymph suspects that Narcissus is the Son of God, and with her supportive companions she approaches the mountainous grove where the shepherd guards his flock after fasting for forty days (an evident allusion to Christ's vigil in the desert). Like in the gospel, Echo-Lucifer tempts Narcissus-Christ by offering him all the riches of the earth: cattle, flowers, minerals, gardens, fruits, pine trees, birds, wild animals, wheat spikes, and the wide variety of countries and navigations that traverse the oceans. Narcissus, as expected, chastises Echo.

Human Nature reappears, conflating past, present, and future: she announces the birth of Christ—who is already allegorically *present* as Narcissus—and then predicts his sacrifice and exalts his beauty in lines evocative of the Song of Songs. (The figurative understanding of history explained in chapter 2 validates this lyrical chronological bending.) Gracia makes her entrance now with another refrain—"dichosa el alma/ que merece hospedarme en su morada" ("happy the soul / that deserves to host me in its home")—and recalls how the serpent induced Adam to disregard her. Grace advises Human Nature to hide among the branches of a tree rising near a fountain—a double reference to the purity of the Virgin Mary and baptismal waters—in order to wait for Narcissus. They climb the tree and stare at each other, hoping that Narcissus will contemplate them, too, while his own features are reflected in the liquid mirror.

Sor Juana's fountain is both a classical *locus amoenus* (a pleasant location) and a medieval *hortus conclusus* (an enclosed garden), a space for pastoral tenderness and virginal pulchritude in which erotic and spiritual exaltations can take their place. As Stephen Hinds explains, Ovid's landscapes are imbued with a "cosmological accent . . . in which the setting may always be more than just a setting."[57] Inspired by Ovidian reminiscences, the fountain-garden is a threshold in which identities are restored into their becoming (which is another way of saying that they are experienced again as history). The Mexican nun conveys this concrescent state through a radical *quasi*-fication of utterance. On three different occasions, the text intensifies its affective impact through the means of echoic segmentation; in those moments, language communicates by disabling its content, by failing to replicate its intended meaning in its entirety. First, Grace and Human Nature praise the benefits of the fountain; then, an angry Echo loses her voice but still tries to talk to Arrogance and Self-Love; finally, the frustrated nymph dislocates Narcissus's melancholic complaints by replicating them in truncated form.

At this point in the *auto*, figure and concept have become inseparable, an effect enhanced by the music that is expected to tie all these iterative sequences together. The poetic form adopted by Sor Juana in two of these echoic scenes is known as the *ovillejo*, a series of questions and answers in which certain words are skillfully rearranged several times and woven into new semantic connotations. After being made relatively popular by Cervantes in *Don Quijote*, Calderón utilized the *ovillejos* in his *autos*, and Sor Juana probably remembered those included by him in his mythological play *Eco y Narciso*.[58] Narcissus hears the lamentations of Echo—who is now hidden inside the hollowed trunk of a tree—and says:

NARCISO Mas, ¿quién, en el tronco hueco
ECO Eco.
NARCISO con triste voz y quejosa,
ECO Quejosa.
NARCISO así a mis voces responde?
ECO Responde.
NARCISO ¿Quién eres, oh voz, o dónde
te ocultas, de mi escondida?
¿Quién me responde afligida?
ECO (Y MÚSICA) Eco quejosa responde.

[NARCISO But who—from this hollowed trunk—echoing
ECO Echoing.
NARCISO with such a saddened and lamenting voice,
ECO Voice.
NARCISO is responding to me through all these sounds?
ECO Sounds.
NARCISO Who are you, tell me, or where are you hiding?
Who is answering me with so much pain?
ECO Echoing Voice Sounds.][59]

Like the Italian *sestina* so dear to Dante and Petrarch, the *ovillejo* is an ingenious combination of symmetric design, verbal recycling, renewal, and predictability. An *ovillejo* is a systematic meditation on the effects of repetition: it produces difference by deploying similarity, and it shows how signifiers and signifieds can be inflected by movement, time, and location. An *ovillejo* is a finely calibrated mapping of anaphor-like relations and directional cues, and as such is particularly invested in stressing the locative elements of verse and the vectorial momentum of poetic language. Poetry, of course, is always attentive to how language marks itself through rhythm, rhyme, cadence, accent, and syllabic counting, but Sor Juana's *ovillejos* are intensifying many of these standard prosodic techniques in order to convey the evasive mechanics of transportation so closely connected to both metamorphosis and transubstantiation. The script is the inscription of an aestheticized concept: *The Divine Narcissus* reassembles an affective network that is being efficaciously performed—even if not being *staged*—by the verbal constructs of the play itself.

Coda: Intercultural Reflexivity

In *Economies of Signs and Space*, Scott Lash and John Urry suggest that film, poetry, television, and painting are forms of affective expertise. We learn from these reflexive practices many of our standards of subjectivity: "Poetic discourse is constitutive of the rituals through which we operate." In late capitalism, poetic rituals are circulated at speeds and distances that were inaccessible to Sor Juana. In contemporary digital media, these aestheticized relays create "mediated universals through which people from . . . many nations communicate. Globalized popular cultures, functioning as poetic discourse [are now] a relatively immediate and internationalized habitus."[60] Popular forms of communication are influential due to the allure of their generative mechanisms; their content is less relevant than the editing strategies and the stylistic preferences they disseminate. More often than not, the main value of these poetic rituals is not representational, but reproductive.

The *auto sacramental* was a popular form of theological entertainment that became globalized as part of the Spanish Empire. As a poetic ritual, its main function was to dramatize a particular type of thinking, one based on allegorical ornamentations, rhetorical complexity, and extravagant financial investments. The relentless reflexivity of the genre was articulated through a deliberate confrontation between concept and figure, a philosophical conflict that could only be fully actualized as theater. In *The Divine Narcissus,* Sor Juana Inés de la Cruz expanded this reflexive genre in order to play again the emergence of her Mexican-Spanish milieu. Sor Juana's *auto* (like some of the song-dances in the *Cantares Mexicanos*) promotes an aesthetic reexperiencing of time and space, a *geochrony* that exposes the itineraries of bodies in motion and the scenarios that reproduce them.

A network is an affective collaboration as much as a series of tasks and reproductive roles. Aesthetic figuration and conceptual intelligibility are hard to distinguish from each other while we are on the move. As we have seen in this book, each relay is both an attractor and a selector energized by our desires and their manifestations as work, as performance. A dramatic script is as good a blueprint for networking as any other. Imaginary bodies and exercised bodies are marked by different intensities, but there is no reason to consider a virtual body more efficacious than a tangible one. The critical approach I have been rehearsing in this book pays special attention to how objects, persons, and territories—the *performations* we both enable and respond to—are posited again and *performed* as intercultural scenarios. A *geochronic* analysis of those scenarios is primarily interested in targeting how shifts of space and time are materialized and promoted by affective entrainments—masquerades, processions, drums, or playwriting.

In *What Is Philosophy?* Deleuze and Guattari define history as "the set of conditions, however recent they may be, from which one turns away in order to become, that is to say, in order to create something new."[61] This is an agonistic understanding of historiography: "Without history, becoming would remain indeterminate and unconditioned, but becoming is not historical."[62] As process, becoming is a story that cannot be told: in order to be narrated, history has to be structured and divided into segments, periodization, places, nations, genders, interruptions—and *geochronies*. To think our becoming more efficaciously we have to focus on the performations of our milieu, the territories that are being made and unmade by our emergence. Deleuze and Guattari are also aware of the potential of geophilosophy to be misread as a cult of location over contingency, and they are particularly careful about stressing the coexistence of nature and chance. We should be able to remain ecologically specific without falling into the trappings of geographic determinism.

Deleuze and Guattari's geophilosophy is a theorization of embeddedness in which nature and body are interconnected parts of an unstable continuum. After all, our body is a moveable *moment-place*, a portable boundary: we dwell in it, we are carried by it through *space* and into *time*, we are always installed in its affective capabilities. For Deleuze and Guattari, geography is a process of *becoming-with*: earth, flesh, and thought are concurrent, not serial. "Space and time are thus never neutral receptacles," argues Guattari. "They must be accomplished, engendered by productions of subjectivity involving chants, dances, stories about ancestors and gods."[63] And Sor Juana's *tocotín* does exactly that—it labors its own time and its own space while enacting a *geochronic* recording of its own history.

Should we consider *The Divine Narcissus* as a *historical* event—another vanishing cut into the ergonic flows of geography? Sor Juana's scientific curiosity is well documented,[64] and her interest in the esoteric teachings of Athanasius Kircher left indelible traces on her writing.[65] Sor Juana was interested in understanding nature with the tools of reason, and Jorge Cañizares-Esguerra has shown how scientific curiosity was linked to an emergent creole mind-set in the colonial baroque.[66] But when Sor Juana selected an indigenous song-dance for her prologue, she was quite consciously tapping into a somatic legacy that was also a milieu, a singularized convergence of vectors that was becoming another (new) Mexico and another (new) Spain, a doubled process that she portrayed as *tocotín* and *ovillejo*, refrains and echoes that changed as they moved while still remaining—or sounding—familiar. Contingency, however, was not exactly an acceptable option in Sor Juana's axiology. *The Divine Narcissus* is a teleological synthesis of Mexican, Jewish, classical, and Christian elements. In Sor Juana's religious worldview, contingency was—when mentioned—no more than a mirage or a miscalculation. All figures are preparations for the return of Christ and the *auto* unhesitatingly supports this goal-oriented narrative. From the perspective of Catholic eschatology, Jerusalem, Athens, Rome, and Tenochtitlán were expected to be absorbed into a dominant Christian essence or *thelos*.

The merit of Sor Juana's *auto* lies in its borrowing of Aztec *tocotines* and Ovidian metamorphosis as tropes for the depiction of the translocalizing effects of transubstantiation. Elaine Fantham describes how in Ovid's poem most human bodies are either reshaped, rearranged, raped, or fused either into each other (like the hermaphrodite) or transformed into animals, flowers, and rocks.[67] These violent shifts of form from human to nonhuman are almost never reversible, and there is only one instance that involves a change from human-made objects into animated beings (Aeneas's ships are morphed into sea nymphs). Narcissus, Human Nature, and Grace overlap their features by reflection (they see each other on the water's surface) but they are not merged into a single shape for too long, and it is Narcissus's desperation at being separated from them again that leads him back to the fountain. The inescapability of their processual state—the fact that they find no respite in their constant becoming away, from, and into each other—signals for Sor Juana the imperfect spiritual condition of these characters, their ambivalent existence between space and place, time and temporality.

When Narcissus dies, an earthquake convinces Echo of his divinity, but the nymph is not easily discouraged and immediately decides to trick Human Nature into forgetting the fate of Narcissus-Christ (a maneuver that will fail at the end of the *auto* due to Christ's resurrection, and the mediatory institution of the Eucharist). Transubstantiation thus solves the conflict between space and place: Christ can now be *everywhere* if we believe so. But this is a dramaturgy of new relations, not a dramaturgy of creation. In *The Divine Narcissus*, emergence is the revelation of something that was hidden due to error or ignorance. Sor Juana convokes history in order to confirm its providential course: the new relation between Aztecs and Spaniards is one more episode in the old story of God's advancing plan. For Sor Juana, intercultural relations are less a question of accessing something *different* than a question of integrating all existing cultural variations into the unifying narrative of Catholicism. Sor Juana was more a historian of subtle assimilations than a chronicler of drastic ruptures.

In *The Divine Narcissus*, change is embraced only to the extent that it encourages or envisions a more harmonious closeness to God. Becoming is here a flaw, a sign of our fallen nature. As I have explained elsewhere,[68] during the baroque period change was considered a problem, not an advantage. Since a world created by a perfect God should have been *right* from the start, it was necessary to justify the constant corruption and renewal of things. From cautious references to Lucretius's *clinamen* to Leibniz's rethinking of matter as a conglomeration of monadic units, baroque philosophers tried to confront the potential incoherence of a reality that seemed to be reemerging all the time. Caroline Walker Bynum claims that around the end of the twelfth century there was in Europe an increasing interest in conceptualizing change as a process in which "an entity is replaced by something completely different. Concerning topics such as digestion and nutrition, for example, theologians now asserted that growth occurs because food really changes into blood and bile in our stomachs and rejected older notions that growth must be a mysterious expansion" of preexisting particles.[69] The theology of the Eucharist was not unaffected by these trends, but the miraculous nature of transubstantiation is always a call for the exceptional. Neither metamorphosis nor transubstantiation creates something out of nothing: both events imply the continuation of something that already exists under other forms. In Ovid, a changed body implies a new relation between its preexisting materials, but not the invention of substantial new ones—what is new in Ovid is shape and articulation, not matter. In the prologue to *The Divine Narcissus*, the refrain changes its content but not its form—a perfect Eucharistic transformation. In the *auto* that follows the *loa*, change is constantly on the verge of happening, but even when it takes place—through mirror reflections or echoic transpositions—it proves to be elusive or short-lived.

Intercultural scenarios are reflexive reassemblings in which certain bodies function as alibis for complete ethnic groups, topographies, languages, and historicized (de)territorializations. What provides room in *The Divine Narcissus* for a *geochronic* stance is Sor Juana's grasping of time and space as a reassembling of affective practices—the fact that, for her, cultural exchanges are inflected by the embodiments they induce, revamp, and participate in. The Mexican nun is deeply sensitive to the epistemic power of somatic entrainments to replicate the emergence of new historical relations, and her vision of intercultural encounters is based on a reflexive presentation of the body as a point where identities meet their own otherness. Sor Juana's sacramental bodies are simultaneously vessel and figure, departure and arrival, channel and action—in other words, emergence.

Performance always demands a confrontation with becoming and a humbling recognition of our limited capabilities to describe that becoming accurately. Intercultural scenarios wrestle their vectors through this impasse by reassembling their networks as performances of collective memory that also articulate new emerging and alterative identities. I hope my readers leave this book with an understanding of how much our identities are marked by what the Greek poet C. P. Cavafy described once as "the secret call / of events that are about to happen."[70] The *about to happen* of the affective historiography I have tried to explore aesthetically and conceptually through these pages is what provides intercultural scenarios with their transformational power. As Sor Juana intuited so well, we are the prepositions we join, the relays we follow and initiate, the figures we translate while life rolls under our feet and around us, all the things we actualize while we write, or wear clothes, and dance, and sing, and finally disappear—until our fellow artists and scholars kindly decide to retrace and revisit the networks we once inhabited.

(Not a) Conclusion

I am not calling the last section of this book a conclusion. As I have shown in the previous pages, closures are transformative transactions, not endings. The demise of the Avila brothers, the processions in honor of the bones, the geochronic energies of Aztec drums, and the refrains of an *auto sacramental* written by a baroque nun can be organized along the lines of an Aristotelian model of beginning, middle, and end—but once we decide to remain in the middle, that model has to be replaced by a narrative of networking. Observing our intercultural scenarios from the middle, we need to attain a methodology than ensures our own mobility, a conceptual outlook in which the middle-in-itself is dynamically experienced as vectors, relays, and translations.

I argue that Bruno Latour's actor-network-theory (ANT) provides us with a point of access to the radical hybridity of everyday life, the persistent performations that support our performances. I also claim that without an understanding of the network as an affective field ANT is nothing more than a sophisticated instruction manual. Objects, humans, and nonhumans are not merely linked pieces in an ecological machine that perpetuates itself—they are *quasi*-entities occupying several functions simultaneously and across different spatial intersections and temporalities. We behave *prepositionally*: our motions are embedded in an environment in which axiology and matter are inextricably connected. Our aesthetic figurations are as relevant to the network as the resources of land and water. Artifacts collaborate with the cognitive entrainments that articulate our somatic relations to the world. A dramatic text is imbued with ergonic forces that can activate its language and hail our responses more than four hundred years after it was written.

Intercultural scenarios recall the mixed qualities of our performations in very specific and localized ways, bringing our becoming back to our perception, pushing our grasp of process out of naturalized occlusions, habits, and ideological controls. But we should also remember that intercultures are *intensified* by new encounters, not invented by them. Every culture is already a plurality of anaphoric movements and modes of existence before the so-called Other arrives. An intercultural historiography will underline the tensions and complexities at work both within and between multiple standards of identity. In order to emphasize our emerging, concrescent process, the intercultural historian will have to retrace the networks of labor that sustain our daily perambulations. These circulatory networks are made of people, objects, animals, costumes, masquerades, rivers, mountains, fountains, texts, drums, song-dances, reliquaries, and scholarly books like the one you are holding right now. Be aware that, by the time you reach the end of this sentence, this book will become a *quasi*-memory that will join *your* becoming by folding another vector and shaping another relay, keeping us together for a while in the middle of our own performative intercultural life.

NOTES

Introduction

1. Shannon Jackson, *Social Works: Performing Art, Supporting Publics* (London: Routledge, 2011), 31.

2. Walter Benjamin, "Analogy and Relationship," in *Selected Writings: Volume I, 1913–1926*, ed. Marcus Bullock and Michael W. Jennings (Cambridge, Mass.: Harvard University Press, 1996), [207–9], 207.

3. Walter Benjamin, *The Origin of German Tragic Drama*, trans. John Osborne (London: Verso, 1977), 175.

4. Ric Knowles, *Theatre and Interculturalism* (London: Palgrave Macmillan, 2010), 61.

5. See Homi K. Bhabha, *The Location of Culture* (London: Routledge, 1994).

6. See Anjali Prabhu, *Hybridity: Limits, Transformations, Prospects* (Albany: State University of New York Press, 2007).

7. Néstor García Canclini, *Hybrid Cultures: Strategies for Entering and Leaving Modernity*, trans. Christopher L. Chiappari and Silvia L. López (Minneapolis: University of Minnesota Press, 1995), 206–63.

8. See Ilona Katzew and Susan Deans-Smith, eds., *Race and Classification: The Case of Mexican America* (Stanford, Calif.: Stanford University Press, 2009).

9. See Marilyn Grace Miller., *Rise and Fall of the Cosmic Race: The Cult of Mestizaje in Latin America* (Austin: University of Texas Press, 2004).

10. See Claudio Esteva Fábregat, *El mestizaje en Iberoamérica* (Madrid: Editorial Alhambra, 1988).

11. See Andrew B. Fisher and Matthew D. O'Hara, eds., *Imperial Subjects: Race and Identity in Colonial Latin America* (Durham, N.C.: Duke University Press, 2009).

12. See R. Douglas Cope, *The Limits of Racial Domination: Plebeian Society in Colonial Mexico City, 1660–1720* (Madison: University of Wisconsin Press, 1994).

13. See Joanne Rappaport, *The Disappearing Mestizo: Configuring Difference in the Colonial New Kingdom of Granada* (Durham, N.C.: Duke University Press, 2014).

14. See Ralph Bauer and José Antonio Mazzotti, eds., *Creole Subjects in the Colonial Americas: Empires, Texts, Identities* (Williamsburg, Va.: University of North Carolina Press, 2009), 1–57.

15. Alessandra Russo, *The Unstranslatable Image: A Mestizo History of the Arts in New Spain, 1500–1600*, trans. Susan Emanuel (Austin: University of Texas Press, 2014), 13, 12.

16. See Peregrine Horden and Nicholas Purcell, *The Corrupting Sea: A Study of Mediterranean History* (Oxford: Blackwell, 2000).

17. See Jürgen Osterhammel, *The Transformation of the World: A Global History of the Nineteenth Century*, trans. Patrick Camiller (Princeton, N.J.: Princeton University Press, 2014).

18. See Susan Toby Evans, *Ancient Mexico & Central America: Anthropology and Culture History* (London: Thames and Hudson, 2008).

19. See Leonardo López Luján, "Water and Fire: Archeology in the Capital of the Mexica Empire," in *The Archeology of Mesoamerica: Mexican and European Perspectives*, ed. Warwick Bray and Linda Manzanilla (London: British Museum, 1999), 32–49.

20. Diana Magaloni Kerpel, *The Colors of the New World: Artists, Materials, and the Creation of the "Florentine Codex"* (Los Angeles: Getty Research Institute, 2014).

21. Russo, *Untranslatable Image*, 247.

22. See Richard Schechner, *Between Theater & Anthropology* (Philadelphia: University of Pennsylvannia Press, 1985); and also Richard Schechner and Willa Appel, eds., *By Means of Performance: Intercultural Studies of Theatre and Ritual* (Cambridge: Cambridge University Press, 1990).

23. Marvin Carlson, "Peter Brook's *The Mahabharata* and Ariane Mnouchkine's *L'Indiade* as Examples of Contemporary Cross-Cultural Theatre," in *The Dramatic Touch of Difference: Theatre, Own and Foreign*, ed. Erika Fisher-Lichte, Josephine Riley, and Michael Gissenweher (Tübingen: Gunter Narr Verlag, 1990), 50.

24. See Patrice Pavis, *Theater at the Crossroads of Culture* (London: Routledge, 1992).

25. See Bonnie Marranca, *Ecologies of Theater: Essays at the Century Turning* (Baltimore, Md.: Johns Hopkins University Press, 1996).

26. See Rustom Bharucha, *The Politics of Cultural Practice: Thinking through Theatre in an Age of Globalization* (Middletown, Conn.: Wesleyan University Press, 2000).

27. See Eugenio Barba, *The Paper Canoe: A Guide to Theatre Anthropology* (London: Routledge, 1993).

28. Patrice Pavis, *Analyzing Performance: Theater, Dance, and Film*, trans. David Williams (Ann Arbor: University of Michigan Press, 2006), 271–302.

29. See Antony Tatlow, *Shakespeare, Brecht, and the Intercultural Sign* (Durham, N.C.: Duke Univesity Press, 2001).

30. See Mita Choudhury, *Interculturalism and Resistance in the London Theater, 1660–1800: Identity, Performance, Empire* (Lewisburg, Pa.: Bucknell University Press, 2000).

31. See Julie Holledge and Joanne Tompkins, *Women's Intercultural Performance: Cultural Double Cross* (London: Taylor and Francis, 2000).

32. See Christopher B. Balme, *Decolonizing the Stage: Theatrical Syncretism and Post-Colonial Drama* (Oxford: Clarendon, 1999).

33. See Jacqueline Lo and Helen Gilbert, "Towards a Topography of Cross-Cultural Theatre Praxis," *TDR: The Drama Review* 16, no. 3 (2002): 31–53.

34. Erika Fisher-Lichte, Josephine Riley, and Michael Gissenweher, eds., *The Dramatic Touch of Difference: Theatre, Own and Foreign* (Tübingen: Gunter Narr, 1990).

35. Erika Fischer-Lichte, "Introduction: Interweaving Performance Cultures—Rethinking 'Intercultural Theatre': Toward an Experience and Theory of Performance beyond Postcolonialism," in *The Politics of Interweaving Performance Cultures: Beyond Postcolonialism*, ed. Erika Fischer-Lichte, Torsten Jost, and Saskya Iris Jain (London: Routledge, 2014), 1–21.

36. See Mark Terkessidis, *Interkultur* (Berlin: Suhrkamp Verlag, 2010), 111–68. I thank Lizzi Stewart for calling my attention to this book. Terkessidis defines the intercultural as an emerging restructuring of society that refuses completion or stability.

37. See Charlotte McIvor and Matthew Spangler, eds., *Staging Intercultural Ireland: New Plays and Practitioner Perspectives* (Cork City: Cork University Press, 2014).

38. Walter Benjamin, *Origin of German Tragic Drama*, 45, 46.

39. Raymond Williams, *Marxism and Literature* (Oxford: Oxford University Press, 1977), 99.

40. Gilles Deleuze and Félix Guattari, *A Thousand Plateaus: Capitalism and Schizophrenia*, trans. Brian Massumi (Minneapolis: University of Minnesota Press, 1987), 105.

41. Williams, *Marxism and Literature*, 132.

42. Michael North, *Novelty: A History of the New* (Chicago: University of Chicago Press, 2013).

43. John H. Holland, *Emergence: From Chaos to Order* (New York: Basic Books, 1998), 4–5.

44. Ibid., 225. Emphasis in the original.

45. Ibid., 231.

46. See Eric Reuland, *Anaphora and Language Design* (Cambridge, Mass: MIT Press, 2011), 123–245.

47. An anaphor can also consist of two different signifiers sharing a common reference: while Venus is for some a *morning* star, for others it is an *evening* one. See Yan Huang, *Anaphora: A Cross-Linguistic Study* (Oxford: Oxford University Press, 2000), 1.

48. "Chaque information nouvelle est la loi d'une étape anaphorique. Chaque gain anaphorique est la raison d'une information nouvelle proposée." See Etienne Souriau, *Les Différents Modes d'existence* (Paris: Presses Universitaires de France, 2009), 108.

49. These productive distributions should not be confused with the Marxist divide between an *überbau* (or superstructure) and its base (or infrastructure). My target here is to theorize becoming as simultaneity, not as strata.

50. William James, *A Pluralistic Universe* (Lincoln: University of Nebraska Press, 1996), 34, 263.

51. "The habitus—embodied history, internalized as a second nature and so forgotten as history—is the active presence of the whole past of which it is the product." Pierre Bourdieu, *The Logic of Practice* (Stanford, Calif.: Stanford University Press, 1990), 56.

52. Niklas Luhmann, *Social Systems*, trans. John Bernarz and Dirk Baecker (Stanford, Calif.: Stanford University Press, 1995), 13.

53. "Emergence is not simply an accumulation of complexity, but rather an interruption and new beginning in the constitution of complexity." Ibid., 23.

54. "Structures capture the reversibility of time because they hold open a limited repertoire of possibilities for choice. One can negate structures, or change them, or with their aid gain security for changes in other respects. Processes, by contrast, mark the irreversibility of time. They are composed of irreversible events. They cannot turn backwards." Ibid., 44.

55. Michel Serres, *The Parasite*, trans. Lawrence R. Schehr (Minneapolis: University of Minnesota Press, 2007), 227.

56. Michel Serres, *The Troubadour of Knowledge*, trans. Sheila Faria Glaser and William Paulson (Ann Arbor: University of Michigan Press, 1997), 5.

57. Ibid., 5.

58. The rubber-ball game (also known as *tlachtli*) was played at two different courts in the ceremonial center of Tenochtitlán: the *tezcatlachco* (or mirror ball court) and the *teotlachco* (or divine court). See Robert S. Santley, Michael J. Berman, and Rani T. Alexander, "The Politicization of the Mesoamerican Ballgame and Its Implications for the Interpretation of the Distribution of Ballcourts in Central Mexico," in *The Mesoamerican Ballgame*, ed. Vernon L. Scarborough and David R. Wilcox (Tucson: University of Arizona Press, 1991), 3–24.

59. See S. Jeffrey K. Wilkerson, "And They Were Sacrificed: The Ritual Ballgame of Northeastern Mesoamerica through Time and Space," in *The Mesoamerican Ballgame*, 45–71.

60. I am aware that the swimmer and the rubber ball game are analogical examples, but at least they are dynamic, not static. Occasionally, some analogies will still be used in this book, but they will not be at the center of my arguments. Serres, *The Parasite*, 225.

61. For a discussion of Latour's career, see Henning Schmidge, *Bruno Latour in Pieces: An Intellectual Biography*, trans. Gloria Custance (New York: Fordham University Press, 2015).

62. The political implications (and misunderstandings) surrounding Latour's work have been carefully explored by Graham Harman in *Bruno Latour: Reassembling the Political* (London: Pluto, 2014).

63. I could have selected Manuel Castells's comprehensive theorization of network societies as a template for this inquiry, especially his conceptualization of networks as spaces of flow and demand. But Castells's enterprise is to explain how global interactions are articulated and maintained through the constant innovations of contemporary technology. In other words, while Castells describes the mechanisms of one specific network (the information age), Latour offers a model that is more general and abstract, a model that can be adjusted more easily across different historical temporalities. See Manuel Castells, *The Information Age: Economy, Society, and Culture, Volume I: The Rise of the Network Society* (Oxford: Wiley-Blackwell, 2010). For a summary of Castells's thought, see Felix Stalder, *Manuel Castells* (Cambridge: Polity, 2006).

64. Bruno Latour, *We Have Never Been Modern*, trans. Catherine Porter (Cambridge, Mass.: Harvard University Press, 1993), 3.

65. Ibid., 78.

66. Ibid., 81.

67. "The ontology of mediators . . . has a variable geometry." Ibid., 86.

68. Bruno Latour, *Reassembling the Social: An Introduction to Actor-Network-Theory* (Oxford: Oxford University Press, 2005), 11.

69. Ibid., 71.

70. The indigenous population found by the Spaniards in Tenochtitlán is still identified as Aztec in most published studies in English, so I will keep that name here. Nevertheless, we should be aware that there are other ways of referring to the Aztecs that can probably be more accurate. Aztec, first of all, is a general name for those groups that emigrated from the legendary lands of Aztlan (north of today's Mexico) to the central valley of Mexico. Mexica (a term I also use) refers to the followers of Huitzilopochtli. (Some people also call them the Culhua-Mexica). And then the people living in Tenochtitlán (not all of them Mexicas, of course) are also known as Tenochca.

71. "Groups are made, agencies are explored, and objects play a role. Such are the three first sources of uncertainty we rely on if we want to follow the social fluid through its ever-changing and provisional shapes." Latour, *Reassembling*, 87.

72. Latour, *Reassembling*, 46.

73. See J. L. Austin, *How to Do Things with Words* (Cambridge, Mass.: Harvard University Press, 1975), 22.

74. Richard Schechner, *Between Theater and Anthropology* (Philadelphia: University of Pennsylvania Press, 1985), 123.

75. Latour, *Reassembling*, 128, 130, 132.

76. See Bruno Latour, *Aramis or the Love of Technology* (Cambridge, Mass.: Harvard University Press, 1996).

77. Latour, *Reassembling*, 55.

78. Latour, *Reassembling*, 9.

79. Allow me a postmodern example: we might disagree about Andy Warhol's stylistic choices (was he truly a painter or a commercial designer?), but it would be harder to justify the presence of his Campbell Soup series in a chemistry textbook unless we were to use his sequential rows of branded cans as an analogy for molecular clusters. There is no serious dispute regarding Warhol being a professional artist, although we are quite sure that he was *not* a professional scientist. Our categories can be fluid, but quite often we *know* what we are talking about.

80. For a fascinating and controversial discussion of this topic, see Quentin Meillassoux, *After Finitude: An Essay on the Necessity of Contingency*, trans. Ray Brassier (London: Bloomsbury, 2008).

81. Bruno Latour, *An Inquiry into Modes of Existence: An Anthropology of the Moderns*, trans. Catherine Porter (Cambridge, Mass.: Harvard University Press, 2013), 20.

82. Ibid., 62.

83. Ibid., 102.

84. Ibid., 79. Emphasis in the original.

85. "Neither the public, nor the common, nor the 'we' exists; they must be brought into being. If the word *performation* has a meaning, this is it." Ibid., 352. Emphasis in the original.

86. See Jeanette Favrot Peterson, *Visualizing Guadalupe: From Black Madonna to Queen of the Americas* (Austin: University of Texas Press, 2014).

87. Latour, *An Inquiry*, 397.

88. See Graham Harman, *Prince of Networks: Bruno Latour and Metaphysics* (Melbourne, Australia: re.press, 2009), 99–116.

89. Graham Harman, *The Quadruple Object* (Winchester, Eng.: Zero Books, 2011).

90. Levi R. Bryant, *The Democracy of Objects* (Ann Arbor, Mich.: Open Humanities, 2011).

91. Jane Bennett, *Vibrant Matter: A Political Ecology of Things* (Durham, N.C.: Duke University Press, 2010).

92. See Sara Ahmed, *Queer Phenomenology: Orientations, Objects, Others* (Durham, N.C.: Duke University Press, 2006).

93. See Paul Connerton, *How Societies Remember* (Cambridge: Cambridge University Press, 1989).

94. See Anders Blok and Torben Elgaard Jensen, *Bruno Latour: Hybrid Thoughts in a Hybrid World* (London: Routledge, 2011), 125–29.

95. See his magnificent synthesis: Manuel DeLanda, *A New Philosophy of Society: Assemblage Theory and Social Complexity* (London: Continuum, 2006).

96. Dwight Conquergood, "Beyond the Text: Toward a Performative Cultural Politics," in *Cultural Struggles: Performance, Ethnography, Praxis*, ed. E. Patrick Johnson (Ann Arbor: University of Michigan Press, 2013), (47–63), 55.

97. See the introduction to Charlotte M. Canning and Thomas Postlewait, eds., *Representing the Past: Essays in Performance Historiography* (Iowa City: University of Iowa Press, 2010), 1–34.

98. Enrique Florescano, *Los orígenes del poder en Mesoamérica* (Mexico, D.F.: Fondo de Cultura Económica, 2009).

99. Roy Strong, *Art and Power: Renaissance Festivals 1450–1650* (Suffolk, Eng.: Boydell, 1984).

100. Jacques Rancière, *The Politics of Aesthetics*, trans. Gabriel Rockhill (New York: Continuum, 2004), 12, 19.

101. Franco Moretti, *Graphs, Maps, Trees: Abstract Models for Literary History* (London: Verso, 2007), 91. Emphasis in the original.

Chapter 1

1. Juan Suárez de Peralta, *Tratado del descubrimiento de las Indias y su conquista* (Madrid: Alianza Editorial, 1990), 183–214. Unless otherwise stated, and in order to avoid an inordinate amount of notes, I have collated the details of the insurrection from this account written in 1589 while Suárez was living in Spain. Born in the late 1530s, his father's original *encomienda* of 900 pesos was inherited by an older brother. Suárez's main sources of income were real estate deals, wheat grinding, and horse breeding. His attitude towards the Indians is generally hostile, but he can also praise their zeal to abstain from sexual intercourse after communion. His admiration for indigenous craftsmanship extracts from him an impressively detailed description of the spinning of *mantas*. He was not indifferent to the nuances of color and texture in masculine clothing, or even the slightly androgynous beauty of young males. See Kathleen Ross, "Gender and Gossip in Criollo Historiography: Juan Suárez de Peralta's *Tratado del descubrimiento de las Indias y su conquista*," in *Creole Subjects in the Colonial Americas: Empires, Texts, Identities*, ed. Ralph Bauer and José Antonio Mazzotti (Chapel Hill: University of North Carolina Press, 2009), 293–312.

2. Brian Massumi, *Parables for the Virtual: Movement, Affect, Sensation* (Durham, N.C.: Duke University Press, 2002), 68–88.

3. Una Chaudhuri, "The Future of the Hyphen: Interculturalism, Textuality, and the Difference Within," in *Interculturalism and Performance*, ed. Bonnie Marranca and Gautam Dasgupta (New York: PAJ Publications, 1991), 193, 196. Emphasis in original.

4. For a detailed description of Tenochtitlán before the arrival of the Spaniards, see José Luis de Rojas, *Tenochtitlan: Capital of the Aztec Empire* (Gainesville: University Press of Florida, 2012).

5. Robert Tomson, *An Englishman and the Mexican Inquisition, 1556–1560*, ed. G. R. G. Conway (Mexico: privately printed, 1927), 20.

6. See Christian Duverger, *El primer mestizaje: La clave para entender el pasado Mesoamericano* (Mexico City: Taurus, 2007).

7. See Ross Hassig, *Time, History, and Belief in Aztec and Colonial Mexico* (Austin: University of Texas Press, 2001); and Elizabeth Hill Boone, *Cycles of Time and Meaning in the Mexican Books of Fate* (Austin: University of Texas Press, 2007).

8. Viviana Díaz Balsera, *The Pyramid under the Cross: Franciscan Discourses of Evangelization and the Nahua Christian Subject in Sixteenth-Century Mexico* (Tucson: University of Arizona Press, 2005). For a summary of the history of missionary theater, see Othón Arróniz, *Teatro de evangelización en Nueva España* (Mexico City: Universidad Nacional Autónoma de Mexico, 1979).

9. See Patricia Lópes Don, *Bonfires of Culture: Franciscans, Indigenous Leaders, and the Inquisition in Early Mexico, 1524–1540* (Norman: University of Oklahoma Press, 2010).

10. The best general summary of these efforts—in spite of its ideological shortcomings—is still Robert Ricard's *La conquista espiritual de Mexico* (Mexico City: Fondo de Cultura Económica, 1986).

11. Michel de Certeau, *The Practice of Everyday Life* (Berkeley: University of California Press, 1988), 93.

12. Born in Mexico in 1532, Martín Cortés y Zúñiga accompanied his egregious father to Spain in 1540 and subsequently served Philip II both as courtier and soldier. He attended Philip's wedding to Mary Tudor in England in 1554 and fought in the battle of San Quintín. In 1548 he married Ana Ramírez de Arellano (she was both his niece and first cousin). Their first son Fernando was born in Spain and remained there when the couple moved to Mexico in 1562. Not too long after their arrival in Mexico Ana gave birth to a second son, Jerónimo. It was probably for this reason that Cortés stayed three months in Campeche before entering Mexico City in early January 1563.

13. During an official visitation in the early 1530s, it was reported that the province of Cuernavaca paid tributes and services to Hernán Cortés by providing his household every second week with maize, chickens, turkeys, rabbits, partridges, tortillas, fruit, salt, peppers, wood, hay, eggs, and cacao beans. Even wet nurses were to be supplied for his servants, and every eighty days a delivery of *mantas*, shirts, bedcovers, and pillows was also expected. See Lesley Bird Simpson, *The Encomienda in New Spain: The Beginning of Spanish Mexico* (Berkeley: University of California Press, 1950), 106–7.

14. Even before leaving Spain, Martín Cortés was splitting hairs with the crown in relation to the number of vassals awarded to his father. Local Mexican authorities interpreted the grant as designating 23,000 people, but the second

marquis preferred to count 23,000 households—a legal trick that would have automatically augmented his demographic and economic influence in the viceroyalty. Philip II kept the census debate unresolved but reclaimed for the crown the Pacific port of Tehuantepec after consoling Cortés with a financial compensation.

15. In 1570—four years after the insurrection—"nearly half of the Estate income derived from the tribute payments," and it remained so, despite inevitable demographic and financial fluctuations, until 1807. See Ward Barret, *The Sugar Hacienda of the Marqueses del Valle* (Minneapolis: University of Minnesota Press, 1970), 9–10.

16. Under the *repartimiento*, Indians were assigned to specific tasks by a local magistrate in response to a petition. The crown was concerned with decreasing Indian demographics under the *encomienda*, but also wanted to avoid any forms of vagrancy. See Silvio Zavala, *El servicio personal de los indios en la Nueva España*, vol. 2 (Mexico: El Colegio de Mexico, 1985), 11–112.

17. Charles V was reluctant to expand the *encomienda* system beyond the Caribbean islands, but Hernán Cortés insisted on offering them to his soldiers. The emperor vacillated between his increasing dependence on colonial revenues to pay for his European wars and his desire—spurned by Las Casas and others—to protect the Indians. Charles also wanted to avoid the growth of a creole seignorial elite overseas. The enforcement of the New Laws of 1542 detonated rebellious outrages in Perú (1544–46 and 1552) and Nicaragua (1548). In New Spain, both Viceroy Antonio de Mendoza and Bishop Zumárraga capped the incipient storm by not obstructing the deployment of a delegation that went to Spain in 1544 and had article 35 repelled. Nonetheless, in 1549 personal services from the Indians were abolished. See Silvio A. Zavala, *La encomienda Indiana* (Mexico: Editorial Porrúa, 1992), 320–416.

18. See Francisco Cervantes de Salazar, *Crónica de la Nueva España* (Madrid: Hispanic Society of America, 1914), 317.

19. Victoria A. Vincent points out how the inventory made after Avila's arrest listed "six taffeta hats, three damask capes, a velvet cape embroidered in gold, and another of blue velvet. He also owned eight surcoats, numerous doublets in expensive fabrics, hose of velvet and satin, many trimmed with gold and silver lace." See Victoria A. Vincent, "The Avila-Cortés Conspiracy: Creole Aspirations and Royal Interests" (Ph.D. diss., University of Nebraska, 1993), 25–26. I am grateful for Vincent's dissertation for providing a well-organized and documented panoramic view of the insurrection.

20. See Suárez de Peralta, *Tratado del descubrimiento*, 206.

21. Charles Gibson, *The Aztecs under Spanish Rule: A History of the Indians of the Valley of Mexico, 1519–1810* (Stanford, Calif.: Stanford University Press, 1964), 64–68, 416–17.

22. See Antonio Sotelo de Betanzo's letter to the king on December 9, 1567, in *Epistolario de la Nueva España, 1505–1818*, ed. Francisco del Paso y Troncoso, vol. 10 (Mexico City: Porrúa e Hijos, 1940), 210–12.

23. The *actas* of the municipal *cabildo* of Mexico City show that the *encomenderos* were already asking Cortés to defend their interest in the Spanish court as early as January 13, 1562. There was another request on April 29 of the same year. See *Actas del Cabildo de la Ciudad de Mexico*, vol. 7 (Mexico: Oficinas Tipográficas de El Socialista, 1877), 18–19, 35–48.

24. It is intriguing that Cortés selected as one of his signature enjoyments an activity that both ecclesiastic and civil authorities associated with urban unrest. Wine was not easy to acquire in Mexico City during those years, and drinking bouts were mostly ascribed to the Indians. In 1545, Philip II himself—always ready to micromanage his kingdoms—saw in the Indians' tendency to drink an invitation to unleash the thinly contained idolatrous tendencies of indigenous communities, and many caciques were accused of investing in their own intoxication a substantial amount of tributary wealth that should have been paid directly to the crown. See Sonia Corcuera de Mancera, *Del amor al temor: Borrachez, catequesis y control en la Nueva España (1555–1771)* (Mexico: Fondo de Cultura Económica, 1994), 262–63. In the second chapter of his chronicle, even Suárez de Peralta sermonizes against the Indian's drinking habits (Suárez, *Tratado del descubrimiento*, 52–53). The monarchy and the church saw drunkenness mostly as an indigenous excess closely connected to their pre-Christian rituals. Before the conquest, the Aztecs monitored alcoholic intake by permitting it mostly as part of periodic devotional practices or family rites like weddings and funerals. (It is assumed that only the elderly and the sick were allowed to drink regularly.) For an overview of this issue, see Henry J. Bruman, *Alcohol in Ancient Mexico* (Salt Lake City: University of Utah Press, 2000). After the victory of the Spaniards, the production of pulque—a beverage made out of fermented maguey sap—became a highly profitable business not devoid of political undertones: some Aztec leaders encouraged the peasants to drink in order to sabotage the evangelic advances of the friars, and Mexico City became a common destination for those Indians who wanted to indulge in alcoholic reveries. For more details, see William B. Taylor, *Drinking, Homicide and Rebellion in Colonial Mexican Villages* (Stanford, Calif.: Stanford University Press, 1979), 28–72.

25. According to Suárez de Peralta, Velasco was ill when Cortés entered Mexico City, but he made an effort to welcome the marquis at the palace. Suárez, *Tratado*, 112.

26. The events presented in this section and the next one come from Manuel Orozco y Berra, *Noticia histórica de la conjuración del Marqués del Valle, Años de 1565–1568* (Mexico: Tipografía de R. Rafael, 1853), 25–30.

27. Between February and September of 1564, Valderrama wrote or drafted no less than eleven reports to the king. If we consider that he had almost no assistants at his disposal, this productivity rate is a testimony to his diligence. Most of his reports coincide in blaming the religious orders for disrupting accurate payments of tributes to the crown by cunningly providing imprecise numbers when the Indians living under their watch were counted by the authorities. In Valderrama's opinion, the friars' sabotage of the census was arranged in connivance with their favorite caciques while the viceroy conveniently looked the other way. Valderrama pointed out that the tributes were not being decreased for compassionate reasons, but to redirect them locally towards the construction of churches or monasteries and the caciques' socializing amusements. Valderrama was alarmed by the openly hostile attitude of some friars who declared that the king was entitled to rule New Spain only by permission of the pope, and he compared the situation to the *comunidades* revolt against Charles V in Castille in 1521. See France V. Scholes and Eleanor B. Adams, eds., *Cartas del Licenciado Jerónimo de Valderrama y otros documentos sobre su visita al gobierno de Nueva*

España: 1563–1565, Documentos para la historia del Mexico Colonial, vol. 7 (Mexico: José Porrúa e Hijos, 1961).

28. On December 31, 1563, following a petition by Valderrama, the *cabildo* of Mexico City welcomed the marquis's older brother, the son of Malinche—also named Martín Cortés—as *alguacil* mayor. The archive suggests that this Martín Cortés attended the *cabildo*'s meetings with certain assiduity at least until April of 1564. The presence of the marquis's mestizo sibling in the *cabildo* coincides with another round of discussions related to the *encomiendas'* perpetuity. On February 4, 1564, the marquis's half-brother was in the *cabildo* when a group of worried citizens presented a petition to the king asking him to grant them perpetual possession of their encomiendas. *Actas del Cabildo*, 163, 176. For a slightly romanticized overview of Malinche's son's life, see Anna Lanyon, *The New World of Martín Cortés* (Cambridge, Mass.: Da Capo, 2003).

29. Alejandro Cañeque, *The King's Living Image: The Culture and Politics of Viceregal Power in Colonial Mexico* (New York: Routledge, 2004), 120.

30. Michael Taussig, *Defacement: Public Secrecy and the Labor of the Negative* (Stanford, Calif.: Stanford University Press, 1999), 50. I thank my friend and colleague Christine Thomas for calling my attention to Taussig's work.

31. Although he says nothing about it, Juan Suárez de Peralta participated in some of these brawls. Suárez is far from a neat, totally reliable informer. In his *Tratado*, he never explains that, due to his marriage with Ana de Cervantes, he was actually related to a family that disliked Cortés, and that Luis de Velasco—the viceroy's son—was part of this group. He never discloses that his father was Juan Suárez de Avila, supportive friend and first brother-in-law of none other than Hernán Cortés. Suárez also fails to mention that in 1529 his father accused Hernán Cortés of killing his wife—our chronicler's aunt. Suárez de Peralta exculpates the first marquis from this crime, thus discrediting the allegations of his own father. For a detailed account of Suárez de Peralta's connections, see Enrique González González, "Nostalgia de la encomienda: Releer el *Tratado del descubrimiento*, de Juan Suárez de Peralta," *Historia Mexicana* 59, no. 2 (2009): 533–603.

32. Vincent, "The Avila-Cortés Conspiracy," 129–30.

33. March was a busy month for the *cabildo* members. Valderrama's approaching departure incited a flourish of discussions in which the internal divisions among the *encomenderos* became increasingly tense. During a reunion at the marquis's house, some *encomenderos* elected a representative to accompany Valderrama to Spain. Another group of *encomenderos* saw that decision as an attempt to step over the legal rights of the *cabildo* itself, and decided to select their own *procurador*, or emissary, instead. This confrontation between several candidates and their supporters boiled through the whole month, and by the time Valderrama left Mexico towards the end of March, no official representative sailed with him. See *Actas del Cabildo*, 271–79. In his narrative, Suárez de Peralta places the Avila brothers' masquerade right after the baptism of the Cortés's twins, but the interrogation records indicate otherwise. By the time the twins were baptized in June 1566, Valderrama had left New Spain. During the interrogations, Avila quite explicitly mentioned Valderrama as being present during the masquerade.

34. A transciption of Avila's interrogation appears in the second half of Orozco y Berra, *Noticia histórica*, 7–9. Some of these documents are now at the Harkness Collection in the Library of Congress (Washington, D.C.), where I read them. The proceedings against the Avila brothers are in HC-M15, Document XIII, Ac 3489A, Container 28.

35. Suárez de Peralta, *Tratado*, 198–99. Curiously enough, Avila fails to mention the Indian costumes and masks used for the masquerade.

36. Vincent, "The Avila-Cortés Conspiracy," 144–233. To my knowledge, this is the only dissertation in English that studies the insurrection by consulting the original archival documents available in Spain. I personally consulted some of the proceedings related to Martín Cortés at the Archivo General de Indias (AGI) in Seville, specially the documents included in Patronato 208, R.1 and Patronato 209, R.1. Interesting details about Cortés's attitudes and arguments can be also read in Patronato 17, R.2 and R.4.

37. See Jody Enders, *Murder by Accident: Medieval Theater, Modern Media, Critical Intentions* (Chicago: University of Chicago Press, 2009).

38. "The disappearance of the object is fundamental to performance." Peggy Phelan, *Unmarked: The Politics of Performance* (London: Routledge, 1993), 147.

39. Taylor specifies at least six nodes of interpretation for a scenario: the location and materials involved; the critical distance produced between recycled roles, and how they can be recast as parody or subversion; the tensions between predictability and surprise; the different systems of signification involved; how distinctions between observers and participants tend to be blurred or eliminated; and how reenactment implies reactivation over duplication. Diana Taylor, *The Archive and the Repertoire* (Durham, N.C.: Duke University Press, 2003), 29–33.

40. Ibid., 54.

41. Latour, *Reassembling*, 37–38, 159.

42. Taylor, *The Archive*, 232–36.

43. Randolph Quirk and Sidney Greenbaum, *A Concise Grammar of Contemporary English* (London: Harcourt Brace Jovanovich, 1973), 143.

44. Manuel Castells, *The Rise of the Network Society* (Oxford: Wiley-Blackwell, 2010), 501.

45. It seems that *mitote* is a Spanish adaptation of the Nahuatl expression *mi'totia* ("he or she dances"). When combined with other words, *i'totia* ("to dance") can also be related to sorcery and enchantment. For information about the *mitote* and Aztec dancing in general, see Barbara E. Mundy, "Indigenous Dances in Early Colonial Mexico City," in *Festivals & Daily Life in the Arts of Colonial Latin America, 1492–1850*, ed. Donna Pierce (Denver: Denver Art Museum, 2014), 11–30.

46. Quoted by John Bierhorst in his *Cantares Mexicanos: Songs of the Aztecs* (Stanford, Calif.: Stanford University Press, 1985), 88–90.

47. Presented to Valderrama, the *Osuna Codex* shows that many Indians resented the excessive amount of work both their own caciques and the Spanish authorities demanded from them. The document is, among other things, a painted inventory of unpaid services rendered by the litigants and their communities. Luis Chávez Orozco, ed., *Códice Osuna* (Mexico: Instituto Indigenista Interamericano, 1947), 14–15.

48. Michel Serres with Bruno Latour, *Conversations on Science, Culture, and Time* (Ann Arbor: University of Michigan Press, 1995), 103, 105.

49. Luis Reyes García, ed., *¿Cómo te confundes? ¿Acaso no somos conquistados? Anales de Juan Bautista* (Mexico City: Centro de Investigaciones y Estudios Superiores en Antropología Social y Biblioteca Lorenzo Boturini, 2001), 185–299.

50. Max Harris, *The Dialogical Theatre: Dramatizations of the Conquest of Mexico and the Question of the Other* (New York: St. Martin's, 1993), 82–94.

51. Patricia A. Ybarra, *Performing Conquest: Five Centuries of Theater, History, and Identity in Tlaxcala, Mexico* (Ann Arbor: University of Michigan Press, 2009), 34–67.

52. Inga Clendinnen, *Aztecs: An Interpretation* (Cambridge: Cambridge University Press, 1991), 213–35.

53. Bernardino de Sahagún, *Historia General de las cosas de Nueva España*, vol. 2 (Madrid: Crónicas de América, 1990), 660–64.

54. Chávez Orozco, *Códice Osuna*, 14–15, 18–19, 24–25. My translation.

55. Alonso de Zorita, an *oidor* who lived in New Spain for many years until his return to Europe in September 1566 (right after the events we are studying here), recounts how Indians were forced into tactics of espionage in order to learn earthenware skills. See Alonso de Zorita, *Historia de la Nueva España* (Madrid: Librería General de Victoriano Suárez, 1909), 299.

56. Enrique Rodríguez-Alegría, Hector Neff, and Michael D. Glascock, "Indigenous Ware or Spanish Import? The Case of Indígena Ware and Approaches to Power in Colonial Mexico," *Latin American Antiquity* 14, no. 1 (2003): 67–81.

57. Suárez de Peralta observed these mugs brought by Avila for the masquerade with something akin to an expert's eye, and in the manuscript of his narrative, he tries to reproduce one of them. On April 10, 1564, four *alfareros* from Cuauhtitlán presented a legal complaint against him. The *alfareros* claimed that, after requiring them to make a series of "jarros, tinajas e alcarrazas," Suárez underpaid their labor. The *alfareros* included an illustrated list of the objects ordered by Suárez. This painted catalog presented by the litigants includes many *jarras* molded as heads of Spaniards and Negroes, and some of them were also ornamented with eagles. Suárez defended himself, saying that the Indians were overcharging him. (See Roberto H. Barlow, "El códice de los alfareros de Cuauhtitlán," *Revista Mexicana de Estudios Antropológicos* 12 [1951]: 5–8.) In his chronicle, Suárez fails to mention a very important detail: in 1564 he was *alcalde mayor* of Cuauhtitlán. In one of his dispatches, Valderrama mentions him as such, adding that he thought Suárez was not particularly talented or "de buenas costumbres." See González González, "Nostalgia de la encomienda," 557–58.

58. When the Spaniards arrived, Cuauhtitlán was already a major provider of pulque. Pottery had become prominent there only after the second half of the fourteenth century. Hernán Cortés gave the lands as an *encomienda* to Alonso de Avila (uncle of our Alonso de Avila). Avila's *encomiendas* in the region included Zumpango, Huehuetoca, and Xaltocan. For an overview of the area's history, see Rosaura Hernández, ed., *Cuauhtitlán* (Mexico: El Colegio Mexiquense, 1996), 11–15.

59. During the interrogations, several potters from Cuauhtitlán declared that although water jars adorned with a crown were already in use in Avila's household, others were also specifically made for the masquerade; see Vincent, "The

Avila-Cortés Conspiracy," 133, note 218. The proceedings include testimony by an Indian potter named Pablo de Santos in which he claimed to own the mold for one of these mugs (Archivo General de Indias, Patronato 203, R.6). During the interrogations, Agustín de Sotomayor said that the Indians from Cuauhtitlán were singing during the masquerade (Archivo General de Indias, Patronato 213, R.1).

60. James Lockhart, *The Nahuas after the Conquest: A Social and Cultural History of the Indians of Central Mexico, Sixteenth through Eighteenth Centuries* (Stanford, Calif.: Stanford University Press, 1992), 14–58.

61. See *Códices Indígenas de Algunos Pueblos del Marquesado del Valle de Oaxaca* (Mexico City: Archivo General de la Nación, Talleres Gráficos de la Nación, 1933).

62. Ross Hassig, *Trade, Tribute, and Transportation: The Sixteenth-Century Political Economy of the Valley of Mexico* (Norman: University of Oklahoma Press, 1985), 145–50, 262–67.

63. Massumi, *Parables for the Virtual*, 70–73.

64. "For Latour, in scientific objects and technological projects, the operations of natural and cultural formations are necessarily intermingled, occupying neither a nature outside of society nor a society outside of nature. To observe the real intermingling of the natural and the social, Latour follows the circulation of quasi-objects . . . entities with indeterminate or multiple references to categories of subject and object." See Bruce Clarke, *Posthuman Metamorphosis: Narrative and Systems* (New York: Fordham University Press, 2008), 47.

65. See Latour, *We Have Never Been Modern*, 51–55. As I explained in the introduction, Latour adopts the concept of *quasi*-entities from the work of Michel Serres.

66. See John Moreland, *Archeology and Text* (London: Duckworth, 2011).

67. See Joseph Roach, *Cities of the Dead: Circum-Atlantic Performance* (New York: Columbia University Press, 1996), 5.

68. Arjun Appadurai, "Introduction: Commodities and the Politics of Value," in *The Social Life of Things: Commodities in Cultural Perspective*, ed. Arjun Appadurai (Cambridge: Cambridge University Press, 1986), 57.

69. Alice Rayner, *Ghosts: Death's Double and the Phenomena of Theatre* (Minneapolis: University of Minnesota Press, 2006), 75, 76.

70. Marvin Carlson, *The Haunted Stage: The Theatre as Memory Machine* (Ann Arbor: University of Michigan Press, 2003), 27.

71. The first meeting between Cortés and Motezuma produced a long genealogy of *mitotes* and other performances that are still active today. For a review of this fascinating topic, see Jesús Jáuregui, "Cortés contra Moctezuma-Cuauhtémoc: El intercambio de mujeres"; and Demetrio Brisset, "Cortés derrotado: La vision indígena de la conquista," both in *Las danzas de la conquista*, vol. I: *México contemporáneo*, ed. Jesús Jáuregui and Carlo Bonfiglioli (Mexico: Fondo de Cultura Económica, 1996), 33–68 (Jáuregui) and 69–90 (Brisset).

72. As a curious note, we should observe that this is exactly what the Earl of Essex intended when he paid for a performance of *Richard II* the day before his rebellion against Elizabeth I in 1601. As in Avila's case, the plan backfired.

73. See Tracy C. Davis, "Performative Time," in *Representing the Past: Essays in Performance Historiography*, ed. Charlotte M. Canning and Thomas Postlewait (Iowa City: University of Iowa Press, 2010), (142–67), 149, 163, 161.

74. When Valderrama was getting ready to leave Mexico, he asked Cortés to stay in the city after his departure. The marquis wanted to move to Toluca, but the *visitador* and the *oidores* insisted that he remain in the capital in case they needed his help to protect themselves. See Vincent, "The Avila-Cortés Conspiracy," 132–33.

75. *Actas del Cabildo*, 283.

76. Bernal Díaz del Castillo attended the 1539 festivities, and he was still amazed many years later at the sumptuousness of the costumes worn by the performers, the profusion of birds flying in the woods, the diversity of animals hunted, the splendors of the food served, and the drinking excesses of some participants. Bernal Díaz del Castillo, *Historia Verdadera de la Conquista de la Nueva España* (Mexico: Editorial Porrúa, 1983), 544–50.

77. For an analysis of this event, see Max Harris, *Dialogical Theatre,* 75–81.

78. There were three *oidores* at that point: Francisco de Ceynos, Pedro de Villalobos, and Jerónimo de Orozco. For more information about the *oidores* and a succinct narrative of the insurrection, see J. Ignacio Rubió Mañé, *El Virreinato*, vol. 2 (Mexico: Fondo de Cultura Económica, 1983), 3–21.

79. *Actas del Cabildo*, 251–52, 286–287, 290, 292–93.

Chapter 2

1. Latour, *Reassembling*, 39.

2. Ibid., 132, 128.

3. Ibid., 108.

4. Ibid., 35.

5. Latour also says that "because they deal with fiction, literary theorists have been much freer in their enquiries about figuration than any social scientist, especially when they have used semiotics or the various narrative sciences. This is because, for instance in a fable, the same actant can be made to act through the agency of a magic wand, a dwarf, a thought in the fairy's mind, or a knight killing two dozen dragons . . . Novels, plays, and films from classical tragedy to comics provide a vast playground to rehearse accounts of what makes us act." Ibid., 53–55.

6. Ibid., 71.

7. Fernando R. de la Flor, "Economía simbólica de la relación y conmemoración fúnebre en el antiguo régimen: Gasto, derroche y dilapidación del bien cultural," in *La Fiesta: Actas del II Seminario de las Relaciones de Sucesos*, ed. Sagrario López Posa and Nieves Pena Suerio (Ferrol: Sociedad de Cultura Valle Inclán, 1999), 121–32.

8. For a discussion of emergence in all its potential angles, see Mark A. Bedau and Paul Humphreys, eds., *Emergence: Contemporary Readings in Philosophy and Science* (Cambridge, Mass.: MIT Press, 2008).

9. See Elizabeth Grosz, "Thinking the New: Of Futures Yet Unthought," in *Explorations in Time, Memory, and Futures Becomings*, ed. Elizabeth Grosz (Ithaca, N.Y.: Cornell University Press, 1999), (15–28), 15, 19.

10. See Rebecca Schneider, *Performing Remains: Art and War in Times of Theatrical Reenactment* (London: Routledge, 2011), 87–110.

11. See Samuel Y. Edgerton, *Theaters of Conversion: Religious Architecture and Indian Artisans in Colonial Mexico* (Albuquerque: University of New Mexico Press, 2001).

12. See David Carrasco, *City of Sacrifice: The Aztec Empire and the Role of Violence in Civilization* (Boston: Beacon, 1999).

13. For a survey of missionary theater and a collection of some of the plays created for it, see Louise M. Burkhart, ed., *Aztecs on Stage: Religious Theater in Colonial Mexico* (Norman: University of Oklahoma Press, 2011).

14. See David Tavárez, *The Invisible War: Indigenous Devotions, Discipline, and Dissent in Colonial Mexico* (Stanford, Calif.: Stanford University Press, 2011).

15. In 1573 Philip II promoted his *Ordinances on the Discovery and Population of Towns*, a document that prescribed how new and old cities were supposed to be built or rearranged. In 1577 the monarch requested Bernardino de Sahagún's writings in order to examine them and prevent their publication. Sahagún saw thirty years of exhausting labor and collaboration with his native interpreters disappear into the remote vaults of the royal archives. For an exploration of Sahagún's work, see Eloise Quiñones Keber, ed., *Representing Aztec Ritual: Performance, Text, and Image in the Work of Sahagún* (Boulder: University Press of Colorado, 2002).

16. See Kelly Donahue-Wallace, *Art and Architecture of Viceregal Latin America, 1521–1821* (Albuquerque: University of New Mexico Press, 2008) 72–99, 170–77.

17. Morales was a zealous provider of religious medals and images for the Indians, and on more than one occasion raised money for the dowries of orphaned girls who wanted to enter a convent. Some people found him arrogant, and slightly disorganized as an administrator. Pedro de Morales, *Carta del padre Pedro de Morales de la Compañía de Jesús: Para el muy reverendo Padre Everardo Mercuriano, General de la misma Compañía. En que se da relación de la festividad que en esta insigne Ciudad de Mexico se hizo este año de setenta y ocho, en la collocación de las Sanctas Reliquias que nuestro muy Santo Padre Gregorio XIII les embió*, ed. Beatriz Mariscal Hay (Mexico: El Colegio de Mexico, 2000), xli–xlvi. All my citations from the *carta* come from this edition.

18. See Gabriel Andrés, "Relaciones extensas de fiestas públicas: itinerario de un 'género,' " in *La Fiesta: Actas del II Seminario de las Relaciones de Sucesos*, ed. Sagrario López Posa and Nieves Pena Suerio (Ferrol: Sociedad de Cultura Valle Inclán, 1999), 11–17.

19. For a comprehensive study of the Horatian trope, see Rensseler W. Lee, *Ut Pictura Poesis: The Humanist Theory of Painting* (New York: Norton, 1967).

20. See Stephanie Merrim, *The Spectacular City, Mexico, and Colonial Hispanic Literary Culture* (Austin: University of Texas Press, 2010), 23–29.

21. See Don Domingo de San Antón Muñón Chimalpahin Quauhtlehuanitzin, *Annals of His Time*, ed. and trans. James Lockhart, Susan Schroeder, and Doris Namala (Stanford, Calif.: Stanford University Press, 2006).

22. Morales, *Carta del padre*, 4.

23. Fray Toribio de Benavente o Motolinía, *Historia de los indios de la Nueva España* (Madrid: Clásicos Castalia, 1985), 192–215.

24. Some secular bones were treated *religiously*, too. The remains of Hernán Cortés were shipped to the second marquis in 1566 (the same year of the insurrection discussed in chapter 1). The bones remained in the church of San Francisco de Tezcoco until 1629, when they were buried again in Mexico City in the convent

of San Francisco during the funeral of Pedro Cortés, the conquistador's grandchild. For a record of the history of these bones, see José Luis Martínez, *Hernán Cortés* (Mexico: Fondo de Cultura Económica, 1990), 778–95.

25. Charlemagne reinforced the semantic power of sacred bones when in 803 he sanctioned the practice of swearing oaths on relics; he even included compartments for them in his own throne. After that, sacred bones became a fundamental aspect of Christian life. A market for relics exploded all over Europe: bones and objects were displayed for cash in fairs and on collecting tours, exchanged for donations, sold to private citizens, borrowed to inspire funding campaigns, and even used as tools for diplomatic manipulations. The need to supply as many remains of saints as possible motivated an international trading network as frantic as recent treasure hunts seen on eBay. The consumers tended to privilege bones from the catacombs of Rome, but Spanish bones were also highly desirable, since martyrs were still being produced there due to the ongoing wars against the Arab kingdoms of the peninsula. Bones were classified as *reliquae insignes* (head, arms and legs), *notabiles* (hands, feet), and *exiguae* (fingers, teeth). See James Bentley, *Restless Bones: The Story of Relics* (Suffolk, Eng.: Constable, 1985), 34–116.

26. "Jerusalem first circulated in the West in the form of its physical fragments—pieces of stone, drops of oil, bits of bone, particles of wood. The city proved a productive source of sacred debris by which the divine might be possessed . . . The particles of Jerusalem that came to lodge in the West as relics provided proximity to the city from which they came." See Annabel Jane Warthon, *Selling Jerusalem: Relics, Replicas, Theme Parks* (Chicago: University of Chicago Press, 1981), 86–127.

27. See Patrick J. Geary, *Furta Sacra: Thefts of Relics in the Central Middle Ages* (Princeton, N.J.: Princeton University Press, 1978), 68–131.

28. The increasing exhumation of bones led to serious and not entirely solved debates and conceptual refinements in an effort to clarify the legal status of all *res sacrae*. See Nicole Hermann-Mascard, *Les Reliques des saints: Formation coutimiére d'un droit* (Paris: Editions Klincksiek, 1975), 313–63.

29. See Seeta Chaganti, *The Medieval Poetics of the Reliquary: Enshrinement, Inscription, Performance* (New York: Palgrave Macmillan, 2008), 19–45.

30. The arrival of relics at a particular church implied a show of God's mercy that underlined the importance of that particular location in the unfolding plans of divine providence. Bishops and religious orders also managed to turn relics into successful sources of revenue and political influence. See Peter Brown, *The Cult of Saints: Its Rise and Function in Latin Christianity* (Chicago: University of Chicago Press, 1981), 86–127.

31. Relics were cherished, among other things, for their capacity to gather crowds. Displays of public affection for relics were not always easy to control. Both Urban II (1099) and Eugenius III (1153) authorized papal bulls that exempted monks from showing relics against their will. See Barbara Abou-El-Haj, *The Medieval Cult of Saints: Formations and Transformations* (Cambridge: Cambridge University Press, 1994), 14.

32. See Catherine Keller, *Face of the Deep: A Theology of Becoming* (London: Routledge, 2003), 12.

33. Giorgio Agamben, *The Kingdom and the Glory: For a Theological Genealogy of Economy and Government*, trans. Lorenzo Chiesa (with Matteo Mandarini) (Stanford, Calif.: Stanford University Press, 2011), xii.

34. Ibid., 41.
35. Ibid., 193.
36. Ibid., 217.
37. Texcatlipoca was the god of omnipresent vision, and his main symbol was a mirror. For a full description of the impersonator's fate, see Carrasco's *City of Sacrifice*, 115–39.
38. Morales, *Carta del Padre*, 108.
39. Fernando Horcasitas, *El teatro náhuatl: Épocas novohispana y moderna* (México: Universidad Autónoma de México, 1974).
40. Othón Arróniz, *Teatro de evangelización en Nueva España* (México: Universidad Autónoma de México, 1979).
41. Louise M. Burkhart, *Holy Wednesday: A Nahua Drama from Early Colonial Mexico* (Philadelphia: University of Pennsylvania Press, 1996).
42. María Beatriz Aracil Varón, *El teatro evangelizador: Sociedad, cultura e ideología en la Nueva España del siglo XVI* (Rome: Bulzoni Editore, 1999).
43. Michael K. Schuessler, *Artes de fundación: Teatro evangelizador y pintura mural en la Nueva España* (México: Universidad Nacional Autónoma de México, 2009).
44. See Maya Ramos Smith, *Actores y compañías en la Nueva España: Siglos XVI y XVII* (Coyoacán, México: Instituto Nacional de Bellas Artes, 2011), 77–97.
45. See Erich Auerbach, *Scenes from the Drama of European Literature* (Minneapolis: University of Minnesota Press, 1984), 11–76.
46. See Bartolomé de las Casas, *Brevísima relación de la destrucción de las Indias*, in *Tratados* (México: Fondo de Cultura Económica, 1965), 67–83. For an English translation, see *A Short Account of the Destruction of the Indies*, trans. Nigel Griffin (New York: Penguin Books, 1992), 45–47.
47. Morales, *Carta del padre*, 220–22.
48. Ibid., 8–9.
49. Curiously enough, in 1574—just four years before the students' procession—during the first auto-da-fé organized by the Inquisition in New Spain, several survivors from Sir John Hawkins's expedition of 1568 were paraded in front of the cathedral, and at least one of them was burned at the stake on that occasion. English bodies were a fresh memory for the population of the city.
50. Juan Sánchez Baquero, quoted in Xavier Gómez Robledo, *Humanismo en Mexico en el siglo XVI: El sistema del Colegio de San Pedro y San Pablo* (Mexico: Editorial Jus, 1954), 37.
51. The Jesuit ideal of effective thinking and affective expression—*ratio et oratio*—saw the writings of Cicero and Quintilian as models that fomented in the students a sense of discipline in which aesthetic sensitivity and a talent for dexterous argumentation were tightly conjoined. Lanuchi wasted no time in implementing his curriculum. In 1575 a tragicomedy was produced as part of a literary contest, and in 1577 a literary celebration honored the festivities of Corpus Christi.
52. Gómez Robledo, *Humanismo en Mexico*, 65–86.
53. Morales, *Carta del padre*, 236.
54. Quoted by Pilar Gonzalbo Aizpuru, *Historia de la educación en la época colonial: La educación de los criollos y la vida urbana* (Mexico: El Colegio de Mexico, 1990), 155–56, note 59.

55. See Clementina Díaz y de Ovando, *El Colegio Máximo de San Pedro y San Pablo* (Mexico: Instituto de Investigaciones Estéticas, 1951), 7–95.

56. Villaseca also paid for the preparation of three silver reliquaries. At least one object related to his philanthropy was still there at the time the Jesuits were expelled from the Spanish Empire in 1797. See Francisco Javier Alegre, *Historia de la Provincia de la Compañía de Jesús de Nueva España*, vol. 1 (Rome: Instituto Historicum S. J., 1956), 229.

57. Morales, *Carta del padre,* 32–33. I have replicated the layout of the poem as I found it in each printed version.

58. The translation appears in Alfred E. Lemmon, S. I., "Jesuits and Music in Mexico," *Archivum Historicum Societas Iesu* 66 (1977): (191–98), 193.

59. Morales, *Carta del padre*, 32–33.

60. See Francisco Cervantes de Salazar, *Crónica de la Nueva España* (Madrid: Hispanic Society of America, 1914), 38–39. The translation is mine.

61. See Robert Stevenson, *Music in Mexico: A Historical Survey* (New York: Thomas Y. Crowell), 8–19.

62. See James Lockhart, *The Nahuas after the Conquest: A Social and Cultural History of the Indians of Central Mexico, Sixteenth Through Eighteenth Centuries* (Stanford, Calif.: Stanford University Press, 1992), 282–83.

63. See W. V. Quine, "Translation and Meaning," in *Quintessence: Basic Readings from the Philosophy of W. V. Quine*, ed. Roger F. Gibson Jr. (Cambridge, Mass.: Belknap Press of Harvard University Press, 2004), (119–68), 163–68.

64. Roland Faber and Andrea M. Stephenson, eds., *Secrets of Becoming: Negotiating Whitehead, Deleuze, and Butler* (New York: Fordham University Press, 2011), 12.

65. Samuel Weber, "A Touch of Translation: On Walter Benjamin's 'Task of the Translator,' " in *Nation, Language, and the Ethics of Translation*, ed. Sandra Bermann and Michael Wood (Princeton, N.J.: Princeton University Press, 2005), 66 (65–78). Emphasis in the original.

66. See Stevenson, *Music in Mexico*, 51–68; 119–122.

67. Walter Mignolo suggests that by imposing Latin orthography upon Nahuatl and other Indian languages the friars had no choice but to find those Indian languages deficient if their sounds did not match the representations of Latin sounds. See Walter Mignolo, *The Darker Side of the Renaissance: Literacy, Territoriality, and Colonization* (Ann Arbor: University of Michigan Press, 1995).

68. See Joseph Errington, *Linguistics in a Colonial World: A Story of Language, Meaning, and Power* (Malden, Mass.: Blackwell, 2008), 22–47.

69. Molina offers "abajador"—from *tlatemouiani* ("el que abaja algo")—as an example of the first case, and the Nahuatl "nino calzascopina" ("descálzome las calzas") as an illustration of the second case. (Molina limited his dictionary to only two areas, Textzcuco and Mexico City.) See Fray Antonio de Molina, *Vocabulario Nahuatl-Castellano, Castellano-Nahuatl* (Mexico: Ediciones Colofón, 1966), 11–14.

70. Alfred North Whitehead, *Process and Reality: An Essay in Cosmology* (New York: Free, 1978), 16.

71. Ibid., 210.

72. Ibid., 108.

73. Ibid., 105.

74. Ibid., 129.

75. Morales, *Carta del padre*, 233–34.

76. See Solange Alberro, *El águila y la cruz: Orígenes religiosos de la conciencia criolla: Mexico, siglos XVI–XVII* (Mexico: Fondo de Cultura Económica, 1999), 87. I strongly recommend reading her section on Indian dances and *mitotes* (40–50) and other Jesuit celebrations (104–11).

77. Patricia Rieff Anawalt, *Indian Clothing before Cortés: Mesoamerican Costumes from the Codices* (Norman: University of Oklahoma Press, 1981). For information about the *huipil*, see 52–55. I also recommend her article "Costume and Control: Aztec Sumptuary Laws," *Archeology* 33, no. 1 (1980): 33–43.

78. For a survey of the *huipil* in contemporary Mexico, see Donald Cordry and Dorothy Cordry, *Mexican Indian Costumes* (Austin: University of Texas Press, 1968), 50–80.

79. See Abelardo Carrillo y Gariel, *El traje en la Nueva España* (Mexico: Instituto Nacional de Antropología e Historia, 1959), 204.

80. Fray Diego Durán, *Historia de las Indias de Nueva España e islas de la Tierra Firme*, vol. 2 (Mexico City: Editorial Porrúa, 1967), 207.

81. See Chloë Sayer, *Costumes of Mexico* (Austin: University of Texas Press, 1987), 73.

82. Cotton (*ixcatl*) was reserved for the elite. The rest of the population used agave, or maguey fabrics (*ixtle*), and even coarser textiles made of yucca. After the conquest, the Spaniards introduced wool and silk. After 1565, satins and velvets were received from China thanks to the Philippine trade. Dyes were extracted from fruits, roots, wood barks, flowers, shellfish, and cochineal (an insect that lived in *nopales*, or prickly-pear cacti). Chapters 1 and 2 of Sayer's book have been an important source for this note.

83. For a modern reader it might be logical to assume that Mexico was performed by a woman, but in spite of the costume described by Morales, that is not necessarily the case here. If the play was acted by students from the Colegio de San Pablo y San Pedro—and so it seems—they were all young males, or boys. A boy wearing a *huipil* in order to represent Mexico appeared in a ceremony in honor of King Charles II in 1677, in the company of "six children richly dressed as Indians performing a Moctezuma dance." See Ilona Katzew, "'Remedo de la ya muerta América': The Construction of Festive Rites in Colonial Mexico," in *Contested Visions in the Spanish Colonial World*, ed. Ilona Katzew (Los Angeles: Los Angeles County Museum of Art, 2011), 166.

84. "Sahagún mentioned ten different designs: the whirlpool design, as if with eyes painted; the turkey with the mat-designed interior; the small face; the twisted weave; broken cords, with husks outlined in black in wide black lines, with the interior diagonal design; the jaguar design; the shiny maguey-fiber cape; the white-flowered design; the wavy design; and nettles." Rieff Anawalt, *Indian Clothing*, 29; for more information about the *tilma*, see 27–33.

85. Tlazolteotl, the "Great Spinner and Weaver," was also linked to childbirth and the cycles of the moon (and, by extension, the menstrual calendar). Xochiquetzal was also depicted with looms and spindles. The intensive manual labors involved in textile production were also seen as a metaphor for sexual intercourse, pregnancy, and the transition from youth (spinning) into adulthood (weaving). Women were buried with their weaving artifacts. See Sharisse D. McCafferty

and Geoffrey G. McCafferty, "Spinning and Weaving as Female Gender Identity in Post-Classic Mexico," in *Textile Traditions of Mesoamerica and the Andes: An Anthology*, ed. Margot Blum Schevill, Janet Catherine Berlo, and Edward B. Dwyer (New York: Garland, 1991), 19–40.

86. See Richard J. Salvucci, *Textiles and Capitalism in Mexico: An Economic History of the Obrajes, 1539–1840* (Princeton, N.J.: Princeton University Press, 1987), 29–30.

87. See Carolyn Dean, *Inka Bodies and the Body of Christ: Corpus Christi in Colonial Cuzco, Peru* (Durham, N.C.: Duke University Press, 1999).

88. See Jonathan D. Spence, *The Memory Palace of Matteo Ricci* (New York: Penguin Books, 1985).

89. See Gauvin Alexander Bailey, *Art on the Jesuit Missions in Asia and Latin America, 1542–1773* (Toronto: University of Toronto Press, 1999), 3–51.

90. For a discussion of potentiality in Agamben's work, see Leland de la Durantaye, *Giorgio Agamben: A Critical Introduction* (Stanford, Calif.: Stanford University Press, 2009), 1–25. For several articles related to Whitehead's notions of becoming, see Faber and Stephenson, *Secrets of Becoming*.

91. Giorgio Agamben, *Infancy and History: The Destruction of Experience* (London: Verso, 2007), 110.

92. For an interesting comparison of Western and Chinese philosophies of becoming, see François Jullien, *The Silent Transformations*, trans. Krzysztof Fijalkowski and Michael Richardson (London: Seagull Books, 2011).

93. Whitehead, *Process and Reality*, 279.

94. Ibid., 280.

95. Certeau, *The Practice of Everyday Life*, 97, 109, 103.

96. See Paul Ricoeur, *On Translation* (London: Routledge, 2006), 10.

97. Morales, *Carta del padre*, 53–55.

Chapter 3

1. See Luis Reyes García, ed., *¿Cómo te confundes? ¿Acaso no somos conquistados? Anales de Juan Bautista* (Mexico: Centro de Investigaciones y Estudios Superiores en Antropología Social, Biblioteca Lázaro Boturini, 2001), 197. The translation from Spanish to English is mine.

2. See Latour, *Reassembling*, 214.

3. See Isabelle Stengers, *Cosmopolitics II*, trans. Robert Bononno (Minneapolis: University of Minnesota Press, 2011), 209.

4. Ibid., 211.

5. David Graeber, *Possibilities: Essays on Hierarchy, Rebellion, and Desire* (Oakland, Calif.: AK, 2007), 76.

6. Brian Massumi, *Parables for the Virtual: Movement, Affect, Sensation* (Durham, N.C.: Duke University Press, 2002), 3.

7. Ibid., 11.

8. Ibid., 20.

9. Latour is interested in discussing what he calls "body talk," the ways in which ideas of the body are mobilized across disciplines and discourses. See Bruno Latour, "How to Talk about the Body? The Normative Dimension of Science Studies," *Body & Society* 10 (2005): 206 (205–29).

10. Males were twenty and females were usually fifteen when they got married. See David Carrasco and Scott Sessions, *Daily Life of the Aztecs* (Santa Barbara, Calif.: Greenwood, 2011), 122.

11. See Jacques Soustelle, *La vida cotidiana de los aztecas en vísperas de la conquista* (Mexico: Fondo de Cultura Económica, 2003), 176–81.

12. See Stevenson, *Music in Mexico*, 26–27.

13. In 1555 the First Mexican Council under Bishop Montúfar tried to curtail the proliferation of Indian musicians, and in 1561 Philip II intervened, calling the Indians' devotion to musical instruments excessive. The Council of Trent (1545–63) rejected the use of percussive or loud wind instruments in the liturgy, giving a boost to the organ and the stringed instruments instead.

14. See Mark Pedelty, *Musical Ritual in Mexico City: From the Aztecs to NAFTA* (Austin: University of Texas Press, 2004), 39–55.

15. Paul A. Scolieri, *Dancing the New World: Aztecs, Spaniards, and the Choreography of Conquest* (Austin: University of Texas Press, 2013), 90–126.

16. See Lourdes Turrent, *La conquista musical de Mexico* (Mexico: Fondo de Cultura Económica, 1996), 46–108.

17. See Ross Hassig, *Time, History, and Belief in Aztec and Colonial Mexico* (Austin: University of Texas Press, 2001).

18. See Stevenson, *Music in Mexico*, 41, 63.

19. Graeber, *Possibilities*, 76.

20. For a summary of the characteristics of these drums and other aspects of Aztec music, see Enrique Martínez Miura, *La música precolombina: Un debate cultural después de 1492* (Barcelona: Paidós, 2004), 115–22, 127–32, 191–228, 217–21.

21. Coatepec was the mountain where Huitzilopochtli was born and his half-sister was dismembered. Pedelty, *Musical Ritual*, 15. Emphasis in the original.

22. Alan Knight, *Mexico: From the Beginning to the Spanish Conquest* (Cambridge: Cambridge University Press, 2002), 160–61. See also 177–92.

23. James Maffie, "Consciousness and Reality in Nahua Thought in the Era of the Conquest," in *Ontology of Consciousness: Percipient Action*, ed. Helmut Wautischer (Cambridge, Mass.: MIT Press, 2008) 97–126, 98.

24. For a survey of Olmec art and ideas, see Richard A. Diehl, *The Olmecs: America's First Civilization* (London: Thames and Hudson, 2004).

25. See Molly H. Bassett. *The Fate of Earthly Things: Aztec Gods and God-Bodies* (Austin: University of Texas Press, 2015).

26. Inga Clendinnen, *Aztecs: An Interpretation* (Cambridge: Cambridge University Press, 1991), 252–53.

27. Miguel León-Portilla, *Pre-Columbian Literatures of Mexico*, trans. Grace Lobanov and Miguel León-Portilla (Norman: University of Oklahoma Press, 1969), 107, 109.

28. As Elizabeth Hill Boone shows, migration histories were a cardinal narrative device for the Aztecs, and there are many extant codices that prove this. But even if we take these migratory narratives—with their prepositional paths often marked by footprints in the codices—as a morphological model for Aztec religious rituals, that does not mean the Aztecs saw them exclusively or primarily as a compendium of dramatic scenes. See Elizabeth Hill Boone, "Migration

Histories as Ritual Performance," in *Aztec Ceremonial Landscapes*, ed. David Carrasco (Niwot: University Press of Colorado, 1999), 121–51.

29. See Suk-Young Kim, *Illusive Utopia: Theater, Film, and Everyday Performance in North Korea* (Ann Arbor: University of Michigan Press, 2010).

30. Coyolxauhqui was defeated by Huitzilopochtli and her scattered body thrown down Coatepec Mountain.

31. See Susan Leigh Foster, "Choreographing History," in *Choreographing History*, ed. Susan Leigh Foster (Bloomington: Indiana University Press, 1995), 8–9.

32. Silvan Tomkins proposed, for example, a distinction between drives and affects. Drives are highly localized needs, like hunger. While the aims of our hunger as *drive* are quite specific—either one eats something, or not—the objects of our taste in food can be *affectively* multiple and malleable (like preferring French cuisine over British cooking). Hunger—a drive—is neither masculine nor feminine, but through history eating habits have been (and still are) closely associated with manners, social status, and even gender. While there are some cognitive predispositions shared by all minds and bodies, those predispositions are expanded and retrained by personal stories. The presence of physiological determinism does not preclude freedom or cognitive modifications; affects are somatic reactions shaped by experience. (Tomkins was trying to strike a balance between Kant and Nietzsche). Tomkins suggested a list of primary affects (interest, enjoyment, surprise, distress, fear, shame, contempt, anger) and co-related them to embodied manifestations that were mostly (but not exclusively) revealed through facial expressions. In his later work, Tomkins elaborated a dramaturgical approach based on the existence of a number of affective scripts. Scripts are particularized scenes—or scenarios—that can be replayed and restored in order to gradually amplify or discard affective tendencies. This trial-and-error mechanism is actualized, more often than not, by a recourse to variations and analogies. For an overview of Tomkins's ideas, see Eve Kosofsky-Sedgwick and Adam Frank, eds., *Shame and Its Sisters: A Silvan Tomkins Reader* (Durham, N.C.: Duke University Press, 1995), 33–74, 179–95.

33. Eve Kosofsky Sedgwick thinks one of the most salient characteristics of Tomkins's affects lies in the fact that they can be autotelic. Contrary to drives, affective cathexis is not exclusively oriented towards reaching a goal outside of itself; it can also have as its object of choice the exercise of its own becoming. It is due to this flexibility that *drives* can be inflected and remobilized by their *affective* routings. Drives are qualified by affects, and affects reframe how drives circulate. We should avoid any attempt at seeing drives and affects as polarized energies; their relation is pedagogical and collaborative, not oppositional. See Eve Kosofsky-Sedgwick, *Touching Feeling: Affect, Pedagogy, Performativity* (Durham, N.C.: Duke University Press, 2003), 1–25, 93–121.

34. See Teresa Brennan, *The Transmission of Affect* (Ithaca, N.Y.: Cornell University Press, 2004), 5.

35. See Sianne Ngai, *Ugly Feelings* (Cambridge, Mass.: Harvard University Press, 2005), 1–37.

36. Massumi, *Parables for the Virtual*, 71.

37. Fray Toribio de Benavente o Motolinía, *Memoriales* (Mexico: Universidad Autónoma de Mexico, 1971), 383–84.

38. Susan Leigh Foster, *Choreographing Empathy: Kinesthesia in Performance* (London: Routledge, 2011), 115–25, 162–63.

39. Fray Diego Durán, *Book of the Gods and Rites and the Ancient Calendar*, trans. Fernando Horcasitas and Doris Heyden (Norman: University of Oklahoma Press, 1971), 290.

40. Pedelty, *Musical Ritual*, 15.

41. All references come from Bernal Díaz del Castillo, *Historia verdadera de la conquista de la Nueva España* (Mexico: Editorial Porrúa, 2004), 66, 352.

42. John Bierhorst, *Ballads of the Lords of New Spain* (Austin: University of Texas, 2009).

43. An excellent summary of the problems confronted by a reader of the *Cantares* can be found in Miguel León-Portilla, *El destino de la palabra: De la oralidad y los códices mesoamericanos a la escritura alfabética* (Mexico: Fondo de Cultura Económica, 1996), 237–332.

44. For Nahuatl vocabulary, I have consulted the following dictionaries: John Bierhorst, *A Nahuatl-English Dictionary and Concordance to the "Cantares Mexicanos" with an Analytic Transcription and Grammatical Notes* (Stanford, Calif.: Stanford University Press, 1985); Frances Karttunen, *An Analytical Dictionary of Nahuatl* (Austin: University of Texas Press, 1983); and Fray Alonso de Molina, *Vocabulario en lengua castellana y mexicana y mexicana y castellana* (Mexico: Editorial Porrúa, 1970 [1571]).

45. For a panoramic account of the *Cantares*, see Amos Segala, *Literatura náhuatl: Fuentes, identidades, representaciones* (Mexico, D.F.: Grijalbo, 1990), 154–278.

46. We know the *huehuetl*—the drum of preference in the *Cantares*—had two tones a fifth apart (one at the center, another at the rim) and so did the *teponaztli* or Aztec xylophone (a fifth and a fourth). There were also some exclamations or interjections (*aya*, *iya*, *huiya*, *ohuaya*), that served as transitions between segments of the song-dances. It has been suggested the Aztecs used a pentatonic scale. See Vicente T. Mendoza, *Panorama de la música tradicional de Mexico* (Mexico: Imprenta Universitaria, 1956).

47. See Gary Tomlinson, *The Singing of the New World: Indigenous Voice in the Era of European Contact* (Cambridge: Cambridge University Press, 2007), 28–92.

48. My debt to Bierhorst's work as translator, editor, and commentator of the *Song of the Aztecs* is extensive, and this chapter would have been impossible without his pioneering scholarship. I certainly find his theorization of the texts as ghost songs fascinating, but his ideas have also been seriously contested. For my analysis of the song-dances, that issue is not a central one. John Bierhorst, *Cantares Mexicanos* (Stanford, Calif.: Stanford University Press, 1985), 39.

49. Bierhorst, *A Nahuatl-English Dictionary*, 383, 384–85. The Nahuatl text says, "mittotia espayolti mittotia in Mexica yn yancuic tlalpano." *Yancuic* means "new," and *tlalpano* is related to the adverb *tlalpan* ("on the ground") and the noun *tlalpanti* ("floor"). Another lexical connection is with the word *tlalli*, which can refer to "earth" and also "clay" or "mortal flesh." The vectorial mapping of the song suggests, as we can see, several convergent and by no means mutually exclusive possibilities.

50. This Martín Cortés is, in my opinion, the second Marquis del Valle, not his older half-brother of the same name. That would date the song after 1562, closer in time to Don Luis's wedding. Still, since the son of Malinche was involved in calming down a riot in 1564, it is evident he was respected by the Indians, too. I doubt, nonetheless, that he would have been considered the equal of two viceroys, as the song seems to imply.

51. It is important to keep in mind that in Miguel León-Portilla's edition of the *Cantares Mexicanos,* song 83 is number 84, and song 68 is number 69. In many ways, León-Portilla's edition is a response to Bierhorst, and their translations can be quite different. As far as I can see, my emphasis on locations and transportations is not deeply affected by this matter. I have checked the original Nahuatl myself to be sure of certain words and expressions, and although León-Portilla and Bierhorst occasionally select a different turn of phrase, the proxemics of the texts are basically similar in both translations. See Miguel León-Portilla, ed., *Cantares Mexicanos*, vol. 2.2 (Mexico: Universidad Nacional Autónoma de Mexico, 2011), 828–85, 1014–37.

52. Antonio de Molina to the painters: "Ya han ido los padres de ustedes a Castilla, han ido los grupos a conversar con el señor de ustedes el Emperador. Y si no lo acepta el Emperador se dirigirán a Roma. Y qué se hará, sopórtenlo entretanto." ("The friars have traveled to Castille already, the groups have gone now to talk to the Emperor. And if the Emperor says no, they will move on to Rome. In the meantime, endure the situation patiently.") (My translation.) Notice the sequence of events: Don Luis was married on June 4; he was attacked by a crowd on July 13; the alleged trip of the friars to Castille is alluded to on August 18 and then again by Molina on September 29, three days after Don Luis's arrest on the 26th of that month. It is entirely plausible to place the song-dance in the vicinity of those weeks. It is possible that a group of friars went to Spain around this period, but I have not been able to find any additional documentation related to this trip. Reyes García, *Anales de Juan Bautista*, 232–33, 255–56.

53. Bierhorst, *Cantares,* 333.

54. León-Portilla, *Cantares*, volume 2.2, 848–51.

55. For Bierhorst, water-pouring can mean "bloodshed," "pouring revenants from heaven," and/or "baptism." Bierhorst, *Cantares*, 480. Emphasis in the original.

56. Ibid., 327, 331, 335, 337.

57. "They also erected artificial trees covered with fragrant flowers where they seated the goddess Xochiquetzalli. During the dance some boys dressed up as birds, and others [dressed] as butterflies descended [from the trees]. They were richly decked with fine green, blue, red, and yellow feathers. These youths ascended the trees, climbing from limb to limb, sucking the dew of the flowers. Then the 'gods' appeared, each wearing robes such as the idols wore in the altars—a man or a woman dressed on the guise of each. With their blowguns in their hands they went around shooting at the 'birds' who were in the trees." Fray Diego Durán, *Book of the Gods and Rites*, 296.

58. Massumi, *Parables*, 86.

59. Bierhorst, *Cantares*, 337.

60. León-Portilla, *Cantares*, volume 2.2, 862–67. It is important to notice that in León-Portilla's edition the name of Don Martín is not explained in the notes.

Bierhorst guesses that the sudden presence of the *wind* reminds the passengers of the earlier travels of Don Martín Ecatl (Ehecatl is the god of wind in the Aztec pantheon). This is a connection I find entirely plausible. If the reference here is not to Don Martín Ecatl, should we consider the possibility that the song-dance is talking about Martín *Cortés*, the son of the conquistador and Malinche, or Martín Momauhti, the alleged brother of Don Luis? In my opinion, the cluster of references to the wind seems to make Bierhorst's interpretation quite possible.

61. See Serge Gruzinski, *The Mestizo Mind: The Intellectual Dynamics of Colonization and Globalization*, trans. Deke Dusinbeerre (New York: Routledge, 2002), 79–132.

62. It is vital to remember that drums were not the only sound involved in the performance of song-dances: among the instruments played we find the *quiquiztli* (conch-shell trumpet); the *ayacachtli* (gourd-shaped rattle); the *chichtli* (whistle flute); the *coyolli* (jingles); or the *tlapitzalli* (vertical flute); not to mention other instruments made of metal or bone that are harder to explain in modern terms. Carlos Chávez, Henry Cowell, Edgar Varése, and John Cage would have been able to compose many of their pieces in Mexica lands.

63. See Fray Jerónimo de Mendieta, *Historia Eclesiástica Indiana* (Mexico, D.F.: Editorial Salvador Chávez Hayhoe, 1945), 86–87.

64. Bierhorst, *Cantares*, 341.

65. León-Portilla, *Cantares*, volume 2.2, 878–81. León-Portilla's edition shows here several important differences from Bierhorst's translation, but the intercultural coexistence of indigenous and Catholic elements I am trying to underline is equally evident in both versions.

66. Saint Cecilia sang while dying; she was beheaded (a death not devoid of implications to a Mesoamerican mind) in Sicily (c. 176–180).

67. At death, all these forces separated. See Alfredo López Austin, *Cuerpo humano e ideología: Las concepciones de los antiguos Nahuas* (Mexico: Universidad Nacional Autónama de Mexico, 1980), 171–262.

68. See Robin Bernstein, *Racial Innocence: Performing American Childhood from Slavery to Civil Rights* (New York: New York University Press, 2011), 73.

69. See Eleanor Wake, *Framing the Sacred: The Indian Churches of Early Colonial Mexico* (Norman: University of Oklahoma Press, 2010), 235–56.

70. Bernardino de Sahagún, *Historia general de las cosas de Nueva España*, vol. 2 (Madrid: Crónicas de América, 1990), 637–39.

71. Sahagún transplanted these flowers to his *Psalmodia Christiana*, a collection of Christian songs in Nahuatl published in 1581 that shows how closely he tried to adapt the stylistic devices of the *Cantares* to his own religious agenda.

72. See Berenice Alcántara Rojas, "In *Nepapan Xochitl*: The Power of Flowers in the Works of Sahagún," in *Colors between Two Worlds: The "Florentine Codex" of Bernardino de Sahagún*, ed. Gerhard Wolf, Joseph Connors, and Louis A. Waldman (Milan: Officina Libraria, 2011), 107–32, 113–15.

73. See Mark Franko, "Mimique," in *Migrations of Gesture*, ed. Carrie Noland and Sally Ann Ness (Minneapolis: University of Minnesota Press, 2008), 251 (241–58).

74. Lorraine Daston, ed., *Things That Talk: Object Lessons from Art and Science* (New York: Zone Books, 2004), 9.

75. See Tzvetan Todorov, *The Conquest of America: The Question of the Other* (Norman: University of Oklahoma Press, 1999).

76. See Lawrence Grossberg, *Dancing in Spite of Myself: Essays on Popular Culture* (Durham, N.C.: Duke University Press, 1997), 13.

77. See David Graeber, *Debt: The First 5,000 Years* (New York: Melville House, 2011), 355–57.

78. See Reyes García, *Anales de Juan Bautista*, 319. My translation.

79. Ethelia Ruiz Medrano speculates that the presence of the mestizo Cortés on the site of the riot indicates a potential link between Don Luis and the insurrection plans uncovered by the Audiencia two years later and already extensively discussed in the first chapter of this book. See Ethelia Ruiz Medrano, "Fighting Destiny: Nahua Nobles and Friars in the Sixteenth-Century Revolt of the Encomendaros against the King," in *Negotiation within Domination: New Spain's Indian Pueblos Confront the Spanish State*, ed. Ethelia Ruiz Medrano and Susan Kellog (Boulder: University of Colorado Press, 2010), 45–78.

80. Quoted by Gruzinski, *The Mestizo Mind*, 149. Don Luis's successor was accused of incest and his candidacy was rejected. See Reyes García, *Anales de Juan Bautista*, 155.

Chapter 4

1. W. B. Worthen, *Shakespeare and the Force of Modern Performance* (Cambridge: Cambridge University Press, 2003), 24.

2. Latour, *Reassembling*, 60.

3. See M. M. Bakhtin, "Forms of Time and the Chronotope in the Novel," in *The Dialogic Imagination*, ed. Michael Helquist, trans. Caryl Emerson and Michael Helquist (Austin: University of Texas Press, 1994), 84–258.

4. See Michel Foucault, "Different Spaces," in *Aesthetics, Method, and Epistemology*, ed. James D. Faubion (New York: New, 1998), 175–85.

5. See Octavio Paz, *Sor Juana Inés de la Cruz o las trampas de la fe* (Mexico: Fondo de Cultura Económica, 1982).

6. See Stephanie Merrim, *Early Modern Women's Writing and Sor Juana Inés de la Cruz* (Nashville, Tenn.: Vanderbilt University Press, 1999).

7. Frederick Luciani, *Literary Self-Fashioning in Sor Juana Inés de la Cruz* (Lewisburg, Pa.: Bucknell University Press, 2004).

8. For a general overview of geophilosophy, see Mark Bonta and John Protevi, *Deleuze and Geophilosophy: A Guide and Glossary* (Edinburgh: Edinburgh University Press, 2004).

9. Gilles Deleuze and Félix Guattari, *A Thousand Plateaus: Capitalism and Schizophrenia,* trans. Brian Massumi (Minneapolis: University of Minnesota Press, 1987), 292–93.

10. This is not the place to discuss the question of immanence and its philosophical implications. I refer the interested reader to Levi R. Bryant, *Difference and Givenness: Deleuze's Transcendental Empiricism and the Ontology of Immanence* (Evanston, Ill.: Northwestern University Press, 2008); and Laura Cull, *Theatres of Immanence: Deleuze and the Ethics of Performance* (London: Palgrave Macmillan, 2012).

11. Gilles Deleuze and Félix Guattari, *What Is Philosophy?* trans. Hugh Tomlinson and Graham Burchell (New York: Columbia Univesity Press, 1994), 85.

12. "The concept is not paradigmatic, but *syntagmatic*; not projected, but *connective*, not hierarchical, but *linking*; not referential, but *consistent*." Deleuze and Guattari, *What Is Philosophy?* 91. Emphasis in the original.

13. "The figure is essentially *paradigmatic*, *projective*, *hierarchical*, and *referential*." Ibid., 89. Emphasis in the original.

14. Ibid., 101–3.

15. Esposito traces a genealogy of Italian philosophy that includes Machiavelli, Giordano Bruno, and Vico as thinkers who emphasized the links between thought, everyday life, the body, and history. See Roberto Esposito, *Living Thought: The Origins and Actuality of Italian Philosophy*, trans. Zakiya Hanafi (Stanford, Calif.: Stanford University Press, 2012), 1–43.

16. Mauricio Beuchot, *The History of Philosophy in Colonial Mexico*, trans. Elizabeth Millán (Washington, D.C.: Catholic University of America Press, 1998), 92–137.

17. William Egginton, *How the World Became a Stage: Presence, Theatricality, and the Question of Modernity* (Albany: State University of New York Press, 2003), 123–66.

18. Sor Juana Inés de la Cruz, *El cetro de José*, in *Obras Completas*, ed. Alfonso Méndez Plancarte, vol. 3 (Mexico: Fondo de Cultura Económica, 1994), 184–200.

19. Sor Juana Inés de la Cruz, *El mártir del Sacramento, San Hermenegildo*, in *Obras Completas*, ed. Alfonso Méndez Plancarte, vol. 3 (Mexico: Fondo de Cultura Económica, 1994), 97–115.

20. For a discussion of the theological issues at work in this *loa* and others, see Mauricio Beuchot, "Los autos de Sor Juana: Tres lugares teológicos," in *Sor Juana y su mundo: Una mirada actual*, ed. Sara Poot Herrera (Mexico: Universidad del Claustro de Sor Juana, 1995), 355–92.

21. See Edward Schillebeeckx, *The Eucharist* (London: Burns and Oates, 2005).

22. See Aristotle, *Physics*, trans. Robin Waterfield (Oxford: Oxford University Press, 2008).

23. For a full rendition of these ideas, see Saint Thomas Aquinas, "The Eucharistic Presence," in *Summa Theologiae*, ed. William Barden, vol. 58 (London: McGraw-Hill, 1965), 53–161.

24. For more details of Suárez's discussion of the Eucharist, see Manuel Quera, "Suárez y la doctrina de la transubstanciación eucarística," in *Francisco Suárez: El hombre, la obra, el influjo*, ed. Jesús Solano (Madrid: Editorial Razón y Fe, 1948), 409–41.

25. For an accessible summary of how the problem of substance was discussed during the baroque period, see R. S. Woolhouse, *Descartes, Spinoza, Leibniz: The Concept of Substance in Seventeenth Century Metaphysics* (London: Routledge, 2003).

26. Ronald Laymon, "Transubstantiation: Test Case for Descartes's Theory of Space," in *Problems of Cartesianism*, ed. Thomas M. Lennon, John M. Nicholas, and John W. Davis (Kingston, Ont.: McGill-Queen's University Press, 1982), 149–70.

27. "Multipraesentia non habet opus replicatione aut penetratione dimensionum. Sed explicanda est per genus praensitiae nullam habens relationem ad

dimensiones, velut si Deus efficeret, ut aliquid immediate operaretur in distans." G. W. Leibniz, *The Leibniz-Des Bosses Correspondence*, ed. Brandon C. Look and Donald Rutherford (New Haven, Conn.: Yale University Press, 2007), 166–67. It is tempting to see Leibniz's *vinculum* as a *soft* theory of gravity!

28. Sarah Beckwith, *Signifying God: Social Relation and Symbolic Act in the York Corpus Christi Plays* (Chicago: University of Chicago Press, 2001), 62–65.

29. "Nam fides non est contra sensum, sed est de eo ad quod sensus non attingit." Aquinas, *Summa Theologiae*, 76–77.

30. Max Harris, *Theatre and Incarnation* (London: Macmillan, 1990), 37.

31. See Francis Clark, *Eucharistic Sacrifice and the Reformation* (Oxford: Basil Blackwell, 1967), 3–205.

32. See James T. O'Connor, *The Hidden Manna: A Theology of the Eucharist* (San Francisco: Ignatius, 2005).

33. See Jonathan Bishop, *Some Bodies: The Eucharist and Its Implications* (Macon, Ga.: Mercer University Press, 1992).

34. Miri Rubin, *Corpus Christi: The Eucharist in Late Medieval Culture* (Cambridge: Cambridge University Press, 2002), 164–287.

35. For a fascinating historical account of this liturgy, see Barbara R. Walters, Vincent Corrigan, and Peter T. Ricketts, eds., *The Feast of Corpus Christi* (University Park: Pennsylvania State University Press, 2006), 3–54.

36. It has been suggested that Sor Juana wrote *The Divine Narcissus* in a bid to replace Calderón as an author of *autos* at the court in Madrid. If that was the case, it is possible she was invested in addressing an Iberian audience more than a Mexican, local one.

37. See Alexander A. Parker, *Los autos sacramentales de Calderón de la Barca* (Barcelona: Ariel, 1983).

38. See Ignacio Arellano, *Estructuras dramáticas y alegóricas en los autos de Calderón* (Kassel: Reichenberger, 2001).

39. The *autos* were actively performed in Spain until the second half of the eighteenth century. Charles III prohibited their production in 1765. Many Spanish intellectuals saw the *autos* as a dangerous remnant of baroque obscurantism, one that exposed the masses to subtle or superstitious ideas they were not ready to assimilate properly. For a literary discussion of the sacramental plays, see Ricardo Arias, *The Spanish Sacramental Plays* (Boston: Twayne, 1980).

40. See Barbara Kurtz, *The Play of Allegory in the Autos Sacramentales of Pedro Calderón de la Barca* (Washington, D.C.: Catholic University of America Press, 1991).

41. There are two versions of this *auto*, one from 1634 and the other from 1663. See Pedro Calderón de la Barca, *El divino Orfeo*, ed. J. E. Duarte (Pamplona: Universidad de Navarra and Kassel: Edition Reichenberger, 1999), 9–150.

42. For a summary of these public events, see Linda A. Curcio-Nagy, *The Great Festivals of Colonial Mexico City: Performing Power and Identity* (Albuquerque: University of New Mexico Press, 2004), 15–66.

43. Sor Juana Inés de la Cruz, *El divino Narciso*, ed. Robin Ann Rice (Pamplona: Ediciones Universida de Navarra, 2005), 139. An English translation is available: *The Divine Narcissus*, trans. Patricia A. Peters (Albuquerque: University of New Mexico Press, 1998). I decided to do my own translations of the play.

44. Sor Juana Inés de la Cruz, *El divino Narciso*, 142. Unless stated otherwise, all translations from the play are mine.

45. Ibid., 172.

46. See Sor Juana Inés de la Cruz, *Villancicos y letras sacras*, in *Obras completas*, ed. Alfondo Méndez Plancarte, vol. 3 (Mexico: Fondo de Cultura Económica, 1994), 17–18, 41–42.

47. Enrique Dussel, "The Bread of the Eucharist Celebration as a Sign of Justice in the Community," in *Beyond Philosophy: Ethics, History, Marxism, and Liberation Theology*, ed. Eduardo Mendieta (New York: Rowman and Littlefield, 2003), (41–52), 47.

48. For a general discussion of this novel see Giulia de Sarlo, "*Suene el tocotín, pues Triunpha María*: Francisco Bramón y su reinvención criolla de temas y formas metropolitanas en el Barroco Novohispano," in *En la región del aire: Obras de ficción en la prosa novohispana*, ed. Trinidad Barrera (Seville: Editorial Renacimiento, 2011), 251–91.

49. Francisco Bramón, *Auto del triunfo de la Virgen y gozo mexicano*, ed. Agustín Yáñez (Mexico: Imprenta Universitaria, 1945), 56–59. My translation.

50. The mestizo qualities of Bramón's piece are discussed by Luis Leal, "El hechizo derramado: Elementos mestizos en Sor Juana," in *Y diversa de mí misma entre vuestras plumas ando*, ed. Sara Poot Herrera (Mexico: El Colegio de Mexico, 1997), 185–200.

51. Félix Guattari, *Chaosmosis: An Ethico-Aesthetic Paradigm* (Sydney: Power Publications, 2006), 26.

52. Félix Guattari, *Schizoanalytic Cartographies* (London: Bloomsbury, 2013), 210.

53. Edward S. Casey, *The Fate of Place: A Philosophical History* (Berkeley: University of California Press, 1998), xii. For a detailed discussion of concepts of space and place, see also 103–79.

54. For a detailed discussion of the fountain, see Elena Granger-Carrasco, "La fuente hermafrodita en *El Divino Narciso* de Sor Juana," in *Y diversa de mí misma*, ed. Sara Poot Herrera, 237–46.

55. Guattari, *Chaosmosis*, 15.

56. Sor Juana, *Divino Narciso*, 197.

57. Stephen Hinds, "Landscape with Figures: Aesthetics of Place in the *Metamorphoses* and Its Tradition," in *The Cambridge Companion to Ovid*, ed. Philip Hardie (Cambridge: Cambridge University Press, 2002), (122–49), 122.

58. Sor Juana herself used the *ovillejos* in several of her *loas* and in individual compositions, too. See Antonio Alatorre, "Perduración del 'ovillejo' Cervantino," *Nueva Revista de Filología Hispánica* 38, no. 2 (1990): 643–74.

59. Sor Juana, *Divino Narciso*, 258–59.

60. Scott Lash and John Urry, *Economies of Signs and Space* (London: SAGE, 1999), 29.

61. Deleuze and Guattari, *What Is Philosophy?* 96.

62. Ibid., 96.

63. Guattari, *Chaosmosis*, 103.

64. See Dario Puccini, *Una mujer en soledad: Sor Juana Inés de la Cruz, una excepción en la cultura y la literatura barroca* (Mexico: Fondo de Cultura Económica, 1997), 69–127.

65. For a fascinating overview of Kircher's influence in the New World, see Paula Findlen, "A Jesuit's Books in the New World: Athanasius Kircher and His American Readers," in *Athanasius Kircher: The Last Man Who Knew Everything*, ed. Paula Findlen (New York: Routledge, 2004), 329–64.

66. See Jorge Cañizares-Esguerra, *Nature, Empire, and Nation: Explorations of the History of Science in the Iberian World* (Stanford,Calif.: Stanford University Press, 2006), 46–95.

67. Elaine Fantham, *Ovid's Metamorphoses* (Oxford: Oxford University Press, 2004), 6–20.

68. See Leo Cabranes-Grant, "The Fold of Difference: Performing Baroque and Neobaroque Mexican Identities," in *Baroque New Worlds: Representations, Transculturation, Counterconquest*, ed. Lois Parkinson Zamora and Monika Kaup (Durham, N.C.: Duke University Press, 2010), 467–84.

69. Walker Bynum claims that it was only at this point in the Middle Ages that change started to be conceptualized as the actualization of something *other* instead of being explained as a gradual adjustment of primal elements or components. Walker Bynum also observes that towards the final decades of the twelfth century, stories of metamorphosis (and alchemy, vampires, or werewolves) became notoriously fashionable. See Caroline Walker Bynum, *Metamorphosis and Identity* (New York: Zone Books, 2005), 25.

70. C. P. Cavafy, "But Wise Men Apprehend What Is Imminent," in C. P. Cavafy, *Collected Poems*, trans. Daniel Mendelsohn (New York: Alfred A. Knopf, 2009), 7.

BIBLIOGRAPHY

Abou-El-Haj, Barbara. *The Medieval Cult of Saints: Formations and Transformations*. Cambridge: Cambridge University Press, 1994.

Actas del Cabildo de la Ciudad de Mexico. Vol. 7. Mexico: Oficinas Tipográficas de El Socialista, 1877.

Agamben, Giorgio. *Infancy and History: The Destruction of Experience*. London: Verso, 2007.

———. *The Kingdom and the Glory: For a Theological Genealogy of Economy and Government*. Translated by Lorenzo Chiesa with Matteo Mandarini. Stanford, Calif.: Stanford University Press, 2011.

Ahmed, Sara. *Queer Phenomenology: Orientations, Objects, Others*. Durham, N.C.: Duke University Press, 2006.

Alatorre, Antonio. "Perduración del 'ovillejo' Cervantino." *Nueva Revista de Filología Hispánica* 38, no. 2 (1990): 643–74.

Alberro, Solange. *El águila y la cruz: Orígenes religiosos de la conciencia criolla: México, siglos XVI–XVII*. Mexico: Fondo de Cultura Económica, 1999.

Alcántara Rojas, Berenice. "In *Nepapan Xochitl*: The Power of Flowers in the Works of Sahagún." In *Colors between Two Worlds: The "Florentine Codex" of Bernardino de Sahagún*, edited by Gerhard Wolf, Joseph Connors, and Louis A. Waldman. Milan: Officina Libraria, 2011.

Alegre, Francisco Javier. *Historia de la Provincia de la Compañía de Jesús de Nueva España*. Vol. 1. Rome: Instituto Historicum S. J., 1956.

Andrés, Gabriel. "Relaciones extensas de fiestas públicas: itinerario de un 'género.'" In *La Fiesta: Actas del II Seminario de las Relaciones de Sucesos*, edited by Sagrario López Posa and Nieves Pena Suerio. Ferrol: Sociedad de Cultura Valle Inclán, 1999.

Appadurai, Arjun. "Introduction: Commodities and the Politics of Value." In *The Social Life of Things: Commodities in Cultural Perspective*, edited by Arjun Appadurai. Cambridge: Cambridge University Press, 1986.

Aquinas, Thomas. "The Eucharistic Presence." In *Summa Theologiae*, edited and translated by William Barden. Vol. 58. London: McGraw-Hill, 1965.

Aracil Varón, María Beatriz. *El teatro evangelizador: Sociedad, cultura e ideología en la Nueva España del siglo XVI*. Rome: Bulzoni Editore, 1995.

Arellano, Ignacio. *Estructuras dramáticas y alegóricas en los autos de Calderón*. Kassel: Reichenberger, 2001.

Arias, Ricardo. *The Spanish Sacramental Plays*. Boston: Twayne, 1980.

Aristotle. *Physics*. Translated by Robin Waterfield. Oxford: Oxford University Press, 2008.

Arróniz, Othón. *Teatro de evangelización en Nueva España*. Mexico City: Universidad Nacional Autónoma de Mexico, 1979.

Auerbach, Erich. *Scenes from the Drama of European Literature*. Minneapolis: University of Minnesota Press, 1984.

Austin, J. L. *How to Do Things with Words*. Cambridge, Mass.: Harvard University Press, 1975.

Bailey, Gauvin Alexander. *Art on the Jesuit Missions in Asia and Latin America, 1542–1773*. Toronto: University of Toronto Press, 1999.

Bakhtin, M. M. "Forms of Time and the Chronotope in the Novel." In *The Dialogic Imagination*, edited by Michael Helquist, translated by Caryl Emerson and Michael Helquist. Austin: University of Texas Press, 1994.

Balme, Christopher. *Decolonizing the Stage: Theatrical Syncretism and Post-Colonial Drama*. Oxford: Clarendon, 1999.

Barba, Eugenio. *The Paper Canoe: A Guide to Theatre Anthropology*. London: Routledge, 1993.

Barlow, Roberto H. "El códice de los alfareros de Cuautitlán." *Revista Mexicana de Estudios Antropológicos* 12 (1951): 5–8.

Barret, Ward. *The Sugar Hacienda of the Marqueses del Valle*. Minneapolis: University of Minnesota Press, 1970.

Bassett, Molly H. *The Fate of Earthly Things: Aztec Gods and God-Bodies*. Austin: University of Texas Press, 2015.

Bauer, Ralph, and José Antonio Mazzotti, eds. *Creole Subjects in the Colonial Americas: Empires, Texts, Identities*. Williamsburg, Va.: University of North Carolina Press, 2009.

Beckwith, Sarah. *Signifying God: Social Relation and Symbolic Act in the York Corpus Christi Plays*. Chicago: University of Chicago Press, 2001.

Bedau, Mark A., and Paul Humphreys, eds. *Emergence: Contemporary Readings in Philosophy and Science*. Cambridge, Mass.: MIT Press, 2008.

Benjamin, Walter. "Analogy and Relationship." In *Selected Writings: Volume I, 1913–1926*, edited by Marcus P. Bullock and Michael W. Jennings. Cambridge, Mass.: Harvard, 1996.

———. *The Origin of German Tragic Drama*. Translated by John Osborne. London: Verso, 1977.

Bennett, Herman L. *Africans in Colonial Mexico: Absolutism, Christianity, and Afro-Creole Consciousness, 1570–1640*. Bloomington: Indiana University Press, 2003.

Bennett, Jane. *Vibrant Matter: A Political Ecology of Things*. Durham, N.C.: Duke University Press, 2010.

Bentley, James. *Restless Bones: The Story of Relics*. Suffolk, Eng.: Constable, 1985.

Bernstein, Robin. *Racial Innocence: Performing American Childhood from Slavery to Civil Rights*. New York: New York University Press, 2011.

Beuchot, Mauricio, O. P. *The History of Philosophy in Colonial Mexico*. Translated by Elizabeth Millán. Washington, D.C.: Catholic University of America Press, 1998.

———. "Los autos de Sor Juana: Tres lugares teológicos." In *Sor Juana y su mundo: Una mirada actual*, edited by Sara Poot Herrera. Mexico: Universidad del Claustro de Sor Juana, 1995.

Bhabha, Homi. *The Location of Culture*. London: Routledge, 1994.

Bharucha, Rustom. *The Politics of Cultural Practice: Thinking through Theatre in an Age of Globalization*. Middletown, Conn.: Wesleyan University Press, 2000.

Bierhorst, John. *Ballads of the Lords of New Spain*. Austin: University of Texas, 2009.

———. *Cantares Mexicanos*. Stanford, Calif.: Stanford University Press, 1985.

———. *A Nahuatl-English Dictionary and Concordance to the "Cantares Mexicanos" with an Analytic Transcription and Grammatical Notes*. Stanford, Calif.: Stanford University Press, 1985.

Bishop, Jonathan. *Some Bodies: The Eucharist and Its Implications*. Macon, Ga.: Mercer University Press, 1992.

Blok, Anders, and Torben Elgaard Jensen. *Bruno Latour: Hybrid Thoughts in a Hybrid World*. London: Routledge, 2011.

Bonta, Mark, and John Protevi. *Deleuze and Geophilosophy: A Guide and Glossary*. Edinburgh: Edinburgh University Press, 2004.

Boone, Elizabeth Hill. "Migration Histories as Ritual Performance." In *Aztec Ceremonial Landscapes*, edited by David Carrasco. Niwot: University Press of Colorado, 1999.

Bourdieu, Pierre. *The Logic of Practice*. Stanford, Calif.: Stanford University Press, 1990.

Bramón, Francisco. *Auto del triunfo de la Virgen y gozo mexicano*. Edición de Agustín Yáñez. Mexico: Imprenta Universitaria, 1945.

Brennan, Teresa. *The Transmission of Affect*. Ithaca, N.Y.: Cornell University Press, 2004.

Brisset, Demetrio. "Cortés derrotado: La visión indígena de la conquista." In *Las danzas de la conquista*, vol. I: *México contemporáneo*, edited by Jesús Jáuregui and Carlo Bonfliglioli, 69–90. México: Fondo de Cultura Económica, 1996.

Brown, Peter. *The Cult of Saints: Its Rise and Function in Latin Christianity*. Chicago: University of Chicago Press, 1981.

Bruman, Henry J. *Alcohol in Ancient Mexico*. Salt Lake City: University of Utah Press, 2000.

Bryant, Levi R. *The Democracy of Objects*. Ann Arbor, Mich.: Open Humanities, 2011.

———. *Difference and Givenness: Deleuze's Transcendental Empiricism and the Ontology of Immanence*. Evanston, Ill.: Northwestern University Press, 2008.

Burkhart, Louise M., ed. *Aztecs on Stage: Religious Theater in Colonial Mexico*. Norman: University of Oklahoma Press, 2011.

———. *Holy Wednesday: A Nahua Drama from Early Colonial Mexico*. Philadelphia: University of Pennsylvania Press, 1996.

Cabranes-Grant, Leo. "The Fold of Difference: Performing Baroque and Neobaroque Mexican Identities." In *Baroque New Worlds: Representations, Transculturation, Counterconquest*, edited by Lois Parkinson Zamora and Monika Kaup. Durham, N.C.: Duke University Press, 2010.

Calderón de la Barca, Pedro. *El divino Orfeo*. Edited by J. E. Duarte. Pamplona: Universidad de Navarra and Kassel: Edition Reichenberger, 1999.

Cañeque, Alejandro. *The King's Living Image: The Culture and Politics of Viceregal Power in Colonial Mexico*. New York: Routledge, 2004.

Cañizares-Esguerra, Jorge. *Nature, Empire, and Nation: Explorations of the History of Science in the Iberian World*. Stanford, Calif.: Stanford University Press, 2006.

Carlson, Marvin. *The Haunted Stage: The Theatre as Memory Machine*. Ann Arbor: University of Michigan Press, 2003.

———. "Peter Brook's *The Mahabharata* and Ariane Mnouchkine's *L'Indiade* as Examples of Contemporary Cross-Cultural Theatre." In *The Dramatic Touch of Difference: Theatre, Own and Foreign*, edited by Erika Fisher-Lichte, Josephine Riley, and Michael Gissenweher. Tübingen: Gunter Narr, 1990.

Carrasco, David. *City of Sacrifice: The Aztec Empire and the Role of Violence in Civilization*. Boston: Beacon, 1999.

Carrasco, David, and Scott Sessions. *Daily Life of the Aztecs*. Santa Barbara, Calif.: Greenwood, 2011.

Carrillo y Gariel, Abelardo. *El traje en la Nueva España*. México: Instituto Nacional de Antropología e Historia, 1959.

Casey, Edward S. *The Fate of Place: A Philosophical History*. Berkeley: University of California Press, 1998.

Castells, Manuel. *The Rise of the Network Society*. Oxford: Wiley-Blacknell, 2010.

Cavafy, C. P. *Collected Poems*. Translated by Daniel Mendelsohn. New York: Alfred A. Knopf, 2009.

Cervantes de Salazar, Francisco. *Crónica de la Nueva España*. Madrid: Hispanic Society of America, 1914.

Chaganti, Seeta. *The Medieval Poetics of the Reliquary: Enshrinement, Inscription, Performance*. New York: Palgrave Macmillan, 2008.

Chaudhuri, Una. "The Future of the Hyphen: Interculturalism, Textuality, and the Difference Within." In *Interculturalism and Performance*, edited by Bonnie Marranca and Gautam Dasgupta. New York: PAJ Publications, 1991.

Chávez Orozco, Luis, ed. *Códice Osuna*. Mexico: Instituto Indigenista Interamericano, 1947.

Choudhury, Mita. *Interculturalism and Resistance in the London Theater, 1660–1800: Identity, Performance, Empire*. Lewisburg, Pa.: Bucknell University Press, 2000.

Clark, Francis. *Eucharistic Sacrifice and the Reformation*. Oxford: Basil Blackwell, 1967.

Clarke, Bruce. *Posthuman Metamorphosis: Narrative and Systems*. New York: Fordham University Press, 2008.

Clendinnen, Inga. *Aztecs: An Interpretation*. Cambridge: Cambridge University Press, 1991.

Códices Indígenas de Algunos Pueblos del Marquesado del Valle de Oaxaca. Mexico City: Archivo General de la Nación, Talleres Gráficos de la Nación, 1933.

Connerton, Paul. *How Societies Remember*. Cambridge: Cambridge University Press, 1989.

Conquergood, Dwight. "Beyond the Text: Toward a Performative Cultural Politics." In *Cultural Struggles: Performance, Ethnography, Praxis*, edited by E. Patrick Johnson. Ann Arbor: University of Michigan Press, 2013.

Corcuera de Mancera, Sonia. *Del amor al temor: Borrachez, catequesis y control en la Nueva España (1555–1771)*. Mexico: Fondo de Cultura Económica, 1994.

Cordry, Donald, and Dorothy Cordry. *Mexican Indian Costumes*. Austin: University of Texas Press, 1968.

Cull, Laura. *Theatres of Immanence: Deleuze and the Ethics of Performance*. London: Palgrave Macmillan, 2012.

Curcio-Nagy, Linda A. *The Great Festivals of Colonial Mexico City: Performing Power and Identity*. Albuquerque: University of New Mexico Press, 2004.

Daston, Lorraine, ed. *Things That Talk: Object Lessons from Art and Science*. New York: Zone Books, 2004.

Davis, Tracy C. "Performative Time." In *Representing the Past: Essays in Performance Historiography*, edited by Charlotte M. Canning and Thomas Postlewait. Iowa City: University of Iowa Press, 2010.

Dean, Carolyn. *Inka Bodies and the Body of Christ: Corpus Christi in Colonial Cuzco, Peru*. Durham, N.C.: Duke University Press, 1999.

de Betanzo, Antonio Sotelo. "Antonio Sotelo de Betanzo al rey Felipe II de España, to King Philip II of Spain, diciembre 9, 1567." In *Epistolario de la Nueva España, 1505–1818*, edited by Francisco del Paso y Troncoso. Vol. 10. Mexico City: Porrúa e Hijos, 1940.

de Certeau, Michel. *The Practice of Everyday Life*. Berkeley: University of California Press, 1988.

de la Cruz, Sor Juana Inés. *The Divine Narcissus*. Translated by Patricia A. Peters. Albuquerque: University of New Mexico Press, 1998.

———. "El cetro de José." In *Obras Completas*, edited by Alfonso Méndez Plancarte. Vol. 3. Mexico: Fondo de Cultura Económica, 1994.

———. *El divino Narciso*. Edited by Robin Ann Rice. Pamplona: Ediciones Universidad de Navarra, 2005.

———. "El mártir del Sacramento, San Hermenegildo." In *Obras Completas*, edited by Alfonso Méndez Plancarte. Vol. 3. Mexico: Fondo de Cultura Económica, 1994.

———. *Villancicos y letras sacras*. In *Obras Completas*, edited by Alfondo Méndez Plancarte. Vol. 3. Mexico: Fondo de Cultura Económica, 1994.

DeLanda, Manuel. *A New Philosophy of Society: Assemblage Theory and Social Complexity*. London: Continuum, 2006.

de Las Casas, Bartolomé. *A Short Account of the Destruction of the Indies*. Translated by Nigel Griffin. New York: Penguin Books, 1992.

———. *Tratados*. México: Fondo de Cultura Económica, 1965.

Deleuze, Gilles, and Félix Guattari. *A Thousand Plateaus: Capitalism and Schizophrenia*. Translated by Brian Massumi. Minneapolis: University of Minnesota Press, 1987.

———. *What Is Philosophy?* Translated by Hugh Tomlinson and Graham Burchell. New York: Columbia University Press, 1994.

de Zorita, Alonso. *Historia de la Nueva España*. Madrid: Librería General de Victoriano Suárez, 1909.

Díaz Balsera, Viviana. *The Pyramid under the Cross: Franciscan Discourses of Evangelization and the Nahua Christian Subject in Sixteenth-Century Mexico*. Tucson: University of Arizona Press, 2005.

Díaz del Castillo, Bernal. *Historia verdadera de la conquista de la Nueva España*. Mexico: Editorial Porrúa, 2004.

Díaz y de Ovando, Clementina. *El Colegio Máximo de San Pedro y San Pablo*. México: Instituto de Investigaciones Estéticas, 1951.

Diehl, Richard A. *The Olmecs: America's First Civilization*. London: Thames and Hudson, 2004.

Donahue-Wallace, Kelly. *Art and Architecture of Viceregal Latin America, 1521–1821*. Albuquerque: University of New Mexico Press, 2008.

Douglas Cope, R. *The Limits of Racial Domination: Plebeian Society in Colonial Mexico City, 1660–1720*. Madison: University of Wisconsin Press, 1994.

Durán, Fray Diego. *Book of the Gods and Rites and the Ancient Calendar*. Translated by Fernando Horcasitas and Doris Heyden. Norman: University of Oklahoma Press, 1971.

———. *Historia de las Indias de Nueva España e islas de la Tierra Firme*. Vol. 2. México City: Editorial Porrúa, 1967.

Durantaye, Leland de la. *Giorgio Agamben: A Critical Introduction*. Stanford, Calif.: Stanford University Press, 2009.

Dussel, Enrique. "The Bread of the Eucharist Celebration as a Sign of Justice in the Community." In *Beyond Philosophy: Ethics, History, Marxism, and Liberation Theology*, edited by Eduardo Mendieta. New York: Rowman and Littlefield, 2003.

Duverger, Christian. *El primer mestizaje: La clave para entender el pasado Mesoamericano*. Mexico City: Taurus, 2007.

Edgerton, Samuel Y. *Theaters of Conversion: Religious Architecture and Indian Artisans in Colonial Mexico*. Albuquerque: University of New Mexico Press, 2001.

Egginton, William. *How the World Became a Stage: Presence, Theatricality, and the Question of Modernity*. Albany: State University of New York Press, 2003.

Eiland, Howard, and Michael W. Jennings. *Walter Benjamin: A Critical Life*. Cambridge, Mass.: Harvard University Press, 2014.

Enders, Jody. *Murder by Accident: Medieval Theater, Modern Media, Critical Intentions*. Chicago: University of Chicago Press, 2009.

Errington, Joseph. *Linguistics in a Colonial World: A Story of Language, Meaning, and Power*. Malden, Mass.: Blackwell, 2008.

Esposito, Roberto. *Living Thought: The Origins and Actuality of Italian Philosophy*. Translated by Zakiya Hanafi. Stanford, Calif.: Stanford University Press, 2012.

Esteva Fábregas, Claudio. *El mestizaje en Iberoamérica*. Madrid: Editorial Alhambra, 1988.

Faber, Roland, and Andrea M. Stephenson, eds. *Secrets of Becoming: Negotiating Whitehead, Deleuze, and Butler*. New York: Fordham University Press, 2011.

Fantham, Elaine. *Ovid's Metamorphoses*. Oxford: Oxford University Press, 2004.

Findlen, Paula. "A Jesuit's Books in the New World: Athanasius Kircher and His American Readers." In *Athanasius Kircher: The Last Man Who Knew Everything*, edited by Paula Findlen. New York: Routledge, 2004.

Fischer-Lichte, Erika. "Introduction: Interweaving Performance Cultures—Rethinking 'Intercultural Theatre': Toward an Experience and Theory of Performance beyond Postcolonialism." In *The Politics of Interweaving*

Performance Cultures: Beyond Postcolonialism, edited by Erika Fischer-Lichte, Torsten Jost, and Saskya Iris Jain, 1–21. London: Routledge, 2014.

Fischer-Lichte, Josephine Riley, and Michael Gissenweher, eds. *The Dramatic Touch of Difference: Theatre, Own and Foreign.* Tübingen: Gunter Narr, 1990.

Fisher, Andrew B., and Matthew D. O'Hara, eds. *Imperial Subjects: Race and Identity in Colonial Latin America.* Durham, N.C.: Duke University Press, 2009.

Flor, Fernando de la. "Economía simbólica de la relación y conmemoración fúnebre en el antiguo régimen: Gasto, derroche y dilapidación del bien cultural." In *La Fiesta: Actas del II Seminario de las Relaciones de Sucesos*, edited by Sagrario López Posa and Nieves Pena Suerio. Ferrol: Sociedad de Cultura Valle Inclán, 1999.

Florescano, Enrique. *Los orígenes del poder en Mesoamérica.* Mexico, D.F.: Fondo de Cultura Económica, 2009.

Foster, Susan Leigh. *Choreographing Empathy: Kinesthesia in Performance.* London: Routledge, 2011.

———. "Choreographing History." In *Choreographing History*, edited by Susan Leigh Foster. Bloomington: Indiana University Press, 1995.

Foucault, Michel. "Different Spaces." In *Aesthetics, Method, and Epistemology*, edited by James D. Faubion. New York: New, 1998.

Franko, Mark. "Mimique." In *Migrations of Gesture*, edited by Carrie Noland and Sally Ann Ness. Minneapolis: University of Minnesota Press, 2008.

García Canclini, Néstor. *Hybrid Cultures: Strategies for Entering and Leaving Modernity.* Translated by Christopher L. Chiappari and Silvia L. López. Minneapolis: University of Minnesota Press, 1995.

Geary, Patrick J. *Furta Sacra: Thefts of Relics in the Central Middle Ages.* Princeton, N.J.: Princeton University Press, 1978.

Gibson, Charles. *The Aztecs under Spanish Rule: A History of the Indians of the Valley of Mexico, 1519–1810.* Stanford, Calif.: Stanford University Press, 1964.

Gómez Robledo, Xavier. *Humanismo en México en el siglo XVI: El sistema del Colegio de San Pedro y San Pablo.* Mexico: Editorial Jus, 1954.

Gonzalbo Aizpuru, Pilar. *Historia de la educación en la época colonial: La educación de los criollos y la vida urbana.* México: El Colegio de México, 1990.

González González, Enrique. "Nostalgia de la encomienda: Releer el *Tratado del descubrimiento*, de Juan Suárez de Peralta." *Historia Mexicana* 59, no. 2 (2006): 533–603.

Grace Miller, Marilyn. *Rise and Fall of the Cosmic Race: The Cult of Mestizaje in Latin America.* Austin: University of Texas Press, 2004.

Graeber, David. *Debt: The First 5,000 Years.* New York: Melville House, 2011.

———. *Possibilities: Essays on Hierarchy, Rebellion, and Desire.* Oakland, Calif.: AK, 2007.

Granger-Carrasco, Elena. "La Fuente hermafrodita en *El Divino Narciso* de Sor Juana." In *Y diversa de mí misma entre vuestras plumas ando*, edited by Sara Poot Herrera. Mexico: El Colegio de Mexico, 1997.

Grossberg, Lawrence. *Dancing in Spite of Myself: Essays on Popular Culture.* Durham, N.C.: Duke University Press, 1997.

Grosz, Elizabeth. "Thinking the New: Of Futures Yet Unthought." In *Becomings: Explorations in Time, Memory, and Futures*, edited by Elizabeth Grosz. Ithaca, N.Y.: Cornell University Press, 1999.

Gruzinski, Serge. *The Mestizo Mind: The Intellectual Dynamics of Colonization and Globalization*. Translated by Deke Dusinbeerre. New York: Routledge, 2002.

Guattari, Félix. *Chaosmosis: An Ethico-Aesthetic Paradigm*. Sydney: Power Publications, 2006.

———. *Schizoanalytic Cartographies*. London: Bloomsbury, 2013.

Harman, Graham. *Bruno Latour: Reassembling the Political*. London: Pluto, 2014.

———. *Prince of Networks: Bruno Latour and Metaphysics*. Melbourne, Australia: re.press, 2008.

———. *The Quadruple Object*. Winchester, Eng.: Zero Books, 2011.

Harris, Max. *The Dialogical Theatre: Dramatizations of the Conquest of Mexico and the Question of the Other*. New York: St. Martin's, 1993.

———. *Theatre and Incarnation*. London: Macmillan, 1990.

Hassig, Ross. *Time, History, and Belief in Aztec and Colonial Mexico*. Austin: University of Texas Press, 2001.

———. *Trade, Tribute, and Transportation: The Sixteenth-Century Political Economy of the Valley of Mexico*. Norman: University of Oklahoma Press, 1985.

Hermann-Mascard, Nicole. *Les Reliques des saints: Formation coutimiére d'un droit*. Paris: Editions Klincksiek, 1975.

Hernández, Rosaura, ed. *Cuauhtitlán*. Mexico: El Colegio Mexiquense, 1996.

Hinds, Stephen. "Landscape with Figures: Aesthetics of Place in the *Metamorphoses* and Its Tradition." In *The Cambridge Companion to Ovid*, edited by Philip Hardie. Cambridge: Cambridge University Press, 2002.

Holland, John H. *Emergence: From Chaos to Order*. New York: Basic Books, 1998.

Holledge, Julie, and Joanne Tompkins. *Women's Intercultural Performance: Cultural Double Cross*. London: Taylor and Francis, 2000.

Horcasitas, Fernando. *El teatro náhuatl: Épocas novohispana y moderna*. México: Universidad Autónoma de México, 1979.

Horden, Peregrine, and Nicholas Purcell. *The Corrupting Sea: A Study of Mediterranean History*. Oxford: Blackwell, 2000.

Huang, Yan. *Anaphora: A Cross-Linguistic Study*. Oxford: Oxford University Press, 2000.

Jackson, Shannon. *Social Work: Performing Art, Supporting Publics*. London: Routledge, 2011.

James, William. *A Pluralistic Universe*. Lincoln: University of Nebraska Press, 1996.

Jáuregui, Jesús. "Cortés contra Moctezuma-Cuauhtémoc: El intercambio de mujeres." In *Las danzas de la conquista*, vol. I: *México contemporáneo*, edited by Jesús Jáuregui and Carlo Bonfliglioli, 33–68. México: Fondo de Cultura Económica, 1996.

Jullien, François. *The Silent Transformations*. Translated by Krzysztof Fijalkowski and Michael Richardson. London: Seagull Books, 2011.

Karttunen, Frances. *An Analytical Dictionary of Nahuatl*. Austin: University of Texas Press, 1983.

Katzew, Ilona. "'Remedo de la ya muerta América': The Construction of Festive Rites in Colonial Mexico." In *Contested Visions in the Spanish Colonial World*, edited by Ilona Katzew. Los Angeles: Los Angeles County Museum of Art, 2011.

Katzew, Ilona, and Susan Deans-Smith, eds. *Race and Classification: The Case of Mexican America*. Stanford, Calif.: Stanford University Press, 2009.

Keber, Eloise Quiñones, ed. *Representing Aztec Ritual: Performance, Text, and Image in the Work of Sahagún*. Boulder: University Press of Colorado, 2002.

Keller, Catherine. *Face of the Deep: A Theology of Becoming*. London: Routledge, 2003.

Kim, Suk-Young. *Illusive Utopia: Theater, Film, and Everyday Performance in North Korea*. Ann Arbor: University of Michigan Press, 2010.

Knight, Alan. *Mexico: From the Beginning to the Spanish Conquest*. Cambridge: Cambridge University Press, 2002.

Knowles, Ric. *Theatre and Interculturalism*. London: Palgrave Macmillan, 2010.

Kurtz, Barbara. *The Play of Allegory in the Autos Sacramentales of Pedro Calderón de la Barca*. Washington, D.C.: Catholic University of America Press, 1991.

Lanyon, Anna. *The New World of Martín Cortés*. Cambridge, Mass.: Da Capo, 2003.

Lash, Scott, and John Urry. *Economies of Signs and Space*. London: SAGE, 1999.

Latour, Bruno. *Aramis or the Love of Technology*. Translated by Catherine Porter. Cambridge, Mass.: Harvard University Press, 1996.

———. "How to Talk about the Body? The Normative Dimension of Science Studies." *Body & Society* 10 (2005): 205–29.

———. *An Inquiry into Modes of Existence: An Anthropology of the Moderns*. Translated by Catherine Porter. Cambridge, Mass.: Harvard University Press, 2013.

———. *Reassembling the Social: An Introduction to Actor-Network-Theory*. Oxford: Oxford University Press, 2005.

———. *We Have Never Been Modern*. Translated by Catherine Porter. Cambridge, Mass.: Harvard University Press, 1993.

Laymon, Ronald. "Transubstantiation: Test Case for Descartes's Theory of Space." In *Problems of Cartesianism*, edited by Thomas M. Lennon, John M. Nicholas, and John W. Davis. Kingston, Ont.: McGill-Queen's University Press, 1982.

Leal, Luis. "El hechizo derramado: Elementos mestizos en Sor Juana." In *Y diversa de mí misma entre vuestras plumas ando*, edited by Sara Poot Herrera. Mexico: El Colegio de Mexico, 1997.

Lee, Rensseler W. *Ut Pictura Poesis: The Humanist Theory of Painting*. New York: Norton, 1967.

Leibniz, G. W. *The Leibniz-Des Bosses Correspondence*. Edited by Brandon C. Look and Donald Rutherford. New Haven, Conn.: Yale University Press, 2007.

Lemmon, Alfred E. "Jesuits and Music in Mexico." *Archivum Historicum Societas Iesu* 66 (1997): 191–98.

León-Portilla, Miguel, ed. *Cantares Mexicanos*. Vol. 2.2. Mexico: Universidad Nacional Autónoma de Mexico, 2011.

———. *El destino de la palabra: De la oralidad y los codices mesoamericanos a la escritura alfabética*. Mexico: Fondo de Cultura Económica, 1996.

———. *Pre-Columbian Literatures of Mexico*. Translated by Grace Lobanov and Miguel León-Portilla. Norman: University of Oklahoma Press, 1969.

Leslie, Esther. *Walter Benjamin*. London: Reaktion Books, 2007.

Lo, Jacqueline, and Helen Gilbert. "Towards a Topography of Cross-Cultural Theatre Praxis." *TDR: The Drama Review* 16, no. 3 (2002): 31–53.

Lockhart, James. *The Nahuas after the Conquest: A Social and Cultural History of the Indians of Central Mexico, Sixteenth through Eighteenth Centuries*. Stanford, Calif.: Stanford University Press, 1992.

Lópes Don, Patricia. *Bonfires of Culture: Franciscans, Indigenous Leaders, and the Inquisition in Early Mexico, 1524–1540*. Norman: University of Oklahoma Press, 2010.

López Austin, Alfredo. *Cuerpo humano e ideología: Las concepciones de los antiguos Nahuas*. Mexico: Universidad Nacional Autónama de Mexico, 1980.

López Luján, Leonardo. "Water and Fire: Archeology in the Capital of the Mexica Empire." In *The Archeology of Mesoamerica: Mexican and European Perspectives*, edited by Warwick Bray and Linda Manzanilla. London: British Museum, 1999.

Luciani, Frederick. *Literary Self-Fashioning in Sor Juana Inés de la Cruz*. Lewisburg, Pa.: Bucknell University Press, 2004.

Luhmann, Niklas. *Social Systems*. Translated by John Bernarz and Dirk Baecker. Stanford, Calif.: Stanford University Press, 1995.

Maffie, James. "Consciousness and Reality in Nahua Thought in the Era of the Conquest." In *Ontology of Consciousness: Percipient Action*, edited by Helmut Wautischer. Cambridge, Mass.: MIT Press, 2008.

Magaloni Kerpel, Diana. *The Colors of the New World: Artists, Materials, and the Creation of the "Florentine Codex."* Los Angeles: Getty Research Institute, 2014.

Mañé, J. Ignacio Rubió. *El Virreinato*. Vol. 2. Mexico: Fondo de Cultura Económica, 1983.

Marranca, Bonnie. *Ecologies of Theater: Essays at the Century Turning*. Baltimore, Md.: Johns Hopkins University Press, 1996.

Martínez, José Luis. *Hernán Cortés*. Mexico: Fondo de Cultura Económica, 1990.

Martínez Miura, Enrique. *La música precolombina: Un debate cultural después de 1492*. Barcelona: Paidós, 2014.

Massumi, Brian. *Parables for the Virtual: Movement, Affect, Sensation*. Durham, N.C.: Duke University Press, 2002.

McCafferty, Sharisse D., and Geoffrey G. McCafferty. "Spinning and Weaving as Female Gender Identity in Post-Classic Mexico." In *Textile Traditions of Mesoamerica and the Andes: An Anthology*, edited by Margot Blum Schevill, Janet Catherine Berlo, and Edward B. Dwyer. New York: Garland, 1991.

McIvor, Charlotte, and Matthew Spangler, eds. *Staging Intercultural Ireland: New Plays and Practitioner Perspectives*. Cork City, Ire.: Cork University Press, 2014.

Meillassoux, Quentin. *After Finitude: An Essay on the Necessity of Contingency*. Translated by Ray Brassier. London: Bloomsbury, 2008.

Mendieta, Fray Jerónimo de. *Historia Eclesiástica Indiana*. Mexico, D.F.: Editorial Salvador Chávez Hayhoe, 1945.

Mendoza, Vicente T. *Panorama de la música tradicional de Mexico*. Mexico: Imprenta Universitaria, 1956.

Merrim, Stephanie. *Early Modern Women's Writing and Sor Juana Inés de la Cruz*. Nashville, Tenn.: Vanderbilt University Press, 1999.

———. *The Spectacular City, Mexico, and Colonial Hispanic Literary Culture*. Austin: University of Texas Press, 2010.

Mignolo, Walter. *The Darker Side of the Renaissance: Literacy, Territoriality, and Colonization*. Ann Arbor: University of Michigan Press, 1995.

Molina, Fray Antonio de. *Vocabulario en lengua castellana y mexicana y mexicana y castellana*. Mexico: Editorial Porrúa, 1970 (1571).

———. *Vocabulario Nahuatl-Castellano, Castellano-Nahuatl*. México: Ediciones Colofón, 1966.

Morales, Pedro de. *Carta del padre Pedro de Morales de la Compañía de Jesús. Para el muy reverendo Padre Everardo Mercuriano, General de la misma Compañía. En que se da relación de la festividad que en esta insigne Ciudad de México se hizo este año de setenta y ocho, en la collocación de las Sanctas Reliquias que nuestro muy Santo Padre Gregorio XIII les embió*. Edited by Beatriz Mariscal Hay. México: El Colegio de México, 2000.

Moreland, John. *Archeology and Text*. London: Duckworth, 2011.

Moretti, Franco. *Graphs, Maps, Trees: Abstract Models for Literary History*. London: Verso, 2007.

Motolinía, Fray Toribio de Benavente o. *Historia de los indios de la Nueva España*. Madrid: Clásicos Castalia, 1985.

———. *Memoriales*. Mexico: Universidad Autónoma de Mexico, 1971.

Mundy, Barbara E. "Indigenous Dances in Early Colonial Mexico City." In *Festivals & Daily Life in the Arts of Colonial Latin America, 1492–1850*, 11–30. Denver: Denver Art Museum, 2014.

Ngai, Sianne. *Ugly Feelings*. Cambridge, Mass.: Harvard University Press, 2005.

North, Michael. *Novelty: A History of the New*. Chicago: University of Chicago Press, 2013.

O'Connor, James T. *The Hidden Manna: A Theology of the Eucharist*. San Francisco: Ignatius, 2005.

Orozco y Berra, Manuel. *Noticia histórica de la conjuración del Marqués del Valle: Años de 1565–1568*. Mexico: Tipografía de R. Rafael, 1853.

Osterhammel, Jürgen. *The Transformation of the World: A Global History of the Nineteenth Century*. Translated by Patrick Camiller. Princeton, N.J.: Princeton University Press, 2014.

Parker, Alexander A. *Los autos sacramentales de Calderón de la Barca*. Barcelona: Ariel, 1983.

Pavis, Patrice. *Analyzing Performance: Theater, Dance, and Film*. Translated by David Williams. Ann Arbor: University of Michigan Press, 2006.

———. *Theater at the Crossroads of Culture*. London: Routledge, 1992.

Paz, Octavio. *Sor Juana Inés de la Cruz o las trampas de la fe*. Mexico: Fondo de Cultura Económica, 1982.

Pedelty, Mark. *Musical Ritual in Mexico City: From the Aztecs to NAFTA*. Austin: University of Texas Press, 2004.

Peterson, Jeanette Favrot. *Visualizing Guadalupe: From Black Madonna to Queen of the Americas*. Austin: University of Texas, 2014.

Phelan, Peggy. *Unmarked: The Politics of Performance*. London: Routledge, 1993.

Postlewait, Thomas, and Charlotte M. Canning. "Introduction." In *Representing the Past: Essays in Performance Historiography*, edited by Charlotte M. Canning and Thomas Postlewait. Iowa City: University of Iowa Press, 2010.

Prabhu, Anjali. *Hybridity. Limits, Transformations, Prospects*. Albany: State University of New York Press, 2007.

Puccini, Dario. *Una mujer en soledad: Sor Juana Inés de la Cruz, una excepción en la cultura y la literatura barroca*. Mexico: Fondo de Cultura Económica, 1997.

Quera, Manuel. "Suárez y la doctrina de la transubstanciación eucarística." In *Francisco Suárez: El hombre, la obra, el influjo*, edited by Jesús Solano. Madrid: Editorial Razón y Fe, 1948.

Quine, W. V. "Translation and Meaning." In *Quintessence: Basic Readings from the Philosophy of W. V. Quine*, edited by Roger F. Gibson Jr. Cambridge, Mass.: Belknap Press of Harvard University Press, 2004.

Quirk, Randolph, and Sidney Greenbaum. *A Concise Grammar of Contemporary English*. London: Harcourt Brace Jovanovich, 1973.

Ramos Smith, Maya. *Actores y compañías de la Nueva España: Siglos XVI y XVII*. Coyoacán, México: Instituto Nacional de Bellas Artes, 2011.

Rancière, Jacques. *The Politics of Aesthetics*. Translated by Gabriel Rockhill. New York: Continuum, 2004.

Rappaport, Joanne. *The Disappearing Mestizo: Cofiguring Difference in the Colonial New Kingdom of Granada*. Durham, N.C.: Duke University Press, 2014.

Rayner, Alice. *Ghosts: Death's Double and the Phenomena of Theatre*. Minneapolis: University of Minnesota Press, 2006.

Reuland, Eric. *Anaphora and Language Design*. Cambridge, Mass.: MIT Press, 2011.

Reyes García, Luis, ed. *¿Cómo te confundes? ¿Acaso no somos conquistados? Anales de Juan Bautista*. Mexico: Centro de Investigaciones y Estudios Superiores en Antropología Social, Biblioteca Lázaro Boturini, 2001.

Ricard, Robert. *La conquista espiritual de Mexico*. Mexico City: Fondo de Cultura Económica, 1986.

Ricoeur, Paul. *On Translation*. London: Routledge, 2006.

Rieff Anawalt, Patricia. "Costume and Control: Aztec Sumptuary Laws." *Archeology* 33, no. 1 (1980): 33–43.

———. *Indian Clothing before Cortés: Mesoamerican Costumes from the Codices*. Norman: University of Oklahoma Press, 1981.

Roach, Joseph. *Cities of the Dead: Circum-Atlantic Performance*. New York: Columbia University Press, 1996.

Rodríguez-Alegría, Enrique, Hector Neff, and Michael D. Glascock. "Indigenous Ware or Spanish Import? The Case of Indígena Ware and Approaches to Power in Colonial Mexico." *Latin American Antiquity* 14, no. 1 (2003): 67–81.

Rojas, José Luis de. *Tenochtitlán: Capital of the Aztec Empire*. Gainesville: University Press of Florida, 2012.

Ross, Kathleen. "Gender and Gossip in Criollo Historiography: Juan Suárez de Peralta's *Tratado del descubrimiento de las Indias y su conquista*." In *Creole*

Subjects in the Colonial Americas: Empires, Texts, Identities, edited by Ralph Bauer and José Antonio Mazzotti. Chapel Hill: University of North Carolina Press, 2009.

Rubin, Miri. *Corpus Christi: The Eucharist in Late Medieval Culture*. Cambridge: Cambridge University Press, 2002.

Ruiz Medrano, Ethelia. "Fighting Destiny: Nahua Nobles and Friars in the Sixteenth-Century Revolt of the Encomendaros against the King." In *Negotiation within Domination: New Spain's Indian Pueblos Confront the Spanish State*, edited by Ethelia Ruiz Medrano and Susan Kellog. Boulder: University of Colorado Press, 2010.

Russo, Alessandra. *The Unstranslatable Image: A Mestizo History of the Arts in New Spain, 1500–1600*. Translated by Susan Emanuel. Austin: University of Texas Press, 2014.

Sahagún, Bernardino de. *Historia General de las cosas de Nueva España*. Vol. 2. Madrid: Crónicas de América, 1990.

Salvucci, Richard J. *Textiles and Capitalism in Mexico: An Economic History of the Obrajes, 1539–1840*. Princeton, N.J.: Princeton University Press, 1987.

San Antón Muñón Chimalpahin Quauhtlehuanitzin, Don Domingo de. *Annals of His Time*. Edited and translated by James Lockhart, Susan Schroeder, and Doris Namala. Stanford, Calif.: Stanford University Press, 2006.

Santley, Robert S., Michael J. Berman, and Rani T. Alexander. "The Politicization of the Mesoamerican Ballgame and Its Implications for the Interpretation of the Distribution of Ballcourts in Central Mexico." In *The Mesoamerican Ballgame*, edited by Vernon Scarborough and David R. Wilcox. Tucson: University of Arizona Press, 1991.

Sarlo, Giulia de. "*Suene el tocotín, pues Triunpha María*: Francisco Bramón y su reinvención criolla de temas y formas metropolitanas en el Barroco Novohispano." In *En la region del aire: Obras de ficción en la prosa novohispana*, edited by Trinidad Barrera. Seville: Editorial Renacimiento, 2011.

Sayer, Chloë. *Costumes of Mexico*. Austin: University of Texas Press, 1987.

Schechner, Richard. *Between Theater and Anthropology*. Philadelphia: University of Pennsylvania Press, 1985.

Schechner, Richard, and Willa Appel, eds. *By Means of Performance: Intercultural Studies of Theatre and Ritual*. Cambridge: Cambridge University Press, 1990.

Schillebeeckx, Edward. *The Eucharist*. London: Burns and Oates, 2005.

Schmidgen, Henning. *Bruno Latour in Pieces: An Intellectual Biography*. Translated by Gloria Custance. New York: Fordham University Press, 2015.

Schneider, Rebecca. *Performing Remains: Art and War in Times of Theatrical Reenactment*. London: Routledge, 2011.

Scholes, France V., and Eleanor B. Adams, eds. *Cartas del Licenciado Jerónimo de Valderrama y otros documentos sobre su visita al gobierno de Nueva España, 1563–1565: Documentos para la historia del Mexico Colonial*. Vol. 7. Mexico: José Porrúa e Hijos, 1961.

Schuessler, Michael K. *Artes de fundación: Teatro evangelizador y pintura mural en la Nueva España*. México: Universidad Nacional Autónoma de México, 2009.

Scolieri, Paul A. *Dancing the New World: Aztecs, Spaniards, and the Choreography of Conquest*. Austin: University of Texas Press, 2013.

Sedgwick, Eve Kosofsky. *Touching Feeling: Affect, Pedagogy, Performativity*. Durham, N.C.: Duke University Press, 2003.

Sedgwick, Eve Kosofsky, and Adam Frank, eds. *Shame and Its Sisters: A Silvan Tomkins Reader*. Durham, N.C.: Duke University Press, 1995.

Segala, Amos. *Literatura náhuatl: Fuentes, identidades, representaciones*. Mexico, D.F: Grijalbo, 1990.

Serres, Michel. *The Parasite*. Translated by Lawrence R. Schehr. Minneapolis: University of Minnesota Press, 2007.

———. *The Troubadour of Knowledge*. Translated by Sheila Faria Glaser and William Paulson. Ann Arbor: University of Michigan Press, 1997.

Serres, Michel, with Bruno Latour. *Conversations on Science, Culture, and Time*. Ann Arbor: University of Michigan Press, 1995.

Simpson, Lesley Bird. *The Encomienda in New Spain: The Beginning of Spanish Mexico*. Berkeley: University of California Press, 1950.

Souriau, Etienne. *Les différents modes d'existence*. Paris: Presses Universitaires de France, 2009.

Soustelle. Jacques. *La vida cotidiana de los aztecas en vísperas de la conquista*. Mexico: Fondo de Cultura Económica, 2003.

Spence, Jonathan D. *The Memory Palace of Matteo Ricci*. New York: Penguin Books, 1985.

Stalder, Felix. *Manuel Castells*. Cambridge, Eng.: Polity, 2006.

Stengers, Isabelle. *Cosmopolitics II*. Translated by Robert Bononno. Minneapolis: University of Minnesota Press, 2011.

Stevenson, Robert. *Music in Mexico: A Historical Survey*. New York: Thomas Y. Crowell, 1952.

Strong, Roy. *Art and Power: Renaissance Festivals 1450–1650*. Suffolk, Eng.: Boydell, 1984.

Suárez de Peralta, Juan. *Tratado del descubrimiento de las Indias y su conquista*. Madrid: Alianza Editorial, 1990.

Tatlow, Antony. *Shakespeare, Brecht, and the Intercultural Sign*. Durham, N.C.: Duke University Press, 2001.

Taussig, Michael. *Defacement: Public Secrecy and the Labor of the Negative*. Stanford, Calif.: Stanford University Press, 1999.

Tavárez, David. *The Invisible War: Indigenous Devotions, Discipline, and Dissent in Colonial Mexico*. Stanford, Calif.: Stanford University Press, 2011.

Taylor, Diana. *The Archive and the Repertoire*. Durham, N.C.: Duke University Press, 2003.

Taylor, William B. *Drinking, Homicide and Rebellion in Colonial Mexican Villages*. Stanford, Calif.: Stanford University Press, 1979.

Terkessidis, Mark. *Interkultur*. Berlin: Suhrkamp Verlag, 2010.

Tobi Evans, Susan. *Ancient Mexico & Central America: Anthropology and Culture History.* London: Thames and Hudson, 2008.

Todorov, Tzvetan. *The Conquest of America: The Question of the Other*. Norman: University of Oklahoma Press, 1999.

Tomlinson, Gary. *The Singing of the New World: Indigenous Voice in the Era of European Contact*. Cambridge: Cambridge University Press, 2007.

Tomson, Robert. *An Englishman and the Mexican Inquisition, 1556–1560*. Edited by G. R. G. Conway. Mexico: Privately printed, 1927.

Turrent, Lourdes. *La conquista musical de Mexico*. Mexico: Fondo de Cultura Económica, 1996.

Vincent, Victoria A. "The Avila-Cortés Conspiracy: Creole Aspirations and Royal Interests." Ph.D. diss., University of Nebraska, 1993.

Wake, Eleanor. *Framing the Sacred: The Indian Churches of Early Colonial Mexico*. Norman: University of Oklahoma Press, 2010.

Walker Bynum, Caroline. *Metamorphosis and Identity*. New York: Zone Books, 2005.

Walters, Barbara R., Vincent Corrigan, and Peter T. Ricketts, eds. *The Feast of Corpus Christi*. University Park: Pennsylvania State University Press, 2006.

Warthon, Annabel Jane. *Selling Jerusalem: Relics, Replicas, Theme Parks*. Chicago: University of Chicago Press, 1981.

Weber, Samuel. "A Touch of Translation: On Walter Benjamin's 'Task of the Translator.'" In *Nation, Language, and the Ethics of Translation*, edited by Sandra Bermann and Michael Wood. Princeton, N.J.: Princeton University Press, 2005.

Whitehead, Alfred North. *Process and Reality: An Essay in Cosmology*. New York: Free, 1978.

Wilkerson, Jeffrey K. "And They Were Sacrificed: The Ritual Ballgame of Northeastern Meso-America through Time and Space." In *The Mesoamerican Ballgame*, edited by Vernon Scarborough and David R. Wilcox, 45–71. Tucson: University of Arizona Press, 1991.

Williams, Raymond. *Marxism and Literature*. Oxford: Oxford University Press, 1977.

Woolhouse, R. S. *Descartes, Spinoza, Leibniz: The Concept of Substance in Seventeenth Century Metaphysics*. London: Routledge, 2003.

Worthen, W. B. *Shakespeare and the Force of Modern Performance*. Cambridge: Cambridge University Press, 2003.

Ybarra, Patricia A. *Performing Conquest: Five Centuries of Theater, History, and Identity in Tlaxcala, Mexico*. Ann Arbor: University of Michigan Press, 2009.

Zavala, Silvio A. *El servicio personal de los indios en la Nueva España*. Vol. 2. Mexico: El Colegio de Mexico, 1985.

———. *La encomienda Indiana*. Mexico: Editorial Porrúa, 1992.

INDEX

Page numbers in **boldface** refer to illustrations.